Opium, State, and Society

Opium, State, and Society

*China's Narco-Economy and
the Guomindang, 1924–1937*

Edward R. Slack, Jr.

University of Hawai'i Press
HONOLULU

Library of Congress Cataloging-in-Publication Data

Slack, Edward R., 1963–
    Opium, state, and society: China's narco-economy and the Guomindang, 1924–1937 /
Edward R. Slack, Jr.
        p. cm.
    Includes bibliographical references and index.
    ISBN 0–8248–2278–1 (cloth: alk. paper)—ISBN 0–8248–2361–3 (pbk.: alk. paper)
        1. Opium trade—Government policy—China. 2. Opium habit—China. 3. Chung-kuo
kuo min tang. 4. China—Politics and government—1928–1937. I. Title.

HV5840.C6 S54 2001
363.45'0951—dc21   00–042315

Cover illustration: *From a poster printed by the National Anti-Opium Association for their "Anti-
Opium Week" in October 1930. The art is by Zhi Mo.*

Designed by inari.

Printed by the Maple-Vail Book Manufacturing Group

To Kwang-ching Liu, the epitome of a *junzi*

Contents

Acknowledgments

FIRST AND FOREMOST, I would like to thank the Slack Foundation, my mother Carol and my father Edward, for their moral and financial support. Without the latter, my research for this book in Taiwan, in the People's Republic of China, and at Stanford University would have been impossible. Another important person who made this effort attainable was Kwang-ching Liu. My manuscript evolved from a seminar paper I wrote for him in 1993 while he was the Burns Chair for the Department of History at the University of Hawai'i. Professor Liu's insightful comments and encouraging guidance kept my spirits from flagging during the Dantean descent known as the writing process, and I am sincerely appreciative of having had the opportunity to get to know him personally. I would also like to thank Daniel Kwok for his sagacious advice and invaluable assistance as chair of my dissertation committee. In similar fashion, I am grateful for all of the input from Tien-yi Tao, Jerry Bentley, and Sen-dou Chang. Many thanks to the two scholars that reviewed my manuscript for the University of Hawai'i Press: your constructive criticisms of the early draft were invaluable.

Parts of chapters 2 and 4 of this book are also included in a chapter titled "The National Anti-Opium Association and the Guomindang, 1924–1937," in the volume *Opium Regimes: China, Britain, and Japan, 1839–1952*, edited by Tim Brook and Bob Wakabayashi (Berkeley: University of California Press, 2000).

Among those deserving recognition for their roles in the publication process are Idus Newby for his generosity and assistance, especially for his much needed editing skills, Jim Kraft for his economic expertise, and Lin Weihong and Xing Yitian for getting me a room at the Academia Sinica in Taiwan. Mahalo to my colleague and friend Chen Zhongping, to Daniel Cole at the University of Hawai'i Center for Chinese Studies, to Mark Tan at Stanford, and to the librarians at the East Asian Language Collection of the Hoover Library.

In Taiwan, I would like to thank Zhang Yufa at the Academia Sinica for his kindness and generosity, as well as Jiang Jing at the Guomindang Central Archives, and Hou Kunhong and the secretaries at the Guoshiguan. At the Institute of Modern History Library of the Academia Sinica, Su Bobo performed a tremendous amount of legwork on my behalf, and the staff of the Center for Academic Activities was ever courteous and helpful. My gratitude also to Bengt Olausson of the Sahlgan University Hospital for his enlightening conversations on the effects of morphine on the human body. Just as important were Kelly Yü and Bernard Wathen for their friendship and support in Taibei and all of the bowling alleys I frequented near the Academia Sinica to ward off insanity.

In the People's Republic of China, Chen Yongxiang, director of the Nanjing-Hopkins Center, rendered inestimable services and advice. Li Yuming of the Number Two Historical Archives likewise provided valuable assistance, and the energetic, ever-friendly staff at Di'er facilitated my research efforts immeasurably. Furthermore, I would like to express my thanks to Mary Buck of Harvard University for showing me the ropes in Nanjing and to Henry's Home Café near Nanjing University for great food at a reasonable price.

During the final stages of preparing this manuscript for publication, I was much indebted to the staff of the University of Hawai'i Press. I have the sincerest respect and appreciation for the contributions made by Patricia Crosby, Masako Ikeda, and Susan Stone. Kudos to Amy Amies at Indiana State University for making my amateurish hand-drawn maps suitable for publication.

Last but not least, I need to thank my friends Todd Henderson, Tony McGeehan, Gray McLaughlin, Rainer and Celine Buschmann, Tom Goodman, Barbara Arroyo, John and Jennifer Young, Max and Irene Hahn, and my siblings Shelly and Scott for their support and understanding during a chaotic period of my life.

Note on Romanization

TRANSLITERATING CHINESE CHARACTERS into forms appropriate for English-language text is complicated by the fact that in addition to the standard Mandarin dialect, many regional dialects are spoken in China. Moreover, several methods for carrying out such a task have been developed by both Western and Chinese scholars. In this book I primarily use the *pinyin* system developed in the People's Republic of China. However, for certain people and places I use more familiar Wade-Giles or Cantonese spellings. In such instances, the *pinyin* equivalent is placed in parentheses following these forms.

Weights and Measures

All weights given in tons are based on the British long ton unless otherwise indicated:

$$1 \text{ long ton} = 2,240 \text{ pounds}$$
$$1 \text{ metric ton} = 2,200 \text{ pounds}$$

All weights given in piculs *(dan)* correspond to the following weights in pounds:

1 picul = 133.3 pounds (before 1920s)
= 110 pounds (for National Agricultural Research Bureau data)
= 83.3 pounds (for opium, 1920s–1930s)

All weights given in *liang* correspond to the following weight in English ounces:

$$1 \text{ } liang = 1.33 \text{ ounces}$$

All measurements given in *mu* correspond to the following measurement in English acres:

$$1 \text{ } mu = 0.16 \text{ acre}$$

All monetary figures following the dollar sign are designated in Chinese dollars unless otherwise indicated:

$ = Mexican dollar (1920–1933)
= Nationalist currency (yuan) (1933–1937)

Introduction

THE MOST INTERESTING AND PERPLEXING relationship that ever evolved between a narcotic drug and a culture is the one involving opium and the Chinese people. Opium first appeared in the Middle Kingdom's historical record during the Han dynasty (206 B.C.–A.D. 220). Before the seventeenth century, opium was used as a remedy for diarrhea, malaria, and scores of other ailments. It was ingested orally and never viewed as a social vice or a public health concern by the imperial court.[1]

The benign image of opium changed radically with the arrival of the "red-haired barbarians" from Europe. In the final decades of the Ming dynasty (1368–1644), American tobacco was introduced to China by Portuguese, Spanish, and Dutch sailors frequenting both sides of the Taiwan Strait. The practices of smoking tobacco and cultivating the plant were imitated in southern China and soon spread throughout the empire. Around this time the Dutch began mixing opium with tobacco, and the habit was quickly adopted by the Chinese as well. At the end of the seventeenth century, the popularity of inhaling a blend of opium and tobacco had been supplanted by the smoking of unadulterated opium *(yapian)*.[2]

In 1729, Emperor Yongzheng issued the first opium prohibition edict. Although it technically outlawed the drug, sales and smoking for medicinal purposes were nevertheless legal. The edict's ambiguity and hypocrisy (opium imports were still taxed) precipitated lax enforcement.[3] In the half-century following Yongzheng's proscription, opium smoking proliferated in conjunction with rising imports and expanding domestic cultivation. Beijing increasingly

viewed inhaling opium as a pernicious vice and trafficking in the narcotic a serious criminal offense. As a result, Emperor Jiaqing renewed all preexisting
edicts with harsher penalties for offenders in 1796 and in 1799 promulgated a
new edict that unambiguously prohibited the importation, cultivation, and use
of opium.[4]

During the late eighteenth and early nineteenth centuries, ever-growing
quantities of opium imported from India provided the means for British merchants to reverse a chronic trade imbalance with China. The lucrative contraband trade united "barbarian" merchants with Chinese officials, merchants, and
criminal elements. Thus, the dragon throne was besieged by the related crises of
foreign contamination, growing addiction, and the alarming exodus of silver to
Western merchants who flagrantly defied the laws of the Celestial Empire.
Additional anti-opium edicts in the early 1800s proved equally ineffective.

The flooding of China with silver—most of it mined in the Americas—in
exchange for silk, porcelains, and tea over the course of three centuries had
dramatically altered the nature of imperial finances. In the 1570s, the Single-
Whip tax system was adopted, specifying that all tax payments be made in
units of silver.[5] Land taxes, the largest source of state income, were paid in
copper cash (*qian*) but calculated and transmitted to Beijing in silver taels
(ounces). Originally, the exchange rate between *qian* and taels was 1,000 to 1.
By 1838, however, the rate had risen to 1,650 to 1, resulting in higher payments
for peasants but no real growth in revenue for the state. Although part of the
reason for the exchange disparity was a debasing of copper coins by the Qing
court, opium smuggled into China from India siphoned off silver reserves and
accelerated the metal's appreciation in value.[6]

A combination of the failed anti-opium policies of the past and the troubling
economic conditions of the 1830s set the stage for the first modern debate on the
question of prohibition versus legalization of an illicit drug. During 1836–1838,
proposals on both sides of the issue were solicited by the Emperor Daoguang.
Presenting the argument for legalization was Xu Naiji, vice-president of the
Sacrificial Court. Echoing the views expressed by officials in Canton (Guangzhou), Xu underscored the loss of silver bullion as China's greatest long-term
threat. Under Xu's plan, opium would carry a minimal tax and be sold only by
barter, thereby halting the exodus of silver. Laws against domestic cultivation
would be relaxed in order to curtail foreign imports. Native opium, Xu argued,
was less potent and therefore less addictive. Even though commoners would be
permitted to indulge the habit, smoking by officials, scholars, and soldiers
would be strictly forbidden.[7]

Among those favoring complete prohibition on purely moral grounds were Huang Juezi and Lin Zexu (Lin Tse-hsü). Huang Juezi advocated an extreme solution, asking the emperor to decree the death penalty for all addicts, traffickers, and cultivators.[8] But it was a memorial written by Lin Zexu in July 1838 that caught Emperor Daoguang's eye. Lin, then governor-general of Hubei and Hunan, recommended a state policy combining terror and compassion to eradicate the scourge of opium. All addicts would be given a one-year grace period to be cured of the habit or else face execution at the end of that time. The state would open drug treatment facilities to assist addicts and divide the year into quarters, increasing the severity of punishment at the end of each period to induce compliance among recalcitrant smokers. In Canton, the root of the evil, the traffickers—native and foreign alike—would be dealt with more harshly. Summary imprisonment and capital punishment would be enforced against all those who sold or smuggled opium, regardless of nationality.[9] Emperor Daoguang found Lin's method most appealing, and in early 1839 Lin was appointed imperial commissioner for frontier defense and dispatched to Canton. The ensuing confrontation with Great Britain over the drug trade resulted in the Opium War of 1839–1842 and the humiliating Treaty of Nanjing.

Ironically, the legality of the opium trade was not addressed until some two decades later under the 1858 Treaty of Tianjin and the 1860 Convention of Beijing. A duty of 30 taels was placed on every *dan* (also called the picul, approximately 133.3 pounds) imported to China. The Zhefu Convention of 1876 and the Addendum of 1885 increased the duties to 110 taels per *dan*. By the 1870s, however, the native product was outcompeting foreign opium in the national market. At the height of domestic cultivation in 1905–1906, China produced perhaps seven-eighths of the total world output, providing windfall profits for farmers, merchants, and officials.[10]

The reasons behind the dramatic increase in native production during the last decades of the nineteenth century were economic and patriotic. As Lin Man-houng has documented, China's domestic economy was in shambles following the devastations of the Taiping, Nian, and Muslim insurrections between 1850 and the early 1870s. An unforeseen consequence was that importation of the drug from India was severely disrupted. Chinese farmers soon addressed the supply side of the predicament by planting poppies. In the late 1870s, indigenous production of opium spurred the growth of inter-regional trade networks and functioned as an integrative force for rebuilding the domestic economy.[11] Undoubtedly, another reason was that smoking

Chinese-grown opium could be viewed as a way to strike back at the "foreign devil" at a time when China was increasingly besieged by Western imperial powers.

In the 1880s, foreign missionaries began expressing concern for the destructive effects of opium on Chinese society. At the turn of the century, Qing government officials, returned students who had studied abroad, and Chinese Christians added their voices for a prohibition against opium.[12] The antidrug chorus drew on Confucian morality, Chinese nationalism, and Christian ethics, and the Manchu court responded to it in September 1906 by issuing an anti-opium edict. This ten-year plan called for a phased reduction of the acreage under poppy cultivation and the registration of addicts to monitor consumption. Authors of the plan estimated that 30 to 40 percent of the population were opium smokers.[13]

For the ten-year plan to succeed, the government needed the cooperation of foreign powers, especially Great Britain, which continued to ship large quantities of opium from India to China. Accordingly, the Qing and British governments agreed that effective 1 January 1908, Britain would reduce the importation of Indian opium by 10 percent a year until it ceased altogether in tandem with Qing poppy eradication efforts.[14] After a trial period of three years, the two governments signed a revised agreement to end all Indian imports by 1917, at which time the cultivation, sale, and use of the narcotic was to have been completely prohibited. Complementing the Sino-British effort, the Qing and Republican governments reached anti-opium accords with other foreign nations between 1908 and 1914. During these years, central and local authorities achieved impressive results suppressing the trade and consumption to nonhazardous levels. Even though there was some slackening of enforcement associated with the dislocations caused by the 1911 Revolution, the policy of prohibition survived mostly intact.

Despite this progress, in 1917–1918 large-scale poppy cultivation reappeared, and by 1922 China was producing more than 80 percent of the world's opium.[15] At the Geneva opium conferences sponsored by the League of Nations in 1924–1925, the Chinese delegation walked out in protest and refused to sign an international accord that legalized state-controlled sales of the narcotic in Asia. The central government's policy of de jure prohibition notwithstanding, the opium trade flourished with the complicity and encouragement of local officials throughout the nation.

In the politically unstable milieu of the Warlord Era (1916–1928) and the Nanjing Decade (1927–1937), the Guomindang (National[ist] Party) undertook the daunting tasks of national unification and state building. Following the First Nationalist-Communist alliance of 1923, the Guomindang simultaneously plunged into the vortex of warlord politics and stepped into China's opium quagmire. How the Nationalists reacted to the drug problem and the factors that determined that reaction are the focus of this book.

Before embarking on an investigation of Guomindang opium policy, a thorough study of the narco-economy (i.e., the opium economy) and its effects on state-society relations is essential for providing the proper context. Chapter 1 examines the total economic impact of the opium trade on multiple levels. Peasants, merchants, bankers, warlords, soldiers, government officials, and underworld gangs or secret societies all played prominent roles in the addictive drama that unfolded in the 1920s and 1930s. Chapter 2 takes a holistic approach to comprehending the diverse effects of opium on Chinese society. The physical, psychological, and sociocultural factors involved in acquiring and treating the habit are elucidated, in addition to its consequences for Chinese family life and the social forces working for and against state-sponsored prohibition movements.

Chapters 3 to 5 survey the dynamic evolution of Guomindang opium policy from 1924 to 1937. The twists and turns of policy-making shine a much-needed light on previously unexplored dimensions of the interaction between state and society during this turbulent historical epoch. There have been many assumptions, innuendos, and rumors regarding Nationalist involvement in the opium trade since the 1930s. Based solidly on archival sources and allowing the facts to speak for themselves, this study seeks to ventilate the conjectural haze that has shrouded the subject. It also endeavors to comprehend and analyze Guomindang attempts to deal realistically with an intractable issue under the most inhospitable domestic and international circumstances. Moreover, this study is intended to go beyond a gestalt examination of the relationship between China's narco-political economy and society. In a larger comparative framework, the successes, failures, compromises, and hypocrisies evident in Nationalist antinarcotics strategies could provide valuable lessons to nations that are currently grasping for solutions to their own narcotics paradox.

1 China's Narco-Economy in the 1920s and 1930s

CHINESE FARMERS HAVE CULTIVATED the plant known as *Papaver somniferum* in Latin and *yingsuhua* in Mandarin for at least a millennium. By 1900, the planting of opium was so widespread that it was jokingly referred to as the national flower *(guohua)*.[1] Both late Qing and early Republican governments had virtually eliminated poppy fields from the Middle Kingdom between 1906 and 1917, but opium made a rapid comeback during the Warlord Era and continued to be China's leading cash crop until the early years of Communist rule.

Peasants and Poppies

Peasants have traditionally cultivated the five grains *(wugu)*, which in the twentieth century were wheat, rice, barley, millet, and sorghum *(gaoliang)*. Another "grain," euphemistically referred to by farmers as "black rice" *(heimi)* must be added to that list. After military strongman Yuan Shikai's death in 1916 and the rise thereafter of "warlordism" or "militarism," by the mid-1920s poppy cultivation flourished on a scale comparable to China's peak producing years of 1900–1906, variously estimated between 9,000 and 35,000 tons.[2] At the Geneva opium conferences in 1924–1925, the International Anti-Opium Association of Beijing reported that China was growing at least 15,000 tons of opium annually, which accounted for about 88 percent of global production.[3]

By that time, farmers in almost every province in the republic were cultivating the poppy. Reports of opium planting came from a variety of sources, Chinese and foreign, and by cross-referencing the information in those sources it is possible to identify the regions involved and rank them as sites of heavy, medium, or light cultivation (see Map 1). The centers of heavy cultivation were in the provinces of Sichuan, Yunnan, and Guizhou; those of medium cultivation in Shaanxi, Gansu, Rehe (Jehol), Fujian, Anhui, Henan, Heilongjiang, and Jilin (Kirin); and those of light cultivation in Hubei, Hunan, Suiyuan, Chaha'er, Jiangsu, Xikang, Guangdong, Shandong, Jiangxi, Ningxia, Xinjiang, Hebei, Liaoning, Zhejiang, and Guangxi. Elsewhere, there was no cultivation, or at least no evidence of cultivation.[4]

The poppy has a life span of one farming season; in other words, it is an annual. In full bloom, its flowers are arrayed in a rainbow of colors—red, purple, white, yellow, and pink—that beautifully conceal the dangers of its addictive fruit. Owing to the diversity of climatic and topographic conditions in a nation as large as China, planting and harvesting schedules varied widely. For

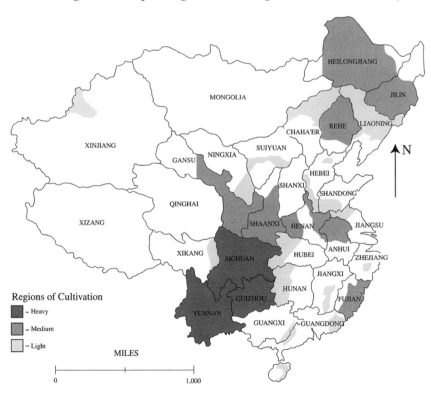

Map 1. Opium Cultivation in Republican China, 1924–1937

example, in Fujian province planting might occur any time between August
and the following January, while in Guizhou planting normally occurred in
late November to early December and harvesting in late March to early
April.[5] Because of the shorter growing season in Manchuria (Liaoning, Jilin,
and Heilongjiang), Rehe, Suiyuan, Ningxia, and parts of Gansu and Shaanxi,
farmers sowed poppy seed in the spring and reaped its yield in September.

Poppies required rich land and heavy fertilization. Manure, night soil (human waste), soybean cakes, and ammonium sulphate were the preferred soil
enhancers. Intensive application of earth enrichment materials was essential
for optimum results, as military regulations posted in 1923 for poppy farmers
in southern Fujian indicated.[6] On the average, farmers fertilized their opium
fields three times a season, compared to twice per season for a crop like wheat.[7]

Cultivating opium was very labor-intensive. According to John Buck's data
from the period from 1929 to 1933, the number of working days farmers spent
per crop per acre was as follows: 129 for tea, 109 for opium, 88 for tobacco, 82
for rice, 40 for millet, 35 for sorghum, 26 for wheat, and 23 for corn.[8] Harvesting required the efforts of an entire farming family, often with assistance from
temporary laborers. Since China had a surplus of cheap labor, swarms of migrants descended like locusts into opium-producing regions at harvest time.[9]
When the prized fruit was ripe, workers did not cut down the plant but incised the bolls or pods of the poppy at dusk, and a white, viscous sap oozed out
of the incision and clung to the bolls, turning a dark brown color after exposure to the air. Early the next morning before dawn, the workers collected this
brown sap in earthenware pots and repeated these procedures until the bolls
were emptied of their narcotic nectar. Expert cutters (who received higher
wages than other workers) could drain a poppy in three to four days, but most
workers and farmers took seven to nine days or even longer to complete the
process.[10] Harvest time thus lasted no more than a week or two.

The worst enemy of the poppy cultivator was inclement weather. Drought
and hailstorms might ruin a crop, but the worst case was rain storms during
harvest time. Rain not only washed sap away before it could be gathered, but
also adulterated the quality and morphine content of what remained, thereby
making it difficult or impossible to sell.[11]

Each *mu* of land (about one-sixth of an acre) yielded on average 50 *liang,* or
4.16 pounds, although yields as high as 200 to 300 *liang* sometimes occurred on
the richest and best-cultivated plots in Sichuan and Yunnan.[12] Peasants
wasted no part of the poppy plant. Although the *yingsuhua*'s stupefying syrup
was its most profitable attribute, farmers gathered the leaves of the plants to

feed the pigs, used the dried stalks for fuel, and threshed the pods for poppy seed, which they pressed for oil, ground for food, or saved to plant next season.

Harvest time in the regions of heavy cultivation transformed normally sleepy villages into bustling, vibrant centers of social and economic activity. Peasants from all directions would besiege local market towns, and the streets would be congested with carts, baskets, and jars brimming with raw opium. Besides the migrant workers who flooded these areas, merchants of all sorts who specialized in certain niches of the narco-economy filled hotels, inns, restaurants, and teahouses to capacity. Other entrepreneurs vending everything from guns to *gaoliangjiu* (sorghum wine) gleefully plied their wares. Storytellers, fortune-tellers, traveling folk operas, and even a few famous theatrical companies would ride this wave of economic prosperity for as long as it lasted, readily accepting raw opium as payment for their services. Buddhist and Daoist priests begging for alms likewise found their bowls of salvation full of opium and narco-dollars.[13]

Farmer Rationale for Planting *Yingsuhua*

Farmers cultivated opium for two reasons: they generally earned more from "black rice" than from other crops; and everyone from landlords, merchants, and military and civil officials to bandits and *tuhao lieshen* (local bullies and evil gentry) encouraged or coerced them to do so. In Anhui province in 1928, peasants were asked why they grew opium rather than wheat, the traditional winter crop in the region. Some of the farmers responded that, during the latter part of the third moon (April), their supply of wheat was usually exhausted, but with a *mu* or two of poppy plants, they could always find someone to advance them wheat to be repaid in opium. Others answered that with several *mu* of poppies they earned extra income to buy new tools and other things. Still others said simply that they had no other way to clear their debts.[14]

Comparing the retail prices of grain and opium further illuminates the thinking behind a farmer's decision to cultivate poppy. In the primary and secondary growing regions and markets during the 1920s and 1930s, one *liang* of raw opium was worth approximately one Chinese (Mexican) dollar. For that amount, a person could purchase 30 to 40 *jin* of husked rice. If just one *mu* of land was planted in poppy, then the 50 *liang* of raw opium could be exchanged for close to 2,000 *jin,* or over 2,600 pounds, of rice.[15]

In 1929, the National Anti-Opium Association sent investigators into 131 counties in eighteen provinces to study the opium problem and collect data concerning the preceding year. They found that the ratio of farmers who planted "black rice" voluntarily to those who did so involuntarily was 25 to 3 (see Appendix Table 1). Although this survey included only a few counties in the heavily producing regions of Sichuan, Yunnan, and Guizhou, the information it contains corresponds to the oral response from a majority of farmers that they could earn more from opium than from any other crop.[16]

Farmers who cultivated opium poppies generally paid higher land taxes than those who did not, though in some areas and some years (between 1917 and 1922) they escaped taxes altogether. The tax on opium had various names such as *miaojuan* (poppy-sprout tax), *yanmiao fajin* (poppy-sprout fine), *zhongyan paizhaoshui* (license tax for planting opium), *diaochafei* (investigation fee), *tianfushui* (land surtax), among others.[17] The agency responsible for collecting the tax likewise had different names in different places but was most often called the Jinyanju (Opium Suppression Bureau), whose name preserved the fiction that opium was de jure illegal. The bureau usually assessed the tax according to the number of *mu* under cultivation, but in places like Sichuan the number of poppy stalks was sometimes the basis of assessment.[18] The land tax on other crops such as wheat or rice was the equivalent of $1 to $3 per *mu* in the late 1920s; it was about $8 for poppy. In some cases, the latter exceeded $30, depending on the rapaciousness of local authorities.[19] This *yin-yang* relationship between profits and taxes was often the principal factor behind individual decisions to plant or not to plant *yingsuhua*.

Republican warlords did all they could to encourage poppy cultivation. To illustrate, in September 1927 Zhang Zongchang (the "Dog-Meat General") established an opium monopoly in Shandong province under the name Quansheng Jinyan Zongju (Provincial Opium Suppression Bureau). Posted on the doors of its branch offices was this notice:

> People of all counties—how much opium do you want to plant? Just report it and pay a small fine on each *mu* of land—$15 to $20—and you can plant as much as you want. If you do this, the people will prosper, the provisions for the troops will be sufficient, opium from foreign nations and other provinces will not flood into Shandong, and those drugs such as morphine "white pills" will gradually be eliminated.[20]

In Zhang's mind, farmers who planted opium were thus patriotic citizens of Shandong. They were also antinarcotics crusaders whose harvest would save the province from *waisheng* (other provinces') opium and harder drugs, and whose taxes would strengthen Shandong against outside attacks.

Farmers forced into cultivating opium were usually at the mercy of warlords or civil or military authorities who desperately needed revenue. In areas where these circumstances prevailed, coercion was pronounced. Other predators, whose activities varied widely according to local circumstances, included bandits, landlords, merchants, *tuhao lieshen,* and village headmen.

Military authorities who cajoled peasants to sow poppies were especially notorious in Sichuan and Fujian between 1924 and 1928, the crescendo of the so-called Warlord Era. During 1924 in Chongqing, Sichuan, warlord Liu Chengxun ordered that the county must devote 100,000 *mu* of land to opium and that areas deficient in poppy cultivation be penalized. Liu also ordered military commanders to dispatch troops to each village and announce that their men would be living off the people of the village until the farmers there paid their opium taxes.[21] Several years later in Fujian, there were reports of violent confrontations between peasants opposed to planting poppies and troops sent to collect opium taxes. In the counties of Putian, Hui'an, and Guankou, warlord soldiers either shot, decapitated, or burned alive peasants who opposed the collection of opium levies.[22]

In some areas authorities disguised the forced cultivation of *yingsuhua* in the form of increased land taxes. When the taxes reached a certain level, only poppies could generate enough income to pay them. This tactic was especially popular in Shaanxi, Gansu, Sichuan, Yunnan, Guizhou, and Fujian. In 1927, authorities in Shaanxi decreed that farmers in every county had to devote a specified acreage to poppies, depending on the size of the county and the amount of arable land in it. Whether individual farmers planted poppies or not, they still had to pay land taxes at opium-cultivation levels. Those who grew opium paid a tax called the *"fakuan"* (fine) to Fakuanju (Fine Collection Bureaus) for "illegally" cultivating the drug. Those who chose not to plant poppy paid a *baidikuan* (barren lands *tankuan*) amounting to the equivalent of $33 per *mu*, which was three times higher than the "fine."[23] Similarly, peasants who failed to plant *yingsuhua* in Wanxian, Sichuan, had to pay a *lanjuan* (laziness levy) that was much higher than the poppy-sprout tax.[24] In both instances, since most peasants could not afford to pay the *baidikuan* or the *lanjuan,* they had no choice but to grow opium.

Other extortionists, whether county magistrates, village headmen, or bandits, developed their own methods of coercion. County magistrates dispatched runners from their yamen (government office) to villages under their jurisdiction instructing peasants to plant opium. In Hubei's Suixian county, the magistrate's yamen provided poppy seeds for the peasants and then taxed them at rates four times higher than for land planted in other crops.[25] Landlords charged oppressive rates of interest on loans to sharecroppers planting poppies and then forced their tenants to sell them their harvest at the lowest prices possible. Bandits who infested the backwaters of Henan, Guizhou, Shandong, Fujian, and other opium-growing regions intimidated peasants into cultivating the drug wherever they could. Thus, exploitation and opium profits coexisted and indeed fed off each other where circumstances permitted.

A recent study by Lucien Bianco investigating the reactions of opium growers to eradication campaigns and unreasonable taxes shines more light on the subject. According to Bianco, although there were scattered reports of peasants resisting orders to cultivate poppy, they were a very distinct minority. Farmers were far more likely to take up arms against local authorities when the latter group attempted to uproot poppy plants, thereby directly threatening the peasants' livelihood. Official avarice in the form of excessive taxation also sparked several violent revolts by opium farmers in the early 1930s, the most sanguinary incidents occurring in Anhui province.[26] When peasant economic interests were directly threatened in the form of enforced prohibition or extortionate levies, they defended their decision—violently if necessary—to sow and reap this valuable cash crop. All things being equal, even when coercion was in evidence, one did not have to twist the farmer's arm too hard to ensure compliance.

Quantifying Opium Performance

Although the data are incomplete and even fragmentary, all of them point to the significance of poppy cultivation in Chinese agriculture. Appendix Table 2 reports the yearly production of opium from 1924 to 1937, divided into high and low estimates. The estimate of at least 15,000 tons by the International Anti-Opium Association for 1924 is the most widely accepted figure for the period of this study. The parallel estimates of the National Anti-Opium Association for 1924 and 1927 appear to be too low. The national association invariably understated the culpability of the Chinese in the opium trade and thus overstated the responsibility of foreigners. It therefore underestimated the yearly production of the drug in China. Dr. Wu Liande (Wu Lien-teh), a founding member of the national association and the source for the original estimate of 7,500 tons in 1924, approximated Chinese production in 1930 at a minimum of 11,875 tons. The reason for the disparity in these two figures was not so much a dramatic increase in opium production between 1924 and 1930 as an increase in the reliability of the statistics.[27]

Similarly, the production figures quoted by Nanjing authorities for the years 1934 to 1937 are excessively low, in part because they exclude the Japanese-occupied areas of Manchuria and Rehe, where opium production sharply increased between 1931 and 1937.[28] When the Guomindang instituted its six-year plan to eliminate opium production in 1934, there was a significant reduction in a few areas of middle and light production, but not enough to make the low official figures acceptable. Perhaps the most reliable numbers for the 1930s were made by U.S. consulates, who estimated that in 1935 China produced 12,000 to 18,000 metric tons of raw opium.[29]

Despite the inconsistencies, it is still possible to use the data constructively. They suggest, conservatively, that the average yearly production of opium was in the range of 12,000 to 15,000 tons from 1924 to 1937. A minimum estimate of 12,000 tons thus seems reasonable, though actual production may have been double this amount in certain years. Tables 3 to 8 (see Appendix) represent the estimated annual production of other important crops in China from 1931 to 1937 and can serve as a basis for comparing the performance of opium in the agricultural sector of the economy.

From these data, it becomes readily apparent why farmers were willing to plant a few *mu* of poppies despite the higher taxes. For the year 1929, the average net profit of $38.50 per *mu* (see Appendix Table 6) exceeded that derived from other crops. By comparison, Lynda Bell estimated that farmers in southern Jiangsu in 1929 had a "net income" per *mu* of $12.72 for rice, $12.99 for glutinous rice, and $3.73 for wheat.[30] Both sets of figures exclude the payment of land taxes, which averaged $8 and reached as high as $25 per *mu* for opium, compared to just $1 to $3 for wheat and rice. Nevertheless, on average farmers earned more per *mu* planting poppy than planting other crops in spite of the higher land taxes, rents, and labor costs incurred.

There were many variables not apparent in the data that could drastically alter the actual income of individual farmers. Opium prices fluctuated according to supply and demand, and in the heavy-producing regions of Sichuan, Yunnan, and Guizhou, prices received per *liang* were generally lower, while average yields were higher and average quality better than elsewhere. Yunnan opium, for example, had a reputation as being the best in China, and in 1925 peasants there received 80 to 90 cents per *liang* in Sichuan currency ($1 = U.S. 40 cents), while those in Sichuan and Guizhou received 50 to 60 cents and 40 cents, respectively.[31]

In addition, prices for crops were relatively high in 1929, but fell dramatically after 1931 owing to the appreciation in silver caused by the global economic depression. By 1933 prices were estimated to be 56 percent below what they had been in 1929.[32] Thus, while opium was a highly valued agricultural commodity that could produce windfall profits, it could just as easily produce impoverishment. That was true for other crops as well. What differentiated opium from the other crops, however, was higher production costs in the form of taxes and rents, over which farmers had no control. Yet despite the risks, many farmers were quite willing to take the gamble.

Opium and Famine

The hardships faced by Chinese farmers were plentiful. They were plagued by disasters both natural—drought, earthquakes, floods, migratory locusts, grasshoppers, early frosts, hailstorms—and of human origin—wars, marauding soldiers, bandits, and greedy bureaucrats. The worst calamities, among them the regular flooding of the Yangtze (Changjiang or Yangzi) and the Yellow River (Huanghe), and in some areas prolonged drought, often resulted in the deaths of millions of people. Surely such uncertainties helped encourage poppy cultivation.

When farmers planted poppy it usually replaced a grain crop such as wheat, rice, corn, or sorghum. According to Buck's data, peasant families consumed 50 to 75 percent of the grain and other food crops they produced.[33] Thus when a prolonged drought struck an area where poppy cultivation cut back food production, as in Yunnan, Guizhou, Sichuan, and Hunan in 1924–1926, the consequences could be disastrous. In the spring of 1925 famine conditions were the worst in Guizhou, where in the month of May approximately 3.5 million people were reportedly subsisting on grass and leaves. Conditions were so bad that some people offered to sell their children for handfuls of rice or corn, and reports of cannibalism circulated in a few towns and villages.[34] In the preceding winter so many farmers had planted opium to the neglect of grain crops that the resulting shortages of rice, corn, and wheat raised prices to levels beyond the ability of most peasants to buy them. Poppy cultivation was not the sole cause of this calamity, but it did demonstrate the potential risks of diverting large tracts of land from food crops to opium.

Edgar Snow, who was in China at the time, described the relationship between opium cultivation and famine during the mid-1930s. While traveling from Xi'an to Mao Zedong's "red redoubt" in Yan'an during 1936, he wrote:

Shensi [Shaanxi] had long been a noted opium province. During the great Northwest Famine [1928–1933], which a few years before had taken a toll of 3,000,000 lives, American Red Cross investigators attributed much of the tragedy to the cultivation of the poppy, forced upon the peasants by provincial monopolies controlled by greedy warlords. The best land being devoted to the poppy, in years of drought there was a serious shortage of millet, wheat and corn, the staple cereals of the Northwest.[35]

Military marauding, bad weather, and opium cultivation thus combined to create famine and amplify its effects. During the sustained period of continual warfare, increased opium production, and natural disasters between 1916 and 1937, the importation of food grains—including rice, wheat, and wheat flour—rose dramatically.[36] The annual total of such imports averaged 328,670 metric tons in 1916–1920, 1,295,560 metric tons a decade later, and 2,142,205 metric tons in 1931–1935 (see Appendix Table 9). If one accepts the estimate that 12,000 tons of opium withdrew at least 6,400,000 *mu* from the acreage available for grain cultivation, the resulting yearly shortfall in grain production was 421,343 metric tons of wheat or 1,059,891 metric tons of rice, or an average of 740,617 metric tons if these totals are combined. Consequently, if annual net food grain imports between 1921 and 1935 averaged 1,251,778 metric tons, then more than half (58 percent) of the shortfall between domestic production and imports resulted from the diversion of farmlands from grain to poppies.

Varieties of Opium on the Market

Opium was commonly referred to as *"tu"* (earth or dirt), because in its raw form it was dark brown in color and had a hard, dry texture. Favored domestic varieties were produced in the provinces of Yunnan *(yuntu)*, Guizhou *(qiantu)*, Sichuan *(chuantu)*, and Gansu *(gantu)*.[37] Within the growing regions, opium was normally named after the county from which it hailed, although in Shaanxi local produce was divided into *shanyan* (mountain opium) and *pingyuanyan* (plains opium), the latter selling for 33 percent more in retail markets.[38]

Most of the Indian opium exported to China was of three types: *datu* (big opium) from Patna, *xiaotu* (small opium) from Malwa, and *geda* from Calcutta. Persian opium was called *"hongtu"* (red opium) after its color, while "black rice" from the vast expanse of land along the Manchuria-U.S.S.R. border sold under the name of *biantu* (border opium).

Opium imported from abroad, especially Indian varieties, was usually more expensive than domestic products. An incomplete list of prices for raw opium in Shanghai in 1930 reveals this trend:[39]

datu	$18 per *liang*
geda	$6 per *liang*
hongtu	$3 per *liang*
yuntu	$2.60–2.80 per *liang*
chuantu	$1.50–1.60 per *liang*
biantu	$1.30–1.40 per *liang*

Opium underwent several stages of processing before it appeared on the market. After processors sorted the opium sap by color and quality, they placed it in a large tub and stirred it for several hours. Once the stirred sap dried sufficiently, it was molded into flattened cakes weighing between 10 and 50 *liang* and called *"shengtu"* (raw opium).[40] *Gantu* sold in neighboring Suiyuan, for example, was packaged in rectangular cakes about nine inches long, six inches wide, and just over an inch thick, weighing 50 *liang* and valued at $100.[41] In these shapes, bulk quantities went to wholesale and resale markets.

In preparation for smoking, *shengtu* underwent a meticulous distillation process, during which time the drug lost approximately 40 percent of its original weight.[42] The raw cakes were first dissolved in water, turning into a dark, viscous soup. Processors skimmed off the flotsam and poured what remained into a copper pot that boiled over a low flame for ten hours or more. The soupy substance simmered until it had a molasses-like consistency, known as *regao* or *tugao* (opium paste), at which point it was ready for smoking. Undercooked, the paste was spongy and unsmokable. Overcooked, it had a burnt, unsatisfactory flavor when inhaled.[43]

Opium Merchants

In Republican China, there was ample opportunity for people from all walks of life to engage in one or more aspects of the opium trade, which had penetrated into all facets of Chinese society. This reality was reflected in a 1929 National Anti-Opium Association survey that characterized those involved in the buying and selling of the drug (see Appendix Table 10). Although the sampling was small, it provides a suggestive historical snapshot of the people who participated in the illicit commerce. Merchants, civil servants, soldiers, and individuals involved in organized crime constituted about 70 percent of the people surveyed and were the most significant contributors to the growth and sustenance of the opium trade.

The primus inter pares among this group was the *yanshang* (opium merchant). There was a hierarchy of merchants who specialized in the various levels of production, transportation, and sale of opium in China. After farmers finished collecting the saplike brown resin from their poppy crops, they commonly sold the resin to merchants known as *"gunzishang"* (rolling merchants). These merchants were active middlemen in tying together the economies of the countryside and the market towns. In some provinces, for example, Sichuan, the *gunzishang* contracted with individual farmers to buy their crop, making a down payment on the purchase price at the time of the agreement.[44] In other regions, *gunzishang* converged on small villages during the harvest season, going house to house buying resin offered for sale by individual farmers, or they accosted peasants en route to larger market towns. The rolling merchants then resold the resin to merchants with enough capital to deal with wholesalers in the large towns or to transport the drug over long distances. They earned their nickname by going to different towns and accumulating ever larger quantities of opium, increasing the amount of profit to be made by "rolling" it back and forth in the rural areas (much as a snowball is made larger by rolling it in the snow).[45] Thus, rolling merchants filled the role of middlemen or brokers between farmers and more affluent opium merchants.

A more important category of entrepreneur in the opium business were the *pifashang* or *hangshang* (wholesale merchants). These merchants had considerable capital and engaged in the buying and selling of raw opium on a large scale. After purchasing sizable quantities, they subdivided the resin into grades based on color, texture, and smell, and then molded it into flat cakes of *shengtu*. These cakes would then be placed in wooden crates containing between 500 and 1,000 *liang* to be sold at wholesale prices to the transport merchants.[46] *Pifashang* also vended smaller amounts to local retailers and kept the native population of smokers well supplied.

Those merchants who undertook shipping vast quantities of the drug over long distances, known primarily as *yunshang* (transport merchants), *yanbang* (opium syndicates), or *zuozhuang* (receiving merchants), were the most highly capitalized of all *yanshang*.[47] The quantities of opium they handled were in the hundreds to thousands of *dan* (1 *dan* equaled 1,000 *liang*), which required large amounts of capital. Such merchants were often partnerships or joint-stock companies. The Guangyun Gongsi in Kunming, the Jiyi Zhuanyun Gongsi in Yichang and Hankou, and the Sanxing Gongsi in Shanghai were examples of such partnerships. Many of the *yunshang* owned and operated wholesale and warehouse firms to facilitate the distribution and sales of their merchandise. Generally speaking, the merchants behind these syndicates were from bustling commercial centers such as Canton, Shanghai, Chongqing, or Hankou. They established firms *(yanzhuang, zuozhuang,* or *yanhao)* in their home cities and then branch offices *(fenzhuang* or *fenhao)* in key production or marketing towns.[48] In terms of both the scale and the scope of their operations, these merchants were regarded as the *yapian dawang* (opium kings) of China.

On the lowest rungs of the opium sales ladder were *lingshoushang* (retail merchants) and *regaoshang* (boiled-opium merchants). Retail merchants purchased opium from wholesale or transport merchants and sold it to the boiled-opium merchants or sold it to their own customers as prepared *regao*. The popular nickname for retail merchants was *"lingjianshang"* (merchants who use scissors to cut opium into little pieces).[49]

Boiled-opium merchants—as their name indicates—processed raw opium into its smokable, pastelike *(gao)* form. In many cities, such as Hankou and Chongqing, they boiled the opium paste on the street in front of their shops and in view of their customers.[50] *Regaoshang* gained notoriety, however, as the proprietors of opium dens, which operated under a babel of names, including *"yanguan"* (opium den), *"tanxinchu"* (discussion parlor), *"tugaodian"* (boiled-opium shop), *"yashi"* (private room, as in a restaurant), *"yanziwo"* (swallow's nest), or the oxymoronic *"jieyansuo"* (opium treatment clinic).[51]

Opium dens cultivated clientele on the basis of status or social class. High-class dens were elegantly decorated, expensive, and usually staffed with attractive female attendants who prepared the pipes for their customers. Dens geared to the lower classes provided only the basics: opium paste, lamps, pipes, and mats to recline on. There were even mobile opium dens *(liudong yanguan)* that serviced the ropemen who pulled junks through the difficult rapids along the upper Yangtze in Hubei and Sichuan provinces.[52]

The Chinese have an old saying *"wushang bujian"* (there isn't a merchant who isn't unscrupulous). Opium merchants were extremely deceptive—or creative, depending on one's viewpoint—with respect to increasing their profits at the expense of their comrades and customers. The most common deception was to adulterate pure opium with other materials. The filler was usually date or jujube paste for color and pig or cow rinds chopped up and blended together for texture. Merchants would steam the unadulterated raw opium and cut it into smaller pieces, then add the filler as the patties were re-molded by hand into their original shape. Another method was to cut a hole into the *shengtu*, scrape out a goodly amount of pure product, replace it with filler, and seal the hole with part of what was extracted.[53]

Statistical information on all of the groups just discussed is incomplete and of problematic reliability. In a 1928 survey, the National Anti-Opium Association identified three categories of opium entrepreneur operating in the coastal city of Xiamen (Amoy), Fujian, and offered some basic information about each category. The first category, *zuozhuang* (receiving merchants), numbered between twenty and thirty firms, with capitalization ranging from a low of $300,000 to $400,000 to a high of $2 million to $3 million. The second category was *pifa* (wholesale merchants), who purchased their goods from the *zuozhuang*. There were more than one hundred *pifa* firms operating in the city, each with capital of about $100,000. The third category was *yanguan* (opium dens). The dens bought from the wholesalers, boiled opium for customers, and provided smoking paraphernalia. The National Anti-Opium Association estimated that seven hundred licensed dens were operating in Xiamen at the time of the survey.[54] Although these data represented only one city, Xiamen can serve as a microcosm of the trade in large municipalities throughout China.

Transit Routes and Regional Markets

Since the most intensive cultivation of "black rice" occurred in China's interior and the biggest markets were in cities situated along the coast and in the Yangtze River valley, transporting opium was an essential and lucrative part of the business. In Republican China, many aquatic arteries—especially the Yangtze and the Xijiang (West River)—were flooded with opium. It may be no exaggeration to say that, at the height of the trade, there was not a single steamer or junk plying the Yangtze that did not have some quantity of opium on board.[55] In fact, the primary activity of the Chinese navy at the time was to protect maritime shipments. Little wonder critics called its fleet of vessels the "Opium Navy."[56]

Transporting opium overland by rail or by animal and coolie caravans was also important. Railways were cheap and efficient, especially in such provinces as Manchuria, Hebei, Henan, Shandong, Jiangsu, Hubei, and Hunan, where trunk lines connected major cities, or in Yunnan, where a single line linked Kunming with the French colonial port-city of Haiphong. Animal and coolie caravans were more widespread in the southwestern and northwestern provinces of Yunnan, Guizhou, Sichuan, Shaanxi, and Gansu, where the terrain was often difficult and the roads poor. Owing to the underdeveloped state of transportation in the rugged countrysides of China, opium's high value per unit of weight made it an ideal export product for those provinces.[57]

To simplify the complicated networks of water, rail, and road routes that connected production areas with key market towns, China can be divided into three "opium macroregions"—to apply G. William Skinner's terminology loosely (see Map 2).[58] Among these three regions, the most significant arteries ran along the Yangtze River, stretching from Sichuan to Shanghai, and from

Map 2. China's "Opium Macroregions" in the 1920s and 1930s

Yunnan and Guizhou through Guangxi province following the West River and its tributaries to Canton. Control over these two routes and corresponding macroregions was essential to Nanjing's state-building and political centralization efforts after 1928.

The Yangtze River Region

The Yangtze was by far the principal route in terms of shipping tonnage. During the 1920s, opium *lijin* stations (the *lijin* [*likin*] was an internal transit tax) dotted the banks of the river from Sichuan to the terminus near Shanghai. *Lijin* stations, also called opium suppression bureaus, collected taxes on opium in transit for warlords who controlled the major ports along the river. The key *lijin* stations along the upper and middle Yangtze were located at Yibin, Chongqing, Fuling, Wanxian, Yichang, and Hankou (see Map 3).

The largest producer of opium in Republican China, Sichuan exported some 6,000 tons through the Yangtze River route in 1925 alone.[59] Opium provided Sichuan's numerous warlords with ample revenue to sustain their interprovincial wars well into the 1930s. Naturally, control of shipments to markets downriver was vital to their survival. The warlord Liu Wenhui at Yibin operated a fleet of four small steamers under the name of the Xinhua Shiye Gongsi (New China Industrial Company) and monopolized the transport of opium downriver to Chongqing.[60] In similar fashion, Liu Xiang— who dominated the regions surrounding Chongqing—purchased steamships

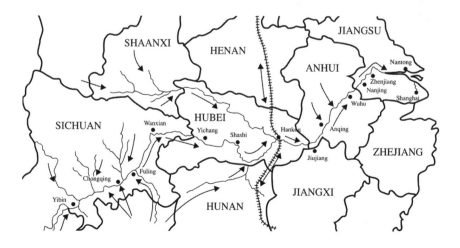

Map 3. The Yangtze River Route

and organized the Minsheng Shiye Gongsi (People's Livelihood Industrial Company), which transported about half of the 500 tons taxed and exported to Yichang each month.[61]

Yichang is located in western Hubei, less than one hundred miles from the Sichuan border. A dozen or so companies there were in the business of transporting and warehousing opium. The largest of them was the Jiyi Zhuanyun Gongsi (Transport Company for the Succor of Yichang), which maintained two large warehouses and operated at least three steamers on the Yichang-to-Hankou run. In the early 1920s, the Jiyi Zhuanyun Gongsi collected opium transit taxes for local warlords. To increase government income, in 1924 the Junjing Jianchachu (Military-Police Supervisory Office), headquartered in Hankou, established a station in Yichang to supervise merchant tax collection.[62] In 1925, the *lijin* station brought in approximately $8,400,000 for local authorities.[63]

If Shanghai was the world's narco-capital in the 1920s, Hankou was a close second. Situated at the confluence of the Han and Yangtze rivers, Hankou was the biggest wholesale market and transshipment point for opium coming from the areas of heavy and medium cultivation in the west. As the terminus of the Beijing-Hankou Railway, the city also received opium from Shaanxi, Gansu, Manchuria, Rehe, and Henan.

In 1928, there were 60 major opium transport and wholesale companies, 600 retail firms, and over 1,700 licensed opium dens operating in Hankou.[64] The agency responsible for collecting transit taxes was the Military-Police Supervisory Office, established by military governor Xiao Yaonan in 1924, who was also a major stockholder of the Jiyi Zhuanyun Gongsi.[65] This *lijin* station provided revenue for the warlord Wu Peifu, who at the time was fighting Zhang Zuolin in the Second Zhili-Fengtian War.[66] Opium taxes collected by the Military-Police Supervisory Office in Hankou and Yichang together generated perhaps $20 million to $30 million annually for military leaders in Hubei.[67] Another factor facilitating trade in Hankou was the Hanyang Arsenal, which sold weapons to Sichuan, Guizhou, and any other province's warlords in exchange for native produce.[68]

The final stage in the Yangtze River route was the leg from Hankou to Shanghai. Once shipments passed through Hankou, portions of the cargo were unloaded at Jiujiang in Jiangxi; Wuhu and Anqing in Anhui; and Nanjing, Zhenjiang, and Nantong in Jiangsu before traversing the Huangpu River to Shanghai. Additionally, ample amounts of Anhui product fed into the opium pipeline. Shanghai was not only the largest market for homegrown "dirt" coming down the Yangtze, but also the chief entrepôt for indigenous and foreign opium arriving from Canton, Qingdao, Dalian, Xiamen, Jilong (Keelung), Vladivostok, Hong Kong, Haiphong, Saigon, Calcutta, Bombay, Bushire, Istanbul, and other ports.

The route to the streets of Shanghai was more complicated than the distribution networks along the upper and middle Yangtze, which were largely under military control. The conspicuous involvement of secret societies and underworld groups, warlord rivalries that included pitched battles for control of Shanghai, and the presence of foreign-administered settlements in the municipality created a mercurial environment conducive to narcotics smuggling.

The three most prominent criminal organizations vying for control of drug trafficking along the lower Yangtze route were the Green Gang (Qingbang), the Red Gang (Hongbang or Hongmen), and the Brothers and Elders Society (Gelaohui).[69] At the time of the 1911 Revolution, the Green and Red gangs consolidated their power in the lower Yangtze region. As a result of expanding ties between the two factions, they became widely known as the Qinghongbang (Green-Red Gang). Their influence grew with the addition of members from the more powerful ranks of society, including the military, the police, the bureaucracy, and the professions. By the early 1920s, the secret societies and underworld syndicates had become synonymous with Shanghai's opium trade.[70]

The Brothers and Elders Society was active in Yunnan, Guizhou, and Sichuan under the name of the Paogehui (Long-Robed Brothers Society). When Paogehui shipments arrived in Hankou, the Red Gang oversaw their delivery to Shanghai.[71] After 1923, when drug shipments neared the city, the Green Gang, from its headquarters in the French Concession and with military and police protection, directed the transportation, storage, and sales of opium. Secret societies had contacts with each other at key ports along the Yangtze and arranged in advance where shipments were to be landed. They occasionally colluded with lower-level military authorities to avoid paying taxes at the opium *lijin* stations and split the resulting profits accordingly. When the opium trade became large and complex in the mid-1920s, regional military commanders in the Shanghai area, among them Lu Yongxiang and Sun Chuanfang, became dependent on the Green Gang to manage the opium business in the municipality for them.[72]

From late 1919 to October 1925 (except for a brief period in 1924), Shanghai was under the military control of Lu Yongxiang. Early in his tenure, Lu established a system for shipping and protecting opium cargoes with the assistance of Chaozhou opium merchants. These merchants from Guangdong province used a real estate company—the Joint Prosperity Trading Corporation (Jufeng Maoyi Gongsi)—as a front for their illegitimate activities. They capitalized the company at $10 million through the sale of shares to interested parties.[73] The company imported, exported, and wholesaled opium, from which Lu and his associates received perhaps $5 to $30 million annually for activities protected by Lu's forces. In 1923, French Concession gangster Huang Jinrong became the major stockholder in the Joint Prosperity Trading Corporation, and profits rocketed to $50 million in the following year.[74]

By 1925, a new, more powerful opium syndicate appeared in the French Concession called the Three Prosperities Company (Sanxing Gongsi).[75] The company name referred to the three leaders of the Green Gang—Huang Jinrong, Zhang Xiaolin, and Du Yuesheng, respectively.[76] The firm's shareholders were Chaozhou opium wholesalers, leaders of the Green Gang, Chinese warlords, and French colonial administrators.[77] With protection from French gendarmes and the Chinese military, the Three Prosperities Company dominated the opium trade in Shanghai and its environs (see Figure 1).

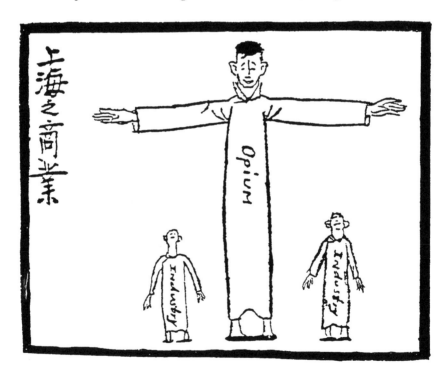

Figure 1. The caption reads "Commerce in Shanghai." The resemblance of "Mr. Opium" to Du Yuesheng is uncanny. Source: *China Critic,* 29 January 1931, 110.

In addition to their links to the Shanghai underworld, Chinese military and naval officials established independent ventures. Sun Chuanfang, for example, created a monopoly in the city of Nantong at the mouth of the Yangtze, which the press referred to as the "Nantong Combine." The military monopoly had an estimated eight hundred retail outlets in central and northern Jiangsu.[78] Naval commanders, among them Yang Shuzhuang, used Shanghai's Jiangnan Arsenal as headquarters for their own lucrative operations. The only time naval gunboats opened fire was to ward off ships from Maritime Customs or "pirates" who threatened cargoes they were protecting.[79] Although control of the Chinese city of Shanghai had changed hands several times before the Guomindang conquered it during the Northern Expedition in 1927, the complicity of military officials, opium merchants, underworld organizations, and foreign administrators kept the Chinese and foreign-controlled sectors of the municipality in a narcotic stupor through the 1930s.[80]

Generally speaking, there were two methods for moving opium downriver from Sichuan to Shanghai. The first and most popular was the quasi-legal system that provided military protection for shipments that paid transit duties at each *lijin* station. Revenue stamps attesting to the payment of taxes and official passports *(huzhao)* guaranteed safe passage through each checkpoint. The accumulating layers of taxation were revealed in the retail prices of opium markets along the Yangtze. To illustrate, consider the hypothetical shipment of *yuntu* from Chongqing to Shanghai in 1925. Yunnan opium cost 80 cents per *liang* at its origin and wholesaled for $1.20 in Chongqing. At Wanxian, Yichang, and Hankou, shippers paid transit taxes on each *dan* of opium transported. After the shipments had reached Hankou, an ounce of *yuntu* had a market value of $2.30. By the time it hit the streets of Shanghai, Yunnanese opium that sold for $1.20 in Chongqing was worth $2.80, an appreciation in value of 133 percent as a result of Yangtze transit taxes collected by local warlord governments.[81]

It was a desire to avoid onerous duties and reap large profits in Shanghai, however, that encouraged smuggling and tax evasion. This method was the preferred modus operandi of the underworld syndicates. One way to move large amounts of opium downriver duty-free was to hire a steamer and pay only the freight charges. When approaching the *lijin* stations, cargoes were unloaded a good distance upriver and carried by coolies or animals on shore. The ship then passed inspections by Maritime Customs or a local opium suppression bureau, and later reloaded the cargo at some point downriver.[82]

An alternative method was to eliminate the shipping charges altogether and move smaller quantities covertly. Chinese crewmen aboard foreign and domestic steamers often hid opium in coal bunkers, secretly built compartments, or placed inside legitimate cargo, especially large barrels of tung *(tong)* oil, paint, or kerosene. Passengers also concealed packets of opium in their luggage or on their person. Even foreign gunboats, which often employed Chinese stokers, deckhands, and engine room crews, might be unsuspecting partners in the trade. In 1920, smugglers used the American gunboat U.S.S. *Palos* to transport a cache of opium worth more than $1 million; and in 1929 inspectors found a shipment of opium aboard the British gunboat H.M.S. *Pater*.[83]

The "Guangxi Corridor"

The second most traveled route for Chinese opium was the Guangxi Corridor, the main avenue for shipping goods produced in Yunnan and Guizhou through the province of Guangxi to Canton (see Map 4). The primary collection and distribution centers in Yunnan were Kunming (Yunnanfu), Mengzi, Guangnan, Kaiyuan, Fuyuan, and Funing. Opium reached these centers via caravans of packhorses and porters accompanied by military escorts. From the

Map 4. The Guangxi Corridor

Yunnan-Guangxi border, the caravans hauled the drug to Bose on the Youjiang (Right River) in western Guangxi. After paying the transit tax at Bose, the interested parties shipped their opium through *lijin* stations in Nanning and Wuzhou, where additional duties were paid before entering Guangdong province and following the Xijiang to Canton.[84]

In November 1922, shippers in Kunming formed the Guangyun Gongsi (Guangdong Transport Company) to ship "native goods" to Canton. They capitalized the company at 1,200,000 Yunnan dollars, with 700,000 dollars provided by warlord Tang Jiyao and the remainder furnished by local and Cantonese merchants.[85] The company originally shipped large amounts of opium on the Kunming-Haiphong Railway through French Indochina.[86] The French Catholic Mission, Banque de l'Indochine, and Banque Industrielle de Chine represented French interests in Kunming and cooperated with provincial authorities and the Guangyun Gongsi in the transportation of *yuntu* by rail to Haiphong and then by steamer to Canton.[87]

After France signed the 1925 Geneva Opium Accord, Indochinese officials halted this *rue des stupéfiants*, but resourceful shippers accommodated to the change. They continued to use the French railroad to transport opium to points just above the Annam border, from which they hired packhorses and coolies to carry the opium under military escort into Guangxi. At Jingxi, the cargo could either be shipped through Longzhou following the Zuojiang (Left River) to Nanning or carried overland to the seaport at Dongxing for shipment to Canton.[88]

Guizhou likewise exported a great deal of opium through the Guangxi Corridor, but a goodly portion of *qiantu* also reached Hankou by way of the Yangtze through Sichuan or via Hunan province to the east. The chief opium markets in Guizhou were Guiyang, Zunyi, Anshun, Tongren, Dushan, and Rongjiang. Shippers transported *qiantu* over rugged terrain by packhorses and porters southward to the Guangxi border and then along the tributaries of the West River to the Guangdong border, paying *lijin* taxes at Liusai, Du'an, and Wuzhou before arriving in Canton.

In the early 1920s, bandits frequently attacked opium caravans in Guizhou as they ventured south toward the Guangxi border. Concerned merchants approached Guizhou warlord Peng Hanzhang in 1925, offering him 30 percent of their profits for military escorts. Peng agreed at once and dispatched some of his best units to guard the caravans.[89] Popularly nicknamed *"shuangqiang-bing"* (soldiers who carried two weapons, i.e., a rifle and an opium pipe), they were nevertheless effective against the brigands. Thereafter, Guizhou's warlords maintained their positions by protecting and taxing the opium trade.[90]

Guangxi warlords also turned the taxation of opium transported through their province into a political asset. Because of the duties collected at key cities along the Xijiang and its tributaries, they became potent political forces in national politics.[91] Between the late 1920s and 1936, before warlords Li Zongren and Bai Chongxi of the "Guangxi Clique" accepted Nanjing's authority, the provincial government received approximately one-third to one-half of its annual revenues from transit taxes on opium.[92]

The final leg of the journey for "black rice" traveling through the Guangxi Corridor was down the Xijiang from Wuzhou to Canton, making that historic city the third largest market for opium in China. *Lijin* stations from the western border to the Boca Tigris fort in the Pearl River Delta ensured various Guangxi, Yunnan, Hunan, and Guangdong warlords a lucrative means to support their activities in the region. After the Guomindang established its revolutionary base in Canton, they also tapped into the wealth flowing down the West River. Domestic opium likewise made its way to Canton via Fujian, Hunan, and Jiangxi provinces, while foreign varieties arrived aboard steamships from the Middle East, India, and Southeast Asia.

In sum, opium and its derivatives flowed as easily along the rivers, roads, and railways of China as morphine molecules flowed through the arteries, veins, and capillaries of its addicts. The scope and scale of the narco-economy was staggering, even by today's standards.

Chinese Currency and Banking

During the Warlord Era and for a good portion of the Nanjing Decade, the exchange of goods in China was not unlike trade between independent states. Thoroughfares leading into regions controlled by militarists were dotted with *lijin* stations, which functioned like frontier customs houses. Moreover, the territory of each warlord had its own currency, which changed when warlords changed and the value of which depended on various circumstances— including its acceptability and convertibility—in the banking system. To understand the financing of the narco-economy, it is therefore necessary to understand China's currency and banking systems.

Politics in 1920s China was decentralized, fragmented, at times chaotic, and highly resistant to the forces of centralization. The same was true of the currency. "China had unquestionably the worst currency to be found in any important country," wrote one contemporary foreign observer.[93] "Chinese currency," wrote another, "forms the most complicated mixture of heterogenous mediums of exchange, from a weight to a coin, that has ever existed in any one country."[94] For the opium trade to function as it did, warlords, government officials, merchants, bankers, and underworld organizations had to adapt to the financial as well as the political chaos in the country. In doing so, they integrated the opium business into existing frameworks of local, national, and even international finance.

China's domestic currency was based chiefly on silver and secondarily on copper. Silver was the medium of exchange used for large-scale commercial transactions, and it was the unit for government accounting procedures and foreign exchange.[95] Until 1933, the basic unit of silver was the tael, the Chinese ounce also known as the *liang*, a unit of weight as well as a degree of purity. However, no nationally recognized weight or degree of purity defined the tael, which therefore varied in value across the country.[96] In October 1923, to illustrate, there were forty-three different exchange rates for the tael quoted in the *Chinese Economic Bulletin* for important trading centers.[97]

As a result of this condition, coin taels were not used in ordinary commercial transactions. Instead, the medium of exchange was the silver dollar—the "Mexican-Chinese" dollar as it came to be known in the 1920s—called the *yuan* in Mandarin. By 1925, all taxes, railway fares, and postage stamps were officially denominated in *yuan*.[98] Between 1924 and 1928, the exchange rate between silver dollars and the tael was about 1.5 to 1 in major cities.

Although Mexican-Chinese dollars had become the most widely accepted form of currency, day-to-day retail transactions were usually made with copper coins known as "cash" *(qian),* the value of which was pegged to the tael. Theoretically, one silver tael equaled one thousand units of cash, but in reality the relative value of the two units varied widely. Because of such things as the adulteration of copper used in cash and daily fluctuations in the value of a local tael in relation to other taels and to foreign currency, the value of the tael varied between 800 and 2,800 units of cash.[99]

Adding to this variety, in 1916 provincial governments began issuing paper money and coinage. Between 1916 and 1928, seventeen provinces printed and coined currencies of their own, and many warlords issued paper notes to their troops called *"junyongpiao"* (soldier scrip) without going through the provincial banks that normally handled such matters.[100] In addition, the two national banks in Beijing, the Bank of China and the Bank of Communications, as well as foreign banks issued notes of various denominations that circulated in this maelstrom of money. According to one source, perhaps thirty thousand different issues of paper currency, most of them denominated in *yuan*, circulated in China at one time or another between 1900 and 1935, most of them issued without specie reserves and without having to meet any legal requirements.[101] Even opium served as a form of currency in the major growing regions of southwest and northwest China, where it could be exchanged for grain, cloth, salt, or weapons.[102]

Opium and Republican Banking

Understanding how the opium business penetrated Chinese banking is imperative to comprehending how the narco-economy functioned in such an unpredictable financial environment. Transport merchants, wholesalers, warlords, and underworld organizations participating in the commerce dealt in large sums of capital. They used small native banks *(qianzhuang),* modern incorporated banks *(yinhang),* national banks, and foreign banks as depositories of funds, to transfer funds, and as sources of credit.[103] Many of the large opium firms themselves got into banking activities either to facilitate the handling of their own funds or as secondary sources of income.[104]

To illustrate how this system worked with a hypothetical example, an opium merchant in Hankou on his way to Chongqing to purchase a quantity of *chuantu* would take with him a *huipiao* (remissions note) from a local bank. In Chongqing, he could take the note to a native or a modern bank and cash it in at a discounted rate for local currency, exchange it for a local bank note, or use it to pay an opium firm for purchases. If he followed the latter course, when the note came due (usually five to ten days after the date of issue) the local opium firm might resell it to merchants traveling to Hankou or cash it in at a native, modern, or foreign bank in Chongqing.[105] All of these transactions included the practice of discounting *(zhekou),* whereby the face value of the note was rarely accepted. Given the large amount of paper scrip in circulation, much of it worthless, the reputation of a bank's solvency or a provincial government's stability determined the real value of its notes within local and national markets.

To expedite financing of the opium economy, opium merchants established more than a quarter (27.5 percent) of all the native banks founded in Shanghai between 1912 and 1926.[106] By the mid-1920s, Shanghai was not only the biggest narcotics market in the world, it was also China's most important commercial and financial center, and many of its banks had little or nothing to do with the opium business. However, since all bank accounts were cleared daily in the *zonghui* (a clearinghouse in which native and modern banks settled accounts until 1933), drug dollars became enmeshed with capital earned by other businesses. As a result, the "dirty money" was "laundered" every day. If opium merchants owned perhaps a quarter of all native banks in Shanghai in the mid-1920s, the drug influence on banking in other centers of the trade, whose economies were less diversified than that of Shanghai, must have been sizable indeed.

Modern banks likewise had key roles in financing the opium trade. For example, the provincial bank of Yunnan was the Fudian Yinhang (Wealthy Yunnan Bank), located in Kunming. From 1920 to 1927, warlord Tang Jiyao used it to store large sums of tax monies collected by his provincial opium suppression bureau. The Fudian Yinhang actively lent money to opium merchants such as the Guangyun Gongsi, for which it made remittances and accepted deposits. It also dealt with French banks entangled in the trade.[107]

Tang eventually cornered most of the silver in Yunnan, which he deposited in the Wealthy Yunnan Bank until he transferred it to accounts in Hong Kong with the British-operated Hong Kong and Shanghai Bank. As this occurred, the Wealthy Yunnan Bank issued large sums of worthless paper currency, and economic conditions in the province deteriorated accordingly. In March 1927, the *China Weekly Review* ran a piece on the province under the apt title "Yunnan: A Land of Opium and Bad Money." When Tang lost power later that year, he had about US$10 million for his retirement in Hong Kong, although he did not live long enough to enjoy it.[108]

Warlords' use of national or regional modern banks to finance their drug trafficking was a ubiquitous practice. For instance, the Bank of China—the national government's exchequer—became an unwitting participant. In late 1923, officials of the Bank of China in Beijing were puzzled by large shipments of silver dollars from the capital to its Baotou branch, totaling much more than was needed to finance the normal trade of the city, which consisted mainly of wools and animal hides. Dispatching one of its officers to investigate the matter, the bank learned that the money was being used to finance the trade in opium. The officer discovered that warlord Ma Fuxiang was encouraging drug sales in the area to offset his military expenditures and had collected nearly $2 million in taxes that year as a result.[109] Similarly, in 1925 the International Anti-Opium Association identified the Nantong branch of the Huihai Shiye Yinhang (Overseas Exchange and Industrial Bank) as a depository for money earned from Sun Chuanfang's Nantong Combine. For this the Overseas Exchange and Industrial

Bank was nicknamed the "Opium Bank," a monniker that was widely applied to modern and native banks during this period.[110]

Opium also affected local finances in other ways. Gilbert King worked for the American Oriental Bank of Sichuan in Chongqing, deep in the heart of opium country. In April 1925, King witnessed a sudden jump in interest rates on commercial loans from 9 percent to 16 percent. A Chinese comprador told him that the reason for the jump was the demand among opium buyers (*gunzishang*) in Fuling for silver dollars to make down payments to farmers for their opium crop. The situation became so critical that these merchants offered Chongqing bankers $103 for each $100 in silver dollars delivered to Fuling. Consequently, an exodus of silver ensued, draining the supply of specie in Chongqing and causing interest rates nearly to double.[111]

Opium trafficking similarly affected exchange rates. Three weeks after the incident involving the flight of silver from Chongqing, the exchange rate between Shanghai and Chongqing taels suddenly dropped from 1,000:1,080 to 1,000:1,012. The cause of the drop was the sale of 60 tons of Yunnan opium downriver. Chongqing merchants had sold *yuntu* worth over $2 million to Shanghai merchants, and the resulting inflow of silver dollars to Chongqing caused the exchange rate to fall by 6.3 percent.[112] In Yunnan, the connection between provincial currency, the opium trade, and exchange rates was just as strong as it was in Sichuan. During the month of March in 1928, the value of the Yunnan currency against the U.S. dollar rose 14 percent. The reason for the rise was news that opium that had been sitting in collection centers for six months because of civil war and banditry was finally going to market through the Guangxi Corridor.[113]

In addition to banking, the opium economy also influenced other businesses, including insurance. Chinese and foreign companies insured policy holders against fire in opium dens, wholesale firms, and retail shops, and even against loss of opium shipments in transit. In the early 1930s, to illustrate the latter, the Hubei-Hunan Special Tax Clearance Office approached a British company about underwriting a shipment of opium from Hankou to Shanghai for $1 million. The British refused to issue the policy not on moral grounds but because the vessel transporting the opium was of questionable seaworthiness.[114]

The trade in opium thus had a major impact on the Chinese economy. In 1926, Tang Shaoyi, honorary chairman of the National Anti-Opium Association, stated, "China spends yearly $800,000,000 in locally produced opium and $200,000,000 in imported opium and other narcotics."[115] In 1933, another Chinese source estimated the opium traffic at $2 billion annually.[116] Whatever the validity of these figures—and the National Anti-Opium Association was conservative in its estimates of the opium trade—they suggest the size of the opium economy. The accepted estimate of the republic's gross domestic product for the year 1933 is around $29 billion.[117] If one splits the difference between the two speculations regarding the sum spent annually on opium ($1.5 billion) and compares that figure with the estimated gross domestic product above, then conservatively speaking, the opium business accounted for approximately 5.2 percent of China's gross domestic product. All of these figures are estimates—educated guesses, really. But it is evident that in China during the 1920s and 1930s there was a large-scale commerce in a drug that profoundly impacted Republican economics, society, and politics.

2 The Effects of Opium on Chinese Society

OPIUM'S INFLUENCE ON CHINESE SOCIETY was not simply an economic and political matter. The drug also affected the way Chinese interacted with each other socially and therefore sociologically. To better comprehend the pervasive influence of opium on Chinese society, it is imperative to probe how deeply it had penetrated into the minds, the bodies, and even the organizational life of its citizens.

Opium Smoking as Ritualistic Behavior

One of the cardinal precepts of Confucian tradition is that of *li*, which can be variously translated as ritual, etiquette, propriety, or ceremony: the external exemplification of gentlemanly behavior. Perhaps one reason for the drug's popularity was that inhaling opium smoke was a ritualistic act. Smokers routinely observed certain protocols in order fully to enjoy opium's narcotic effects. Smoking rarely occurred in solitude; it was an experience shared with other people in a setting of human interaction. Whether the setting was the yamen of a government official, a restaurant, one's own residence, or even the omnipresent opium den, the act of smoking was a shared social experience.

Equally important in individual settings was the kind of opium to be consumed. Individual tastes varied according to location and social standing. Most consumers could afford only cheap domestic varieties—predominantly Sichuanese—while others could afford mixtures of those varieties with more expensive foreign opium. For example, in Canton Persian opium was rarely inhaled unadulterated. Local palates demanded that it be combined with Yunnan, Guizhou, or Fujian blends.[1] The really affluent consumers preferred the most expensive Indian imports, while the poorest could only afford a pernicious mixture of opium ash, sesame cake, jujubes, and pork rinds known as *liaozi* (synthetic opium).[2] Although smoking was the preferred delivery system for the narcotic, some people chewed opium like tobacco, some beat it into a paste and swirled it on their tongues, while others mixed it with water or wine and consumed the drug in liquid form.[3]

Smoking opium was time-consuming, and it required proper paraphernalia. The basic implements were a pipe, an oil lamp, and a long, thin needlelike device called the *"yanzhen"* (opium needle). For addicts as opposed to recreational or social smokers, the amount of time spent in individual acts of smoking was determined by age, the length and degree of dependency, and the intensity of the physical and/or psychological craving for the drug.

In preparation for smoking, the smoker or an attendant poured a small dab of the dark brown *tugao* onto a bamboo leaf, lit an oil lamp (preferably castor or vegetable oil), and then rolled some of the boiled opium onto the *yanzhen* and twirled it over the flame. The *tugao* immediately fizzled into a large brown bubble, with much of the moisture in the paste evaporating. The smoker or attendant then popped the bubble by rubbing it against a bamboo leaf, leaving a small, dry bead. This procedure was repeated until the bead became the size of a large pea, at which point the opium was ready for smoking.

The smoker (or attendant) then heated the brass or pewter bowl on the pipe *(yanqiang)* over the lamp and in a single motion thrust the *yanzhen* into the bowl and withdrew it, leaving the opium clinging to the side of the bowl. The smoker then placed the stem of the pipe in his or her mouth and, with the bowl positioned directly over the flame at an inverted angle, inhaled the smoke until the opium stopped burning. After the last draught, the smoker gulped down a cup of strong tea and lay back to rest as the narcotic took effect. The process described above lasted approximately five to ten minutes per pipeful, and since the average addict inhaled ten to twenty pipefuls a day, the amount of time addicts spent smoking ranged between one and three hours daily or longer in extreme cases.[4]

Opium's Effects on the Human Body

The substance that produces the euphoric state associated with opium use is morphine, named after the Roman god Morpheus, who was responsible for creating dreams.[5] Many great Western writers, among them Edgar Allan Poe, Thomas De Quincey, Samuel Taylor Coleridge, and John Keats, wrote celebrated works under the influence of opium.[6] For some Chinese, the dreamlike state produced by the drug would bring them closer to unlocking the secrets of Daoist mysticism. To quote from an addict who happened to be a Chinese doctor: "With opium, I feel the absolute and nameless condition described by the Taoist mystic, Chuang-tzu, sometimes known as Chuang Chou. This man fell asleep and dreamed he was a butterfly, flitting through the sunshine, free and happy. Upon awakening, he became himself again, the veritable Chou, but he did not know whether he had been Chou dreaming he was a butterfly, or a butterfly dreaming it was Chou."[7]

The percentage of morphine in opium was determined by the soils in which the poppies grew. The Nationalist government conducted laboratory tests on samples of domestically grown raw opium and published their morphine content as follows: Gansu, 13.90 percent; Yunnan, 10.90 percent; Guizhou, 10.70 percent; Sichuan, 6.96 percent; Shaanxi, 5.70 percent.[8] Imported Indian opium contained roughly 10 percent morphine, while Persian and Turkish varieties held between 11 percent and 15 percent.[9]

What happens when morphine enters the bloodstream has been the subject of considerable research since the 1970s, following the discovery of endogenous opioid substances such as endorphins produced by the human body.[10] Endorphins—a contraction of "endogenous morphines"—are inhibitory neurotransmitters. Along with enkephalins and dynorphins, endorphins act to inhibit the release of Substance P (the major neurotransmitter of pain signals) by plugging into opiate receptor sites on Substance P–releasing neurons.[11] In lay terms, endorphins are naturally synthesized painkillers. Besides their analgesic effects, endorphins also produce feelings of euphoria. Long-distance runners, for example, experience this state as endorphins are released to counteract soreness in the leg muscles.[12] Thousands of years before Western medical experts began to study the phenomenon, the Chinese had been stimulating the release of endorphins to relieve pain through the practice of acupuncture.[13]

According to recent studies, the central nervous system of humans in addition to the stomach, intestines, adrenal glands, pancreas, and some other organs, are lined with four types of opioid receptors known as mu, delta, kappa, and sigma. These receptor sites couple with the enkephalins, endorphins, and dynorphins. Because the morphine molecules in opium are almost identical in structure to endorphins, they couple with the mu receptors and mimic the effects produced by endorphins, namely, euphoria and analgesia.[14]

Long-term persistent use of exogenous opiates, including morphine and heroin, upsets the natural biochemical balance of the human body, creating changes that lead to tolerance and dependency (both physical and psychological), and thus addiction. Habitual opium smoking decreases the body's ability to synthesize endorphins, because an oversupply of morphine triggers a near shutdown of endorphin production. In this situation, the mu receptors require increased stimulation—larger amounts of the drug—to function normally. As long as the addict receives this increased stimulation, there is no problem. However, if an addict stops taking the drug, the consequence is a dramatic rise in demand for endorphins normally synthesized by the body. The diminished levels of naturally occurring endorphins are quickly depleted, and the body experiences a biochemical imbalance. Thus, dependence on the drug produces intense physical and psychological cravings—known as withdrawal—due to the lack of morphine in the blood system.[15]

In the 1920s and 1930s, the physical and psychological effects of long-term addiction were readily apparent in a *yangui* (opium addict). In the most severe cases, the addict's face was jaundiced, the cheeks were sunken, and the eyes appeared dull and listless. Habitual smokers lost their appetites and thus lost weight and physical strength. Bodily functions became impaired, resulting in chronic constipation and sexual impotence. Mental powers, at first enhanced by the stimulation of neurons in the hippocampus of the brain, gradually became stunted, leading to a diminished attention span and the loss of short-term and long-term memory.[16] The extent to which these symptoms appeared in individual users depended on variables such as the level of addiction, the rate of metabolism, and the overall health of the individual. Provided an addict had the resources to sustain the habit, he or she could reach old age with no visible side effects other than chronic constipation, listlessness, or emaciation.

The effects of opium withdrawal, however, were intense and excruciatingly painful. After eight to ten hours without the drug, an addict began to experience the physical discomfort of withdrawal. The first symptoms included weakness and dizziness, followed by profuse sweating and watery discharge from the eyes and nose. At the end of the first twenty-four hours, an individual experienced severe vomiting, continual bowel movements, uncontrollable sneezing and yawning, as well as insomnia, severe headaches, and writhing abdominal pains.[17] Finally, the mind experienced serious hallucinations and bouts of dementia.[18]

Current scholarly literature reveals disagreement regarding the distinctions between the archetypal emaciated and jaundiced addict and others who were in various degrees dependent on the drug, on the one hand, versus the larger number of recreational and social smokers, on the other hand, who showed no signs of addiction whatsoever. R. K. Newman's excellent reevaluation of late-nineteenth-century stereotypes rightfully acknowledges the influence of anti-opium propaganda from the period and its ability "to establish itself as axiom."[19] Historical perceptions have been and continue to be colored by such blatantly prejudiced accounts in foreign and Chinese sources from the Republican period as well. Such prejudice was especially apparent in the 1930s, when antidrug campaigns shifted their focus away from opium (which was legalized in 1934) to heroin and morphine addiction. Despite the much smaller percentage of people addicted to harder drugs in comparison to opium smokers, the perception of the real scope of heroin and morphine use in China was grossly exaggerated.

Actually, the amount of morphine that entered the bloodstream through the lungs by smoking was significantly less than for those who ingested opium orally or used heroin and morphine. The average amount of morphine in raw Chinese opium was 8 percent of its total weight. When inhaled, a considerable percentage of the morphine remained behind in the bowl as ash or built up as resin inside the stem of the pipe. When exhaled, a goodly amount of morphine not absorbed through the lungs dissipated into the air. Consequently, the opium-smoking addict spent much more time engaged in the smoking ritual to satisfy the craving in comparison to opium eaters or morphine and heroin addicts.[20]

There was—and is—no cure for opiate addiction. When one speaks of dealing with addiction, the operative context is "treatment," not "cure." Addicts who survived the tortuous detoxification were always susceptible to reacquiring the habit, much like a recovering alcoholic. The siren song of opium was difficult for the addict to ignore, conditioning behavioral patterns to obtain the drug by any means possible. Following the 1911 Revolution in Sichuan, for example, the strict enforcement of prohibition by local authorities created a huge demand for the clay pots in which raw opium had been stored. After decades of use by merchants, the drug had permeated the pores of the earthenware containers to such an extent that they were ground into a powder and swallowed by addicts to satiate their cravings. A small package of the powder sold for almost a half-day's wage.[21]

In the 1920s and 1930s, treatment for addiction was still in its infancy. Both Western and Chinese doctors were then experimenting with diverse methods in hopes of finding a cure. Many of the methods they tried were primitive, some of them deadly, and all of them ineffective. The various treatments lasted from eight days to six months, depending on the health and age of the addict and the degree of addiction.[22] The three standard treatments during this time were sudden withdrawal, gradual withdrawal, and the use of other drugs or natural ingredients to purge the system of morphine.

In sudden withdrawal—known today as going "cold turkey"—an addict was locked in a padded room and given nothing but food and water until detoxification occurred naturally.[23] This method was sheer torture for the addict and was deemed inhumane by most doctors. As a result, it was not a popular treatment. Gradual withdrawal involved a process of weaning the addict off of the narcotic. During the weaning process, the amount of morphine introduced into the system was reduced over a period of four to ten weeks. The major pitfall with this procedure was that it prolonged the agony of patients who suffered from the symptoms of withdrawal and thereby increased the temptation to smoke.[24] Other treatments consisted of injecting poisons such as hyocsine hydrobromide, strychnine, or belladonna into the bloodstream to purge morphine from the system. Many addicts died from such treatments.[25] Further methods included the use of barbiturates or other painkillers during the period of withdrawal, or feeding patients egg yolks and beans, which purportedly created a distaste for opium.[26]

Whatever the method, recovery from addiction often meant the reappearance of the ailments that caused the addiction in the first place. China not only lacked adequate medical facilities and doctors to treat these diseases but was extremely deficient in addiction detoxification centers. Missionary-run hospitals and clinics were too few to have any effect, and not until 1934 did the Nationalist government undertake a meaningful effort to combat addiction.

Reasons for Opium Smoking

Why was opium smoking so widespread? Given the significance of this question, historians have given it surprisingly little attention. Contemporary documentary evidence seems to suggest three basic answers to the question:

opium was used as a "cure" for physical maladies and ailments, or as a stimulant; as a commodity to facilitate social intercourse *(yingchoupin)*; or when visiting prostitutes *(wannong)*, gambling, or whiling away the time *(xiaoqian)*.[27]

Many Chinese regarded opium as a panacea for illnesses, ailments, and other maladies. Although it was merely an analgesic that blocked the neural transmission of pain from the affected area to the brain, most people associated the cessation of pain with a medicinal "cure." Many such people acquired the habit, and the result was widespread opium addiction. Of a thousand patients in a Shanghai opium treatment clinic in 1935–1936 whom investigators asked why they had become addicted to opium, 88.3 percent responded that it was because of a preexisting physical condition. Altogether this sample of addicts listed twenty-seven maladies for which they smoked the drug, the five most frequently listed being gastric diseases, abdominal pains, pulmonary hemorrhaging, rheumatoid arthritis, and diarrhea.[28]

Opium merchants were clever enough to use the myth of opium's curative powers to increase demand for the substance. In 1925, for example, Hong Kong authorities seized raw opium smuggled into the territory from Fujian. The labeling on the cakes read: "These cakes can keep away malaria and foul air, stimulate the spirits, and moisten the throat and tongue. They are as efficacious as gods in curing all kinds of extraordinary and difficult diseases."[29]

One reason for the medicinal use of opium was the relative scarcity of hospitals and physicians in Republican China. In 1929, there were only 519 modern hospitals in the entire country; and in twenty provinces in 1933, the number of government hospitals was a mere 579 staffed by only 3,001 Western-trained doctors.[30] Because China had a population of perhaps five hundred million in these years, one can readily see that modern medical care was not an option for the overwhelming majority of people. Traditional Chinese medicine was available, but it seems to have been of little or no effect in treating opium addiction.

For occasional users as distinct from addicts, opium had a use not unlike that of coffee. For them, opium increased mental energy for a short time, and the euphoria experienced was somewhat analogous to spiritual rejuvenation.[31] Contemporary accounts describe how elderly people used it from time to time to revive their spirits.[32] For the addict, however, opium was a stimulant that rejuvenated energy levels depleted by an absence of the drug from the body. Addicts engaged in strenuous physical labor, such as rickshaw coolies, used it regularly as an antidote to exhaustion and muscular pain.[33]

A second reason for the popularity of *Papaver somniferum* was its social dimension.[34] According to a 1932 report from missionaries in the Lianghu (Hubei and Hunan) region, "at funerals, weddings, or feasts, on any occasion when many guests are invited, a number of rooms is prepared for smoking with beds, pipes, lamps and opium provided for all smokers. This is done openly. Opium is provided as a matter of course, just as is wine."[35] "Lighting of the lamps" was often standard protocol for merchants discussing business, which explains why teahouses, restaurants, brothels, and other sites of business transaction provided the service to patrons.[36]

Members of local elites across the nation considered opium smoking a sign of refinement and status. When officials or business people of equal or higher status called on members of the middle or upper classes, they often—perhaps generally—expected to be offered opium as an act of hospitality. Missionaries and foreign entrepreneurs who turned down such offers frequently found county officials and those doing business with them engaged in the smoking ritual.[37]

So widespread and conventional did opium smoking become that one could gauge the relative wealth of a household by the number and types of opium pipes on display, especially in western China. Well-off households showcased tortoiseshell, ivory, and jade pipes in rooms where they entertained guests. In the words of Nationalist general Yu Da, "opium smoking was ubiquitous, and when guests arrived it was required to entertain them with opium. If there was no opium in the house, then this signified that the social status of that family was not high. . . . The more affluent households had one or two expensive pipes; if they had three, then you could be certain it was a very prominent family."[38] By the 1930s, opium smoking was a symbol of wealth, status, "face," and cultural refinement among elites, and had become a ritualized custom of transcendent significance. It is thus understandable that opium smokers looked down on heroin and morphine addicts. The latter group hid their activities from the public, receiving or giving themselves injections in comparative isolation. Such depraved, individualistic acts lacked the social graces associated with civilized gentlemanly behavior.

A Typology of Opium Smokers

Attempting to assemble a profile of opium smokers in Republican China during the 1920s and 1930s is difficult. There are, however, two useful contemporary sources that shed light on the subject. In 1929, the National Anti-Opium

Association conducted a study of the drug problem in nineteen provinces. The ages and occupations of smokers appear in Appendix Table 11.

Although the National Anti-Opium Association data are generally reliable, they are not flawless. The survey included no description of the methods used to arrive at these figures, and even the calculations contained errors. The data were most likely based on observation and discussions with missionaries and Chinese Christians in the provinces.[39] In terms of categorizing smokers by occupational groupings, the study focuses overwhelmingly on elites, who were only a small percentage of the total population.

Another set of data, this one from the Nationalist government, is more reliable. According to information compiled by the Judicial Yuan for the year 1931, of the 27,435 persons arrested as opium offenders, the majority (53 percent) were between the ages of twenty-one and forty (see Appendix Table 12).[40] Of the occupations listed, the top four were merchants (19 percent), laborers (18.7 percent), farmers (16.7 percent), and those engaged in shipping and transportation (8.3 percent) (see Appendix Table 13). Regarding the socioeconomic and educational backgrounds of the individuals, 65 percent could be classified as living below the poverty line, while over 61 percent were illiterate (see Appendix tables 14 and 15).

Interpreting the Nationalist government's data is also problematic. The well-off people used wealth and personal connections to work out arrangements with law enforcement personnel, and anecdotal evidence suggests strongly that members of the middle and upper classes, especially merchants and civil officials, disproportionately used the drug.[41] Nevertheless, it seems safe to say that opium smoking was widespread among all classes and occupational groups in Republican China, in all age groups among adults, and among women as well as men. Given the demographics of the country, the "average" smoker was no doubt a poor, illiterate farmer or coolie, though rates of smokers were no doubt highest among literate groups living above the subsistence level, especially among local elites.

How many addicts were there? The short answer is that no one knows. There are no precise statistical data on the subject. According to a 1929 study conducted by the National Anti-Opium Association, addicts constituted 3.84 percent of the population surveyed.[42] That percentage out of a total population of 500 million would produce more than 19 million addicts. In December 1934, Nanjing's Ministry of the Interior estimated that there were 30 million opium, heroin, and morphine addicts in the country but did not elaborate on the specifics for each category.[43]

Given the sheer number of contemporary accounts that indicate a much larger smoking population, both of these estimates are almost certainly too low. The National Anti-Opium Association and the Nationalist government tended to underestimate the use as well as the production of opium, and in many areas of the country—especially in heavy cultivation regions—the proportion of addicts was certainly higher than the estimates above indicate. For example, the National Anti-Opium Association itself estimated that over half the populations of Sichuan, Yunnan, and Gansu smoked opium in the early 1930s.[44] Furthermore, the widespread use of opium smoking on social occasions suggests that the majority of smokers were not addicts. Unfortunately, no such distinction is made in the sources. Despite the limitations imposed by the data, these factors together suggest that the total number of smokers and addicts must have been at least 10 percent of the total population and may have been much higher. If that was indeed the case, a more realistic figure would have been fifty million or more smokers, including addicts.

Opium, Familial Life, and Morality

Commonly held assumptions regarding opium permeated the popular consciousness in a very chaotic period of Chinese history. Citizens who appeared normal and exhibited no criminal or socially stigmatized behavior before smoking opium were darkly transformed into liars, swindlers, thieves, robbers, muggers, pickpockets, beggars, prostitutes and ne'er-do-wells (see Figure 2). Opium dens, moreover, encouraged this deviant behavior, for many of them doubled as pawnshops where stolen merchandise was quickly and conveniently changed into cash.[45] As a consequence, the lower-class addict was frequently caught in a vicious cycle, or perhaps a downward spiral, that for many ended in broken homes, imprisonment, or even death.

Further reinforcing the immoral stereotype associated with opium use were the people who most profited from the trade, such as warlords, *jianshang* (wicked merchants), secret society members, gangsters, and *tuhao lieshen*, or traitorous countrymen and foreign devils who wished to perpetuate imperialist domination of the motherland. A description by the National Anti-Opium Association in 1927 is a case in point:

> Why aren't [our nation's merchants] content with engaging in legitimate business activities? Why are they so willing to serve as the slaves of foreigners? As

Figure 2. The main caption reads "Opium and Society." The descriptions within read from the top clockwise "beggars, pickpockets, robbers, and thieves." Source: *Jinyan banyuekan* (Opium Suppression Fortnightly) 1.1 (June 1936): iii.

the running dogs of warlords? As those who injure both the people and the nation? As the pariahs of the marketplace? ... Most [opium merchants] are *jianshang* who only understand seeking profits and don't care about the public's welfare. They curry favor with imperialists and warlords, and entice our male and female countrymen to smoke opium with devastating consequences.[46]

Opium was thus viewed by many as an important factor behind the erosion of the bonds that held an increasingly fraying society together. The "glue" that had performed this role for millennia was the familial unit. According to the traditional Chinese worldview, society was hierarchically and patriarchally organized by sex, kinship, and social function: males were superior to females, elders to juniors, the literate minority to the illiterate majority.[47] For over two thousand years, the Confucian state had indoctrinated the ethical precepts of China's greatest sage into every aspect of public and private life. The foundation of the Confucian social order was the extended family, and the relationships between family members were deemed sacrosanct.

Nevertheless, as traditional Chinese society was challenged by the multiple threats of Western thought, religion, economics, politics, and familial relations, Confucian notions regarding family matters came under intense scrutiny and criticism in the early twentieth century. The New Culture and May Fourth movements iconoclastically challenged the legitimacy of patriarchal domination by attacking such traditional practices as foot binding, arranged marriages, concubinage, and the belief that women should submissively serve their male counterparts without question. Furthermore, Western-style marriages and divorces were becoming more popular in the treaty ports by the 1930s and accelerated the unraveling of the traditional social fabric that for so long had bound Chinese families together.

Although the majority of the population—especially in the rural regions—resisted altering the fundamental essence of Chinese culture, reformers and traditionalists alike agreed that opium posed the greatest threat to family solidarity. Three main areas of concern were the economic security, psychological well-being, and morality of the household.

The average family in China had to live within its means, like families anywhere else in the world. However, in the world's most populous nation—and one of the poorest—the productivity of each member of the household was qualitatively more essential to the survival of the family unit. Generally speaking, smoking opium was an expensive habit. If a household of modest income had just one person who was addicted to the drug, it could drastically alter the lifestyle of the entire family. In economic terms, not only would it lose a productive member in regard to labor and decreased income, but expenditures would rise beyond the capacity of the other members to make up the difference.

An average family from Guangxi province in the early 1930s provides an excellent case study. Under normal circumstances, opium addicts required 30 cents daily or $108 annually to satisfy their habit. According to data from that period, the average yearly cost of living per person was $50, which included the basic requirements of food, clothing, and shelter. If the individual was working, he or she could earn or contribute at least $50 in crops, handicrafts, or some form of manual labor. If a household had just one person who was addicted, as opposed to the social or casual smoker, the loss of yearly income for the family would be over $200 ($50 for food, clothing, and shelter; $50 in lost income; $108 in opium).[48] Accordingly, one *yangui* withdrew three times as much capital from the household as the other members. Even if an addict was able to stay gainfully employed, he or she still siphoned off over $100 from the collective that could not be replaced. In contrast, affluent and middle-income households could sustain such expensive habits, and in fact were more likely to, especially when it was deemed a matter of proper social etiquette to offer important guests a pipeful of dreams. Reports that affluent households often encouraged their sons to smoke in order to prevent them from getting into trouble were not uncommon.[49]

An opium addict's pernicious influence on the household was felt in ways that were not as easily quantifiable. The psychological well-being of the family unit was imperiled by a habitual smoker's day-to-day presence. Changes in mood and character were directly related to the amount of morphine in the body, and the altered behavioral patterns that challenged the existing definitions of what was socially acceptable presented new threats to family solidarity.

Under the headline "Never Live with an Opium Smoker," a story from Shanghai's *Xinwenbao* in late 1927 is a case in point. Wang Quanlin was the proprietor of a foreign goods store. He and his wife, Wang Zhongshi, had been married for over seventeen years and had produced several sons and daughters together. However, Zhongshi became addicted to opium several years earlier. She no longer assisted her husband in the family store, but instead spent all day long reclining and smoking opium to the neglect of her household duties. Many times Quanlin admonished his wife to seek treatment but to no avail. Later, his fifteen-year-old son and ten-year-old daughter imitated their mother's behavior and became addicted to the pipe.

Mr. Wang began taking more severe measures against his spouse. Since smoking was technically illegal, he reported Zhongshi to the local authorities, who arrested and fined her on several occasions, but these punishments did not stop his wife from smoking opium. Her addiction was so acute that she began to stay away from home for days on end, only to return looking disheveled and asking for money, then refusing to tell her husband where she had been. Finally, Mr. Wang had reached the end of his rope, and he contacted a lawyer, who filed for divorce on grounds of endangering the children and absence from home.[50]

The last and most noxious effect of opium on Chinese families was the degradation of morality. A popular saying from northern China went "When men become addicted to opium, they destroy their families and become lascivious; when women become addicted to opium, the belt holding up their trousers slackens [indicating loss of both weight and virtue]."[51] Under the physical and psychological yokes of addiction, men commonly sold their property and possessions to procure the drug and even sold their own flesh and blood.

Examples of unethical behavior by *yangui* run riot through the anti-opium tracts, newspapers, and other literature of the Republican period. For instance, during the 1920s in Anhui's Huaiyuan county, a young lady surnamed Zhang hailed from a prominent literati family. She was locally renown for her artistic talents, especially poetry, calligraphy, and painting. Her older brother became an addict and bought the drug on credit from local den operators, who demanded repayment and threatened to cut off his supplies and do bodily injury. Therefore, the addict conspired with the den owners *(laoban)* to sell his younger sister to a brothel in the large city of Bengbu and thereby erase his debts. Knowing that his sister would not willingly go along with the scheme, the elder Zhang deceptively informed her that a very prominent family in Bengbu had been impressed with her artistic accomplishments and desired to employ her as a domestic to supervise the affairs of the household. She thereupon traveled with her elder brother to Bengbu ostensibly for an interview, but once inside the bordello, Miss Zhang immediately understood that she would be practicing less celebrated arts for a while.[52]

Young girls from poor families were commonly mortgaged to opium dens and served as female attendants—known colloquially as "flowers" *(hua)*—for $100 or more, depending on their looks. They could regain their freedom only after paying back the divan owner by one of two methods. The first was to serve as a waitress preparing opium pipes for patrons. For this service, a girl received 25 percent of the cost per pipeful (20 to 40 cents), or five to ten cents, and it would take a long time to repay the debt. The second way was to sell her body and split the fee with her boss, a more remunerative and speedier solution, but more hazardous to her health.[53]

In memoirs and interviews with people who lived during the Republican era are descriptions of primarily lower-class men who willfully sold their wives and children to others for money to satisfy their cravings for the drug. There were cases of husbands drawing up short-term contracts with other men to rent out their wives for several months at a time or even for half-month rentals. It was also not unheard of for addicts to sell their elderly parents to work in sweatshops or perform other physically demanding work.[54]

Confucian bonds of propriety—most notably filial piety—were thus easily severed by the *yangui*. In late 1930 an addict named Wang Bafang used filial piety as a ruse to transport opium from Gansu to Hebei province. Wang's father had been a minor military official stationed in Gansu and had passed away three years earlier. Under the pretext of bringing his father's remains back to the family cemetery for reburial, Wang Bafang traveled to Gansu, placed his father's body in a coffin, and then made his way slowly back to Hebei in a horse-drawn carriage. Wang was arrested en route when local gendarmes discovered the "filial son" had been vending opium from the coffin and had concealed a sizable quantity of the drug inside his dearly departed father's skull.[55]

In the early 1930s, equally repugnant acts by *yangui* struck at the heart of traditional culture. In one such account, addicts desecrated the graves of cemeteries in the city of Anda in northern Manchuria, stealing clothing from the corpses and selling them for money to purchase drugs.[56] Such depraved and immoral behavior was taken as further proof that opium and other narcotics poisoned the minds of *yangui*.

Opium and Other Vices

By the 1920s and 1930s, opium had acquired the notoriety of being one of Chinese society's most pernicious vices. In fact, the narcotic was commonly grouped together with gambling (*dubo*) and prostitution (*changji*) under the rubric of *"yanduchang."* It is not surprising that opium was synonymous with prostitution and gambling for the mere fact that it was widely available in these other dens of iniquity.

At first there had been clearly distinguishable barriers between the "three evils." It was during the late Qing period that operators of the opium divans realized that providing beautiful female attendants and games of chance for patrons increased their profits. Soon afterwards, gaming establishments and bordellos took notice and liberally vended the drug as an added incentive to lure customers. Additionally, the average person from any municipality in China, be it small or large, could not help but notice the close physical proximity of *yanduchang* establishments in certain neighborhoods.

To quote from a National Anti-Opium Association source on the relationship between brothels and opium smoking, "As a rule, the first thing people do after entering a brothel is to smoke opium."[57] Apparently, there were several reasons for such behavior, emanating from popular myths concerning the mixing of sex and opium. First, the pipe was supposed to stimulate sexual arousal and prolong its pleasures.[58] Second, the purported medicinal properties of the narcotic included a prophylaxis against sexually transmitted diseases. Unbeknown to the bordello clientele, the mere act of sharing an opium pipe with prostitutes and other patrons was hazardous to their health. The pipes served as agents of transmission for a host of maladies, including syphilis, tuberculosis, and pyorrhea.[59]

There seem to have been two reasons for mixing gambling and opium. On the one hand, many gamblers believed that their altered mind-states would enable them to commune with the *dushen* (gods of gambling) and improve their luck. At the same time, the entrepreneurs of gambling dens knew that smoking would stupefy their customers and earn them more money.[60] In the West today, many casino operators ply their customers with complimentary alcoholic beverages, but the result is still the same.

Opium and Civil Society

The term "civil society," a Western-based concept rooted in the historical experiences of emerging European nation-states in the 1700s and 1800s and transplanted to other areas of the world, has been a popular heuristic tool for historians of modern China since the late 1980s. In this work, civil society will denote a form of associational life among private individuals institutionalized in the shape of voluntary and professional associations that were more or less autonomous from the state. Professional associations (*fatuan*) were primarily based on occupational specialization, while voluntary associations (*xiehui* or *tuanti*) centered on social issues and concerns such as religion, education, kinship, relief for the poor, and social vices. Such public bodies could assume managerial or extrabureaucratic authority over society on behalf of the state or even claim to represent the will of the people on equal terms with the state, with or without the state's consent.[61]

The roles of voluntary and professional associations in the late Qing and early Republican periods, and their impact on politics at local and national levels have received much scholarly attention in recent years. However, defining the boundaries within which such associations operated is not an easy task in light of the constantly changing nature of the relationship between state and society, often in response to changes occurring in state and society themselves. During the Warlord Era and the Nanjing Decade, the chaotic twenty-one years (1916–1937) that bore witness to the fragmentation of state power and attempts to recentralize, the zone of interaction between state and society was particularly dynamic.

David Strand's book *Rickshaw Beijing* opened a window through which others could observe the vitality and political influence of professional associations—ranging from chambers of commerce to night-soil guilds—in a major city like Beijing during the 1920s.[62] Similarly, Joseph Fewsmith's work *Party, State, and Local Elites in Republican China* examined the important political role of merchant associations in Shanghai from 1890 to 1930.[63] These works and others leave open the possibility that nonprofessional public associations could, in turn, measurably influence Chinese politics in large municipalities.

The impact of opium on China's emergent civil society of the 1920s and 1930s is a story yet to be told. My focus below on the formation of professional and voluntary associations around the issue of opium—for or against; regulatory, predatory, or defensive—is an attempt to bridge this historical gap. I analyze the reasons and motivations for their formation and chronicle their inner workings when possible. But more important, I attempt to reveal how the Chinese version of civil society was at once similar and different from that of the West. The zone of interaction between state and society in which these forces converged, cooperated, and contended at the local and national levels exposes the complicated web of relations between state and society over the issue of opium during this important transitional era.

Opium Merchant Professional Associations

With such a dramatic rise in the cultivation, sale, and use of the narcotic after 1916, the opium business was becoming increasingly profitable and competitive. Local warlord administrations were becoming more dependent on opium as an invaluable source of revenue to cover their escalating civil and military expenditures. As competition intensified between opium merchants, the first opium merchant professional associations made their appearance in the early 1920s.

A prime example of this development was the Hankou Teye Gonghui (Hankou Special Business Association), established in 1922. The Hankou Teye Gonghui was originally composed of thirty-two opium transport and wholesale companies. According to the association's organizational regulations, member transport merchants were forbidden to sell opium to non-member wholesalers, and member wholesalers could not travel to other regions to purchase their merchandise. All large-scale purchases abroad by constituent transport merchants had to be bid openly before the Special Business Association. Prices for the drug sold in the local market by member wholesalers were to be publicly displayed at its headquarters. Moreover, limits for gross profits realized on sales to and by Special Business Association members were set at 10 percent for *yunshang* and 10 to 15 percent for wholesalers.[64] By regulating the competition between themselves, the most prosperous opium transport and wholesale firms were thus able to monopolize the trade in Hankou. As a result, smaller wholesalers and retailers were forced to purchase their goods from Special Business Association merchants.

In the mid to late 1920s, Special Business Association imitators were openly functioning throughout China.[65] Their existence was one indication of the level of legitimacy the opium trade had attained in spite of a national prohibition of the drug. As will be discussed in more detail in the following chapters, the opium transport and wholesale merchants assumed tax collection duties on behalf of local administrations. When the Guomindang established its monopoly along the Yangtze in the 1930s, opium merchant *fatuan* cooperated with the primary tax-collecting organs of the Nationalist government in their respective municipalities. The Hankou Teye Gonghui, for example, changed its name to the Hankou Teye Qinglihui (Hankou Special Business Clearance Association) in 1930, with special business associations in other cities following suit.[66]

The *yapian dawang* maintained their market dominance by getting elected as executive committee members and presidents of various special business associations, and expanded their influence over local society by cultivating good relations with local military and civil authorities. By negotiating tax rates, collecting taxes on behalf of local governments, and monopolizing the wholesale trade of local markets, leaders of the associations earned potent political capital as well. Chao Dianzhi in Hankou and Du Yuesheng in Shanghai, for instance, both used their position as president of local special business associations to obtain appointments in government tax-collection agencies or even seats on local "opium suppression" committees.[67] Furthermore, warlords and local officials commonly formed partnerships with the opium kings in joint-stock transport, wholesale firms, and modern and native banks involved in financing the trade.[68] As the personal and institutional ties that bound the state and special business associations together increased, so did the power of opium merchant professional associations within that realm between state and society.

Like their wealthier counterparts, boiled-opium merchants also formed *fatuan*. The impetus for doing so, however, was more a matter of self-preservation than of self-regulation. Lacking the capital resources and political influence of the transport and wholesale merchants, *regaoshang* were commonly the victims of excessive taxation and the ubiquitous "squeeze" exacted by local authorities. In response to such pressures from above, opium den operators (who formed the largest number of opium merchants in any given market) joined together and formed "protective" professional associations, using their sheer numbers and the threat of boycotts to keep militarists and their administrators at bay.

Two examples of this phenomenon come from Fujian and Sichuan, respectively. In June 1927, the Fuzhoushi Jinyanju (Fuzhou Municipal Opium Suppression Bureau) announced four new monthly levies to be paid by local opium merchants. According to the National Anti-Opium Association report, Fuzhou had more opium dens than any other city in Fujian province. Three of the four new taxes—relating to den licenses, lamp fines, and monopoly sales fees—were to be borne by the smoking establishments. The boiled-opium merchants reacted to the government's decision by organizing a Yaopinshang Keyou Gonghui (Medicinal Merchants Friendship Association) to oppose collectively the new duties imposed by local authorities.[69]

Before the spring of 1928, the over three thousand licensed *yanguan* in Chongqing, Sichuan, each paid a monthly fee called the *"hongdeng fajin"* (red-lamp fine) to the local opium suppression bureau. The red-lamp fine was assessed according to the volume of business and the clientele of the establishment. Dens with five lamps or fewer paid a fine based on each lamp; dens with more than five lamps, however, paid only a maximum fine for five lamps. In early 1928, the new head of the opium suppression bureau, Huang Jiechu, desired to increase revenues derived from the dens. To accomplish this task, he abolished the old method and instituted a new levy of one tax ticket per lamp *(yideng yi-piao)*. In response to the threat that this new system posed to their profits, the den proprietors formed a Regao Tongyehui (Boiled-Opium Merchants Guild), boy-cotted the new taxes, and demanded a reinstitution of the old levy system.[70] In each of the preceding cases, the boiled-opium merchants who had previously been politically inert and isolated came together en masse and formed "protec-tive" professional associations that compelled local authorities either to abolish the new taxes or to lighten the burden of each tax imposed.

Pro-opium Voluntary Associations

As local governments had become increasingly addicted to opium taxes by the early 1930s, the problem of corruption and abuse of power by tax officials and leading opium merchants became more apparent. In many instances, such be-havior severely curtailed essential services provided by local governments. The circumstances surrounding the creation of a protective voluntary associ-ation in Yichang during the early 1930s presents an intriguing view of the op-erations of China's multifaceted civil society.

A letter from a public body calling itself the "Committee Representing All Vocations in Yichang Working Vigorously to Recover the Police and Educa-tion Special Tax Surtax" to Nanjing's minister of finance, T. V. Soong (Song Ziwen), in 1932 is to the point. This body was composed of the following sev-enteen municipal organizations: the Yichang County Guomindang Head-quarters, the Public Security Bureau, the Bureau of Education, the First District Civil Affairs Office, the First District Defense Corps, the Chamber of Commerce, the Agricultural Association, the Educational Association, the Lawyers Association, the Newspaper Reporters Association, the Reconstruc-tion Promotion Committee, the Militia Rehabilitation Committee, the Dock-workers Union, the National Salvation Association, representatives from the fifteen branch Public Security Bureaus, representatives from the various Civil Affairs Offices, and representatives from various primary schools.[71]

According to this letter, the Police and Education Special Tax Surtax *(gong'an jiaoyu teshui fujuan)* collected by members of the Yichang Special Business Clearance Association on behalf of Nanjing's Yichang Branch Spe-cial Tax Clearance Office brought in about $150,000 every month. Each *dan* of raw opium was assessed a surtax of $60, on top of the normal transit taxes worth $600. However, the Yichang municipal government was receiving only

$20,000 monthly (13.3 percent of that collected), the remainder being embezzled by tax officials and Yichang Special Business Clearance Association merchants. As a result of such corrupt activities, local education, police work, military training, road construction, and even economic relief to the poor had been suffering from fiscal deprivation. The letter was a manifesto to T. V. Soong declaring that this ad hoc association was going to take over collection of the surtax from officials and merchants beginning 1 June 1932 "so that every cent of public money that is taxed is accounted for."[72]

Other nonprofessional pro-opium bodies would have to be classified as predatory voluntary associations lacking legitimacy in the eyes of the public and the law. Perhaps their closest social counterparts would be bandit groups or underworld associations similar to the Red and Green gangs, since they engaged in the same sort of criminal activities (i.e., extortion and protection rackets). Although the scale and scope of their operations were much smaller, the desired objective was identical.

In north China's farming villages, gangs of *yangui* became the greatest threat to social order outside of bandits and roaming warlord soldiers. Impoverished addicts would often steal farmers' crops and exchange them for opium. In addition to foodstuffs, agricultural tools and machines were also targeted and pawned at local opium dens. Since north China has an arid climate, irrigation is essential to peasant survival. Understandably, the use of the *shuiche* (waterwheel) to irrigate fields was imperative. Short of cash and needing to satisfy their cravings, groups of addicts would purloin the water cups on the wheels or the entire wheel itself, and ransom them back to the farmers. In some regions, the *yangui* would organize themselves into Shuichehui (Waterwheel Associations) or Qingmiaohui (Green Sprouts Associations) that would "protect" farmers' irrigation equipment or crops during harvest time in exchange for tidy sums to support their habit. Should households refuse the services of such associations, crops and equipment would disappear, and occasionally fires would be deliberately set, destroying other valuable property.[73]

Anti-opium Voluntary Associations

Ever since the widespread production, trafficking, and use of opium resurfaced following Yuan Shikai's death in 1916, Christian missionaries had been at the forefront of the battle against opium. In early 1918, the British physician Dr. W. H. Graham Aspland spearheaded an effort by Protestant missionaries against the Lazarus of narcotics by organizing the International Anti-Opium Association. The espoused goals of the association were "to secure restriction of the production and use of opium, morphia, heroin, cocaine and allied drugs to legitimate uses in all countries" and "to assist in procuring comprehensive legislation and its adequate enforcement, prohibiting the planting and culti-vation of poppy throughout Chinese territory."[74] Within a year of its found-ing, the association had established twenty branch associations in eleven Chinese provinces, primarily in treaty ports such as Shanghai, Tianjin, Hankou, and Shenyang.[75] The association also began publishing an English-language quarterly titled *Opium Cultivation and Traffic in China*, containing reports on the narcotics problem in the republic from its branch associations and foreign missionaries.

Attempting to gain international support for its efforts, the International Anti-Opium Association unsuccessfully lobbied American, French, and Brit-ish leaders at Versailles to include an antidrug clause in the final draft of the 1919 treaty. They were more successful, however, in convincing the League of Nations to create an Advisory Committee on Trafficking in Opium, which sought to halt the excess production of opium and its derivatives—the latter catalyzed by the enormous casualties resulting from World War I. Within China, the International Anti-Opium Association pressured the various war-lord governments in Beijing to pass detailed laws against the sale and cultiva-tion of opium and even managed to attract important Beijing politicians such as Xu Shichang, Li Yuanhong, and Cao Rulin to serve as members.[76]

Despite such achievements, the International Anti-Opium Association failed to popularize its message among the Chinese masses for the following reason. From 1906 to 1916, the state undertook a serious effort to eliminate opium in China, widely circulating anti-opium literature and rigidly enforc-ing the laws. After the breakdown of central authority during the last year of Yuan Shikai's rule, warlords and local officials actively encouraged poppy cul-tivation and consumption. In virtually every province, opium suppression bureaus and similarly named agencies collected assorted taxes on the drug for local warlord administrations that were reluctant to support any anti-opium activities. Except in the province of Shanxi under Yan Xishan, there were no Chinese-language posters, tracts, or publications distributed to the masses by any state or private interests, although volumes of information were being published by the International Anti-Opium Association in English.

Members of the National Christian Council of China responded to this problem on 4 June 1923 by creating the Antinarcotics Commission (Judu

Weiyuanhui). Although several foreign missionaries—including Aspland—were commission members, the majority were Chinese Christians, as was its general secretary, Dr. R. Y. Lo (Luo Yunyan).[77] According to the National Christian Council, the Antinarcotics Commission was established to fill the void "where the International Anti-Opium Association has been compelled to leave off," in other words, to translate into Chinese the existing reports and literature on opium use, production, and trafficking that had been prepared by the International Anti-Opium Association.[78] To facilitate that all-important task, the commission was originally located in the Beijing headquarters of the International Anti-Opium Association, but later moved into the National Christian Council offices in Shanghai.

Beyond the immediate goal of translating International Anti-Opium Association reports and literature into Chinese, the Antinarcotics Commission also collected data and information concerning drug conditions in China and enlisted the support of other ecclesiastical organizations. More important, this movement was envisioned to transcend its Christian base and gain the support of all Chinese. In the words of its general secretary, the commission sought "to secure . . . the co-operation of Chambers of Commerce, Guilds, other religious bodies, educational associations, government schools, parliaments and provincial assemblies . . . and the press, to educate, mould and arouse public opinion."[79]

China's non-Christian urban elites were similarly concerned with the opium scourge ravaging the nation and worked with the commission to create an all-Chinese public body to deal more effectively with the problem. On 5 August 1924, a group of more than five hundred Chinese, including representatives from thirty-eight leading public organizations, gathered at the General Chamber of Commerce in Shanghai and established the Zhonghua Guomin Juduhui (National Anti-Opium Association of China). The original impetus for the creation of this public body was the upcoming Geneva opium conferences sponsored by the League of Nations (November 1924 to February 1925). On 24 August, the national association issued a manifesto to the entire nation, asking leading public bodies and patriotic individuals to join the crusade against opium and other drugs, and elected Cai Yuanpei, Wu Liande, and Gu Ziren (T. Z. Koo) to act as "people's delegates" at the Geneva opium conferences.[80]

The diversity of voluntary and professional associations constituting the thirty-eight founding organizations of the National Anti-Opium Association was not remarkable given the historical context within which such collaboration took place.[81] The explosion of public associations, political parties, literary journals, and newspapers that informed and mobilized urban populations was at once a reaction and a midwife to the growth of Chinese nationalism during the May Fourth–New Culture climate of the early 1920s.[82] Owing to their distrust of the corrupt warlord governments in Beijing, student associations, chambers of commerce, and banking associations mobilized public opinion and put into practice "popular diplomacy." At the Washington Conference of 1921–1922, for example, the urban elite sent its own delegation abroad to represent "the will of the people" alongside the official Chinese delegation, and the National Anti-Opium Association appeared to be a similar phenomenon.[83]

What was remarkable about the national association, however, was how its genesis was linked to resolving contradictions between the forces of Chinese nationalism and Christianity. The aim of New Culture reformers was to modernize Chinese society, and traditional practices such as foot binding and opium smoking were obvious targets of their efforts. As anti-imperialism also thrived in this emotionally charged atmosphere, Christianity was targeted as one of the most glaring examples of foreign encroachment. Christian missionaries, and often their converts, were protected under the cloak of extraterritoriality, and the ubiquitous presence of Christian schools raised the specter of foreign domination over Chinese education. As a result, many Chinese Christians were caught between the Scylla of their foreign faith and the Charybdis of their "Chineseness" and desperately searched for a way to reconcile both forces without being crushed by one or the other.[84]

The formation of the National Christian Council in 1922 was the first step away from foreign missionary domination toward the light of Chinese nationalism. Although composed of both foreign and Chinese members, the sympathies of its constituency lay squarely with the goals of the Chinese nationalists.[85] The fight against opium, containing both anti-imperialist and iconoclastic elements, was at once a moral and a nationalistic cause that all Chinese (excluding those who profited from it) could rally around. Because the National Anti-Opium Association was constructed around the nucleus of the Antinarcotics Commission and headquartered within the offices of the National Christian Council, it provided Chinese Christians with an important tributary into the mainstream of Chinese nationalism.

What distinguished the National Anti-Opium Association from its predecessors, however, was its staying power. Unlike earlier organizations, it did not dissolve immediately after the Geneva opium conferences, nor was its role solely limited to diplomacy. On the contrary, it grew in size and influence to assume leadership in the populist movement to prohibit drugs in China at a time when local and national governments failed to do so. According to the association's seven-article constitution, its aims were threefold: (1) to enforce the laws prohibiting the cultivation of the poppy and the illicit use, manufacture, and trafficking of opium and other narcotics; (2) to limit the importation of foreign narcotic drugs to the amount required for medicinal needs; and (3) to promote anti-narcotics education and the treatment of drug addiction.[86]

The association was composed of a national committee, an executive committee, an honorary directorate, a secretariat, and hundreds of branch associations. The national committee met annually in Shanghai. Two-thirds of the representatives were appointed by its constituent organs, the remaining one-third "co-opted from leaders in different walks of life who are strong supporters of the anti-narcotics movement."[87] Members of the honorary directorate were notable figures in China's educational, political, business, and legal circles. Tang Shaoyi, Cai Yuanpei, and Shi Zhaoji (Dr. Alfred Sao-ke Sze) were among the honorary directors of the association.[88] Another well-known and respected member of the association's hierarchy was Wu Liande, a Cambridge medical school graduate who headed the Manchurian Plague Prevention Service and served concurrently as an honorary director and chairman of the Ha'erbin branch association.[89] Despite the impressive-sounding positions, for all intents and purposes these men lent their names and prestige to the association for public purposes and played little to no role in the organization's day-to-day activities.

It was in the executive committee and the secretariat that the real power of the association resided, both dominated by members of the National Christian Council. As chairman of the executive committee from 1924 to 1928, Li Denghui (T. H. Lee) had been very active in Chinese civil society. He was both founder and chairman of the World Students Federation (1905–1915); and he served as chairman for both the League of Public Organizations that protested against Chinese ratification of the Versailles Treaty in 1919 and the People's National Federation representing 180 public bodies at the 1922 Washington Conference, in addition to holding directorships with numerous other civic associations.[90] Li's organizational skills and contacts with non-Christian groups benefited the association immensely. Zhao Xi'en (Samuel U. Zau) likewise led a socially active life. He converted to Christianity in the early 1900s and later prospered as a government official, businessman, and philanthropist. Zhao's positions in the Beijing government included civil governorships of Zhejiang and Shandong, while his religious and philanthropic activities ranged from deacon of the Baptist Church to director of the Red Cross Society and Hospital as well as directorships of assorted schools, colleges, orphanages, modern banks, and industries.[91]

The heart of the association was the secretariat. It was headed by a general secretary and contained the four departments of General Administration, Survey and Statistics, Local Organization, and Narcotics Education. The National Anti-Opium Association's first general secretary was Zhong Ketuo (Rev. K. T. Chung), a longtime member of the National Christian Council. He was a former Episcopal rector under the American Church Mission and was well known for his blunt talk and devotion to the anti-opium cause.[92] Zhong served in this capacity until he was succeeded by his longtime assistant Garfield Huang (Huang Jiahui) in late 1928. Huang had been active in Christian organizations and educational institutions since his youth in Xiamen. His résumé included a teaching job at the Anglo-Chinese College in Shantou (Swatow) in 1921–1922, a secretarial post in the National Committee of the YMCA of China (1922–1923), and a post as editorial secretary for the National Christian Council during 1923–1924, and he was a cofounder of the National Anti-Opium Association.[93] In his roles as assistant secretary and general secretary, he edited the association's Chinese- and English-language journals in addition to touring different parts of China to establish branch associations. After his appointment as general secretary in December 1928, Garfield Huang became synonymous with both the National Anti-Opium Association and its work.

The activities of the National Anti-Opium Association were legion. To educate the public on the harmful effects of opium and other narcotics, the association published numerous periodicals, tracts, books, pamphlets, and posters (see Figure 3). Its notable publications included the monthly magazine *Judu yuekan* (Opium, A National Issue), the sporadically issued *Zhongguo yanhuo nianjian* (China Opium Yearbook),[94] and the English-language quarterly *Opium, A World Problem*. The association also worked hard to get Chinese publishers to include information on drugs in their publications, including school primers, and sponsored essay and speech contests among Chinese students in Shanghai and throughout the nation. The resulting mobilization of public opinion had visible impact. When Gu Ziren attended the Geneva opium conferences and addressed the delegates as a representative of the "Chinese people's anti-opium movement," he carried with him a petition signed by 4,265 public bodies representing 4,663,979 Chinese citizens.[95] In autumn 1924, the association declared the last Sunday in September to be "Anti-opium Day." By 1926, the day had

Figure 3. The caption reads "It is the Duty of All Citizens to Work Together and Exert All of Their Energies against the Scourge of Narcotics." Source: *Chinese Recorder* 55.11 (Nov. 1924): 719.

grown into an "Anti-opium Week" celebrated in the first week of October. The National Anti-Opium Association also undertook aggressive organizational drives throughout China, especially in the cities along the Yangtze and in Manchuria. As a result of such efforts, the association grew in size from 188 branch associations in 1924 to 450 in 1930.[96]

In another capacity, the National Anti-Opium Association conducted a number of important studies of the drug situation in China, compiling records for domestic and international audiences. The association chemically analyzed opium "remedies" advertised in Chinese periodicals as cures for addiction and found them generally to be morphine or heroin pills. As word of its work spread abroad, in January 1927 Zhu Zhaoxin (Chu Chao-hsin), Chinese representative to the League of Nations and National Anti-Opium Association honorary vice-chairman, got the League's Opium Advisory Committee to recognize the association for "its cooperation in the task of fighting the opium evil in the Far East."[97]

In working against the opium trade and criticizing those who profited from it, the National Anti-Opium Association found itself confronting Chinese and foreign governments as well as national and international opium cartels. In February 1925, the Beijing government under president Duan Qirui proposed to the legalize the opium trade, since it was in effect quasi-legal throughout the country despite de jure prohibition. The association mobilized public opinion against the proposal, and the sponsors of the legislation—the Fengtian Clique—had to withdraw it.[98] A year later, the National Anti-Opium Association revealed the names of thirty-six opium shops openly operating in the French Concession in Shanghai, and its protests to the French administration resulted in police raids on several of the shops.[99] The association was also a relentless critic of the opium monopolies operating in the Asian colonies of Britain, France, Holland, Portugal, and Japan as well as the "unequal treaties" that protected foreign drug smugglers from Chinese law.

Perhaps the most intriguing features of Republican civil society before the war with Japan were its ambiguity and its flexibility. Although the opium trade was technically illegal under national prohibition laws throughout China in the 1920 and 1930s, local and national governments openly participated in it. They were able to maintain the legal fiction of prohibition by naming tax organs opium suppression bureaus. Similarly, opium merchant guilds existed legitimately as "special business associations" or "medicinal merchants friendship associations" in the same realm as the National Anti-Opium Association. It would be difficult to imagine in the United States today marijuana,

cocaine, heroin, or crystal methamphetamine dealers openly forming professional associations and enjoying the same legal rights as an antidrug association like DARE (Drug Abuse Resistance Education), yet that was the reality
of the times.

The dissimilarities between Republican civil society and the Western
model, and the pitfalls of using the latter to interpret and explain the former
reminds one of the old Chinese parable about the tangerine tree *(juzishu)*.
When the *juzishu* is planted south of the Huai River, it produces tangerines;
when transplanted north of the Huai, it produces the *zhizi* (trifoliate orange),
a thick-skinned, unpalatable fruit that is only good for use in Chinese herbal
remedies. Although the two fruits are similar in outside appearance—like
Chinese and Western civil society—they are very different within.

3 Guomindang Opium Policy during the Height of Warlordism, 1924–1928

IN THE SHANTOU REGION OF GUANGDONG province, people had a saying that might serve as the mantra for Chinese politics in the 1920s and 1930s: "*Xiyapian hui shangyin, chouyapianshui yehui shangyin; yapian yanyin yijie, yapian shuiyin nanjie*" (If you smoke opium, you will become addicted; if you collect opium taxes, you will also become addicted. It is easy to cure someone addicted to opium but difficult to cure someone addicted to opium taxes).[1]

The political and economic milieu in which warlordism functioned set limitations on everyone interested in national political centralization. Unification meant rival leaders and factions liquidating or absorbing each other until a single leader and party dominated the whole of the country. Since this outcome depended chiefly on military manpower and the resources to maintain and use that manpower effectively, it depended on money. To make a long story short, warlords and their organizations solved their money problems, to the extent that they did solve them, by turning to the opium trade. As a major player in the struggle for political survival in the Warlord Era (traditionally observed as 1916 to 1928), the Nationalist Party did likewise. Thus it was that the Guomindang's aspirations for national unification and state building came to be enmeshed in drug trafficking.

The Warlord System

Historians have studied the history of Republican China in considerable depth. The general consensus is that the rise of warlords and warlordism at the expense of a civilian-dominated central government and the concomitant "devolution of power" from centralized bureaucracies to local elites was the culmination of a process that originated in the middle of the nineteenth century. During the failed Taiping Revolution of 1850 to 1864, regional military leaders such as Zeng Guofan, Zuo Zongtang, and Li Hongzhang achieved unprecedented control over large armies and local financial administration, the latter of which they used to divert funds from the central government to their own purposes.[2] In addition, it soon became the custom for local officials or other elites to maintain their own militias for self-defense and for bureaucrats in the central government to delegate responsibility for financial and military matters to those officials or elites.

After the 1911 Revolution began, the ascendancy of regional militarists was acknowledged when Sun Yat-sen resigned the presidency in favor of Yuan Shikai, who subsequently replaced the civilian governors of the provinces with military ones. Yuan's government then systematically uprooted the sprouts of democracy planted by the revolutionaries. It disbanded the elected parliament, rewrote the constitution to augment the president's powers, and undertook a failed effort to make Yuan Shikai emperor.[3]

Despite Yuan's shortcomings, he was the last man in China able to control the militarists. Following his death in 1916, the leading generals in the Beiyang Army began fighting among themselves for control of the new republic. When that occurred, the already strained bonds between centralized bureaucracies in Beijing and provincial authorities, who aligned themselves with one or more of the warring factions, broke down. The result was a fragmentation of political and military power called regional or provincial militarism, though some provinces—especially Sichuan—fragmented internally.[4] From 1916 until the end of the period of this study in 1937, Chinese politics was characterized by continual warfare between competing military factions and political movements, including the Guomindang and the Chinese Communist Party. While the Guomindang and the Communist Party each sought to unify the nation under its own rule, most warlords, as local or military leaders came to be known, fought and otherwise acted to maintain their own power and position. The ensuing era of political disintegration was not unique in Chinese history. However, it did have a unique feature. It took place against the backdrop of rising Chinese nationalism.[5]

Historians have described the phenomenon of warlordism in Republican China in various ways and have dated its beginnings everywhere from the late Qing period to 1916.[6] Traditionally speaking, the date marking its termination is 1928 with the conclusion of the Guomindang's Northern Expedition (Beifa). There is, nonetheless, a consensus that the phenomenon continued after 1928 and hindered Guomindang efforts at political unification and state building. James Sheridan characterizes the persistence of warlord behavior during the Nanjing Decade as "residual warlordism," and other historians cite the examples of Yan Xishan in Shanxi and Long Yun in Yunnan as evidence that such behavior persisted until the end of the Chinese Civil War in 1949.[7]

The term "warlord" is a translation of the two Chinese characters *"junfa"* (a term borrowed from Japan), which together connote military hegemonism. It is a derisive term, originally used only by critics of the warlords, but a term that stuck.[8] A more neutral term for the phenomenon is "militarism," which C. Martin Wilbur has defined as a "system of organizing political power in which force is the normal arbiter in the distribution of power and in the establishment of policy."[9] In any event, warlordism or militarism as a political system was perhaps defined most succinctly by Mao Zedong, who said, "Political power grows out of the barrel of a gun."[10]

To be a warlord one must have command of a personal army and a territorial base from which to extract resources to support the army. According to Jerome Ch'en's count, from 1912 to 1928 more than 1,300 men in China met those two criteria.[11] However, there were absolute criteria that were not always easy to pin down in what was always a dynamic and fluid situation. Warlords often extended their territories and armies by incorporating those of rivals. Expansion also meant delegating responsibilities and authority to underling generals or groups whose loyalties were not always absolute. As a consequence, there were always tensions within warlord confederations, and the larger the confederations, the more likely the tensions would have consequences.

The essential feature of warlordism was what Lloyd Eastman has called the "militarization of politics." According to Eastman: "Following the collapse of Yuan Shikai's government in 1916, contests for power were determined not by popular elections nor by debates in representative assemblies, but by the threat or actual use of military force. Civilian bureaucrats were tools of the militarists, employed in large part to raise revenues for the armies."[12] Eastman cites Chiang Kai-shek (Jiang Jieshi) as a product of this process, a military man who came to dominate the Nationalist Party at the expense of civilian leaders like Hu Hanmin and Wang Jingwei.

Tien Hung-mao also described the process by which Chiang came to dominate the Nationalist government during the Nanjing Decade as the "militarization of the Kuomintang regime."[13] Tien's work demonstrates the militarization of administrative agencies at both national and local levels, and argues persuasively that that phenomenon prevented the Nationalists from developing a modern civil bureaucracy. In Tien's words, "The domination of political power and financial resources by military men, namely Chiang Kai-shek and his colleagues, deprived civilian leaders of the ways and means to establish such [nonmilitary] structures."[14]

In step with the militarization of Republican China, arranging the financial resources necessary to fuel the machines of war was the most vital function of warlord administrations. A by-product of this process was an increasing tax burden on local populations that corresponded to the growth of the men under arms and the level of military activity. In 1916, there were approximately 500,000 soldiers in the republic, and the cost to maintain them was perhaps $153 million. By 1928, when the National Revolutionary Army conquered Beijing, this figure had more than quadrupled to 2.2 million, and the costs of maintaining them had escalated to $800 million. Thereafter, for the period of this study, military expenditures in China continued to escalate (See Appendix Table 16).

Given the voracious appetites of warlord armies, it was probably inevitable that the opium trade would return quickly and massively to Chinese life. For the warlords' purposes the opium trade was an ideal activity. It prospered despite layers of taxation, generated a huge demand and therefore a huge supply, and remained affordable for most potential customers.

The best way to understand Guomindang opium policy from 1924 to 1937 is to see it in the context of this warlord system (see Figure 4).[15] Despite an ostensible effort to destroy the opium trade beginning in 1928, that effort had no real effect except perhaps to strengthen the trade. Not until after 1938, when the war with Japan was well under way, did the trade begin to ebb at all. It was the warlord system, and not the Guomindang itself, that brought the Republican narco-economy to life, and it was the level of military conflict in Chinese politics that sustained it. Conversely, it was the high levels of revenue from the trade that made possible the sustained military conflict.

Not all the major participants in the warlord system were Chinese. After the Japanese Kwantung (Guandong) Army invaded Manchuria and penetrated Inner Mongolia and north China, they behaved much like the Chinese warlords Zhang Zuolin and Zhang Xueliang whom they had replaced. Although their goal was their own—to incorporate large parts of China into an expanded Japanese colonial empire—the Japanese warlords used the opium trade as an essential source of funding for military expansion and occupation. Japanese generals colluded with opium merchants, Japanese bankers, and

Figure 4. The original caption reads "The Patient Star Gazer." Not all the stars in the sky are warlords, but the relationship between opium and their rise and fall is unwittingly portrayed by Sapajou. Source: *North China Herald,* 22 Nov. 1924, 301.

underworld organizations in the same manner as their Chinese counterparts. Japanese militarists established opium monopolies in Manchuria and Rehe as soon as they conquered those regions from 1931 to 1933, actively promoting poppy cultivation in areas under their control.[16]

Still, most warlords were Chinese, and the internal commerce in opium remained primarily in Chinese hands as the Guomindang expanded its influence before the intensification of hostilities with Japan. Viewed through the prisms of warlordism, political centralization, and state building, the dynamics of Guomindang opium policy provide a window that sheds new light on these processes during the 1920s and 1930s. By the time Sun Yat-sen finally had a stable revolutionary base in Canton in 1923–1924, the link between warlordism, opium, and Guomindang political policy had already been firmly established.

The Evolution of Opium Tax-Farming Monopolies

The situation in Xiamen in the mid-1920s illustrates both the ravenous nature of the warlords' appetite for revenue and the tax-farming system. From 1922 to 1924 Cang Zhiping, an ally of the Zhejiang militarists, controlled Xiamen and was responsible for maintaining a military force of 8,000 extraprovincial (*waisheng*) troops. His position in Xiamen was precarious, because armies of native Fujianese there under Sun Chuanfang, Zhou Yinren, and others totaled 72,000 men, and they were loosely allied with Wu Peifu's Zhili Clique, then the archenemy of the Zhejiang militarists.[17] The annual cost of maintaining all of these armies, including the omnipresent graft in tax collection, was perhaps $20 million in 1924.[18]

Cang Zhiping had a Bureau of Finance to handle his fiscal affairs. It farmed out most of Cang's commercial levies to local merchants with the understanding that the warlord would provide the force necessary to collect them. The Xiamen Chamber of Commerce, whose members paid for the right to collect most of the taxes, tried to guard the interests of local businessmen by negotiating with Cang concerning shortfalls in revenue collection and confronting the warlord when levies became overly burdensome.[19]

According to a report compiled by the U.S. consulate in January 1924, residents and business people in Xiamen were paying seventy different kinds of taxes, to which Cang or someone else soon added seven more. The estimated income from these exactions that reached Cang's coffers was just over $38,000 per month.[20] Interestingly, this figure represented less than 40 percent of the actual amount collected in the district, the rest going to brokers or tax farmers.[21] When Cang declared that his monthly expenses were $130,000 and pressed for additional taxes, the inhabitants of Xiamen declared their inability to pay, and merchants began closing their businesses in protest. The Chamber of Commerce acted as intermediary in this dispute and negotiated a solution. It agreed that the people of Xiamen could pay $100,000 per month but no more and that that figure was quite sufficient to meet Cang's administrative requirements. Both sides then decided that the only way to generate the extra revenue needed was to establish an opium monopoly.[22]

Thus, in late January 1924, Cang announced the creation of the Teshe Zhuan-ju (Special Monopoly Bureau) to manage the "strict prohibition of illegal opium sales" in Xiamen.[23] The bureau purchased raw opium at $1.50 a *liang* and sold it for $4.00. It also permitted the cultivation, sale, and smoking of opium—but only by licensed farmers, merchants, and smokers—and assessed various taxes on growers, wholesalers, retailers, and opium dens. The new monopoly realized in excess of $500,000 a month, more than enough to cover the deficits in Cang's accounts and enough to enable him to become militarily venturesome.[24]

This example was symptomatic of the development of opium tax-farming practices by municipal and provincial governments in the 1920s. During the first three months of 1924, the Jiangxi provincial government, Cang's administration in Xiamen, and the Guomindang regime in Canton all publicly announced the creation of so-called opium monopolies and widely circulated regulations governing their operation.[25] This move represented a dramatic change of policy; theretofore, the functioning of the opium trade and the collection of duties on it had been much more discreet. The expansion of the opium traffic, the involvement of military and civil authorities in it, and the increasing fiscal addiction of armed forces to the trade were now everywhere public policy—and knowledge.

The types of opium monopolies instituted by warlords typically combined tax farming and licensing schemes. Jiangxi's monopoly inaugurated in March 1924 operated on a provincial scale. Warlord Cai Chengxun and the Jiangxi Provincial Assembly created a Juduhui (Anti-opium Society) composed of leading military and civilian officials to supervise the transportation and sale of opium. The Juduhui farmed out the purchase, importation, and sales of domestically grown opium to licensed transport, wholesale, and boiled-opium merchants. It was estimated that this monopoly generated $400,000 monthly for Cai's government, with Jiangxi's opium merchants happily pocketing the overage.[26] Other contemporary accounts confirm the turgid mechanics of opium revenue extraction. In 1927, authorities in Fujian's provincial capital of Fuzhou farmed out the collection of poppy taxes for the neighboring counties of Tong'an, Maxiang, and Guankou to several bidders for the sum of $700,000. Actual collections by the tax farmers, however, exceeded $1,100,000.[27]

How much revenue did the opium trade generate for the warlords? There are no precise data on that question, but there are suggestive estimates based on a variety of contemporary sources for important areas of warlord activity. These estimates are too fragmentary to produce an overall estimate, as indicated in Appendix Table 17. The only overall estimate in the reliable literature is that of Herbert L. May, who conducted a yearlong investigation of the opium situation in East and Southeast Asia in 1926 for the Foreign Policy Association of New York, then a think tank for American foreign policy makers. May wrote, "$200,000,000 [Mexican] is a fair guess at the annual stake for which the 'war lords,' provincial governors, high central government officials, and petty politicians have been playing of in late years."[28] Although May acknowledges that his figure is a "fair guess," a comparison between it and the estimated amounts of money available to various warlords suggests that it has value as an approximation of the total size of tax revenues derived from the commerce in opium in the mid-1920s.

Sun Yat-sen, the Guomindang, and Opium in Canton

Since Sun Yat-sen and his writings formed the basis of political legitimacy for the Guomindang in Republican China, a discussion of Nationalist opium policy properly begins with the beloved *guofu* (Father of the Nation). Sun's private as well as public statements over thirty-five years make it clear that he was wholeheartedly committed to the task of eradicating the drug. Born in the aftermath of the Opium Wars and the unequal treaties, Sun lived into the Warlord Era of the 1920s (he died in 1925). Through all these years, he never wavered from his commitment to exorcising the drug demon from the land of his ancestors.

Nevertheless, being committed to an ideal and achieving it were two separate matters entirely. For example, Sun's commitment to democracy was unquestionable, yet to implement that system of government during his lifetime while militarists held the reins of power proved an unreachable goal. When one looks at Sun's statements on prohibition in relation to their actual fulfillment, it becomes clear how the realpolitik of warlordism necessitated certain ideological sacrifices.

In a letter written in 1889, when he was twenty-three years old, Sun imitated Lin Zexu's petition to Emperor Daoguang by comparing the effects of opium on Chinese society to the turmoil created by wild beasts, insects, and snakes in ancient China until they were driven out by the "sages." The young patriot blamed the Qing government for these conditions and emphasized the court's moral responsibility to deal with them effectively. He then noted that his native county in Guangdong had formed associations to encourage people to quit smoking and established clinics to help treat them, and he emphasized that the same must be done throughout the rest of the country without any further delay.[29]

Sun wrote four documents (laws and letters) on opium in 1912, following in the wake of the revolution. One law, titled Jin Yapianyan Ling (Decree Prohibiting Opium Smoking), promulgated on 8 March, stated that opium smokers would be stripped of their civil rights in the new republic and encouraged civic organizations to lead the fight against drugs on the local level.[30] In spite of the harsh rhetoric embodied in the law, its effects were dubious. The 1911 revised accord with Great Britain permitted the importation and sale of Indian opium until the year 1917. Sun thus linked the continued sale of foreign opium to the imcomplete eradication effort in China. Imitating Lin Zexu's letter to Queen Victoria, Sun's May 1912 correspondence to Whitehall titled "A Letter to the People of England on the Sovereignty of Opium Prohibition" argued that all of China's prohibition work would be in vain unless Indian imports were simultaneously curtailed.[31]

The final document comes from 1924, in a completely different context than those of twelve years earlier. No longer were the British to blame for China's drug problems; Indian imports had ceased, and now it was the Chinese themselves who were largely responsible for the illicit trade and their inablility to implement a serious poppy eradication campaign. Sun's view was recorded by a reporter from *Dagongbao* (L'Impartial) on 14 December in Tianjin, when educators from the National Anti-Opium Association had queried the *guofu* about his opium policy. Of all the laws, letters, and interviews concerning opium that were later incorporated under the rubric of the "Thought of Sun Yat-sen," these words were considered his most important statement of Guomindang opium policy and were canonized as Sun's "Judu yixun" (Anti-opium Will):

> In my opinion, the problem of opium suppression in China is synonymous with the problem of good government. For the traffic in opium cannot coexist with a National[ist] government deriving its power and authority from the people. Until political workers in China are in a position to implement civil authority in the administration of government, it will be nearly impossible to prohibit opium completely.[32]

Canton's Opium Monopoly, 1924–1925

By late 1923, Sun's third government in Canton since 1917 was still vulnerably reliant on the good graces of regional warlords and desperate for revenue.[33] In the aftermath of a failed effort to seize control over Canton's Maritime Customs collection in December 1923 and with a petty amount of foreign aid trickling in from the Soviet Union, the Canton regime was living day to day on financial life support.

Despite his commitment to an opium-free China, even Sun Yat-sen could not ignore the fiscal realities of the times. Therefore, on 16 January 1924, he announced the creation of an opium monopoly in Canton in the form of Opium Suppression Regulations (Jinyan Tiaoli).[34] According to the Jinyan Tiaoli, all matters relating to opium suppression were under the jurisdiction of Yang Xiyan, whom Sun appointed opium suppression superintendent (*jin-yan duban*), head of the Jinyan Dubanshu (Opium Suppression Superintendent's Office). Yang had served as minister of finance in 1923 and was still a member of the Canton government's Finance Committee.[35] The Opium Suppression Superintendent's Office was responsible for gathering information on addicts in Canton and "advising" them to purchase a smoker's permit or face criminal prosecution. It also controlled the transportation, storage, and sale of all "opium-cure medicine" (*jieyan yaopin*), as the Guomindang called opium sold under its monopoly, and the apprehension and punishment of violators of the regulations. The office had branches in outlying regions under Guomindang control or nominal influence, and exacted heavy fines from persons selling or importing nonmonopoly opium.[36]

Immediately after the office was created, it encountered difficulties. The first was a conflict between Sun and Yang Xiyan over the prosecution of opium offenders.[37] Another was interference in the collection of tax monies by warlord armies allied with the Canton regime. In February, Sun ordered his generals to prohibit their troops from hijacking revenues under pretext of "military emergencies," and on one such occasion, Yang Xiyan was held ransom for 10,000 ounces of opium.[38] Further exacerbating the situation were many ersatz loyal commanders, most notoriously Yunnanese mercenaries, vending smuggled opium from their home province in direct competition with the monopoly.[39]

Still another stumbling block for Sun's suppression effort was corruption. Since opium revenues were so lucrative, the temptation of embezzlement was strong. A case in point was when Sun dismissed Yang on charges of "not carrying out his duties in an honest manner and wanton corruption."[40] Yang Xiyan had not only abused his powers to extort additional fines from opium offenders but had also misappropriated substantial funds at the government's expense. He was replaced by Lu Diping in late March 1924, and the suppression monopoly thereafter became the sole official source of revenue for Tan Yankai's Hunan troops.[41]

Although on the surface the January 1924 regulations maintained the fiction of government control over all facets of the monopoly, the reality was much different. Opium importation and sales were farmed out to a merchant syndicate that paid the Opium Suppression Superintendent's Office $3,000 daily for issuing wholesale (branch office) and retail (opium den) licenses in addition to collecting other taxes associated with the legal commerce. The number of opium dens licensed (in three classes) to sell the suppression office product in Canton jumped from 473 in February 1924 to perhaps 800 in August.[42] The dens were selling opium paste *(regao)* for $5.50 to $11 a *liang*, depending on the varieties, which included Indian, Persian, Yunnanese, and various mixtures.[43] According to the signs on their doors, the dens were "*tanhuachu*" (discussion parlors), which attracted little attention from uninformed citizens or foreigners.[44] However, the *tanhuachu* operators had already organized their own guild when, in late July 1924, Sun's government levied a surtax on their dens in addition to the lamp tax and license fees they were already paying. The guild decided to protest the new levy by closing down for several days, which so curtailed revenues that the government agreed to rescind the surtax.[45]

The Guomindang's experience with tax collection in Canton was a microcosm of warlord financing in its early years, as government finances were wholly dependent on the Cantonese merchants.[46] The Chamber of Commerce and other merchant *fatuan* prospered from the tax-farming arrangements by extracting much more from local society than they gave to the government for that privilege. Just as in Xiamen, where tax farmers kept about 60 percent of total collections for themselves while remitting the rest to Cang Zhiping's government, similarly, until the power of these *shangren caituan* (merchant syndicates) in Canton was broken and revenue collection bureaucratized, the government could not expect to improve its financial situation.[47]

Sun's government undertook a series of reforms to free itself from the stranglehold of Cantonese merchants. The first step was to create the Central Bank, which soon accumulated one of the largest silver reserves of any bank in China and provided a solid, trusted currency for the regime.[48] Another important measure was the suppression of the Canton Merchants Volunteer Corps in October 1924. This merchant army provided Cantonese merchants (the tax farmers) with the means to resist government attempts to centralize financial administration.[49] A final step was the defeat in June 1925 of Yunnanese mercenaries Liu Zhenhuan and Yang Ximin, whose interference in revenue collection—notably with opium—was a chronic problem.[50]

Despite the state-building initiatives executed by bureaucratic and military means, it appears that there was no concerted effort to purge tax farmers from the opium monopoly machinery until the summer of 1925, a few months after Sun Yat-sen passed away in Beijing. On 1 August, a revised set of Opium Suppression Regulations was promulgated.[51] The regulations announced a new commitment to end the opium trade in four years. Under this four-year plan, all addicts were to be cured of their habit by means of a smoker's permit scheme that mandated a 25 percent decrease in annual consumption monitored by local authorities.

The revised Opium Suppression Regulations again gave the Opium Suppression Superintendent's Office jurisdiction over the monopoly. More important, the Ministry of Finance replaced the Hunanese generals as the party responsible for handling the revenues generated by the "suppression" effort. Although the revised regulations announced that all opium dens (*tanhuachu* and *yanguan*) were prohibited, they actually represented an attempt by the Canton regime to dominate the sales of all opium paste through its own distribution network at the expense of the well-organized boiled-opium merchants.[52]

The Opium Suppression Superintendent's Office was divided into two departments: Inspection and Monopoly Sales. The Inspection Department included sections concerned with inspection and arrest, public information, licensing, and treatment; and the Monopoly Sales Department contained sections concerned with procurement, manufacturing, security, sales, and administration.[53]

The interaction between the reorganized Opium Suppression Superintendent's Office and the commercial and wholesale merchants of Canton illuminates the system of opium control implemented by the Guomindang in August 1925. On 8 August, Opium Suppression Superintendent Fan Qiwu signed a contract authorizing the Anhua Gongsi (Peaceful China Company) to purchase and transport to the Opium Suppression Superintendent's Office in Canton one thousand cases of Persian opium for the ensuing year. Titled "Chengban texu caiyun yantu heyue" (A Contract to Undertake the Specially Approved Purchase and Transport of Raw Opium), the document is an invaluable testament to the ties between governments and opium merchants in the 1920s.[54]

The contract stipulated the procedures for transporting and delivering opium to the suppression office. The Anhua Gongsi merchants first had to contact the office and receive a *huzhao* (passport) specifying the number of cases, weight, and destination of the shipment (see Figure 5). If the shipment was overweight, the inspectors would confiscate the overage. Nor could the vessel transporting the shipment sell any opium en route to Canton. If the

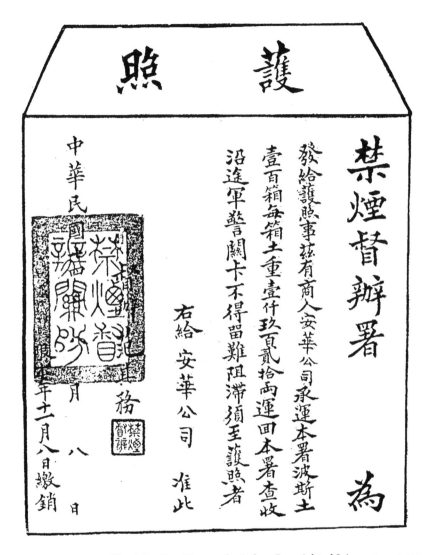

Figure 5. Passport issued by *duban* Fan Qiwu to the Anhua Gongsi dated 8 August 1925, permitting the shipment of one hundred cases of Persian opium to the Opium Suppression Superintendent's Office in Canton. Source: Guomindang Central Archives, Document No. 442/54.1.

army, navy, or native customs officials interfered with a shipment, the company was to report the interference to the Opium Suppression Superintendent's Office to reclaim it. Moreover, if any loss resulted from confiscation or interference, the office was held liable. When a shipment approached Canton, at either Yangjiang or Taishan, the company had to inform the office of the impending arrival. The office would then dispatch a gunboat and troops to protect it. All taxes, charges, and other expenses normally levied on opium shipments into Canton were to be waived on shipments covered by the contract. In addition, the costs of escorting the shipments were to be borne by the Opium Suppression Superintendent's Office.

The contract dealt at length with the obligations of each party concerning the quality of goods to be delivered. For one thousand cases of Persian opium, each case weighing 1,920 *liang* (160 lbs.), the Opium Suppression Superintendent's Office agreed to pay $4,250 per case in silver dollars. The opium itself had to be at least 70 percent Persian, which was verified by chemical analysis, and the remaining 30 percent usually consisted of domestic southern varieties preferred by Cantonese smokers.

After the company delivered the opium, the office tallied its weight, analyzed the morphine content, processed it into opium paste, and attached tax stamps to it. Following government inspection of the paste, the Anhua Gongsi stored the *regao* in its own warehouse under the supervision of the Opium Suppression Superintendent's Office and delivered specified amounts of it to the branch agencies, for which the company charged 5 percent daily interest for storing the goods.

Finally, if the government arbitrarily canceled the agreement before the company had fulfilled it, Canton was responsible for the resulting losses to the Anhua Gongsi. If the company failed to fulfill the terms of the contract, it forfeited the $5,000 *baozhengjin* (bond or deposit) paid to the government to ensure compliance with the contract. Furthermore, if the Anhua Gongsi defaulted and lost the deposit, it was responsible for losses incurred by the government up to a maximum of $30,000.

It appears on the surface that the contract with the Anhua Gongsi was a good deal for the government. In a year under the contract, the Ministry of Finance was to pay the company $4,250,000 plus storage fees of $212,500 for 1,920,000 *liang* of raw opium, about $2.30 per ounce. Since opium lost about 40 percent of its weight in the boiling process, the selling price of *regao* had to be much higher than $2.30 an ounce. In fact, *regao* made from Yunnanese opium sold for around $5 an ounce, from Persian around $11, from Indian $13 an ounce, and mixtures of the sort the suppression office produced about $8 an ounce.[55] At $8 a *liang*, retailing 1,152,000 *liang* of opium paste would gross at least $9,216,000, or around $5 million net, not including income from the sale of smoker's permits. The actual profits of the government are unknown, but according to T. V. Soong, the monopoly earned just over $520,000 for the four months it operated.[56] In late November 1925, the government terminated its contract with the Anhua Gongsi, then abolished and replaced the Opium Suppression Superintendent's Office with the Jinyan Zongchu (Opium Suppression Office), an agency within the Ministry of Finance.[57]

Why the failure? Because Canton and its environs were so inviting a market that the government and the Anhua Gongsi could not enforce the monopoly. Too much opium entered Guangdong province overland from Guangxi, Hunan, Jiangxi, and Fujian, or by sea from a myriad of Asian ports for the government to corner supply or keep unlicensed merchants, retailers, and den operators from plying their trade. Another factor was that coolies and lower-class smokers—the largest consumption groups—could not afford the prices of the Opium Suppression Superintendent's Office. As a result, by late October the monopoly had sold only 4,500 smoker's permits.[58]

For these reasons Soong recognized the failure, abolished the Opium Suppression Superintendent's Office, and reestablished a traditional tax-farming system that encouraged everyone to profit from the trade, thereby increasing state revenues.[59] The Nationalist government maintained that method of "opium suppression" until late 1928.

T. V. Soong's Bureaucratization of Tax Collection, 1925–1926

The appointment of Soong as Minister of Finance in September 1925 facilitated the trend toward rationalizing and bureaucratizing the regime's financial administration. It is therefore logical to conclude that Soong had a hand in the failed Opium Suppression Superintendent's Office–Anhua Gongsi monopoly established in August that year. Generally speaking, Soong applied his Harvard training to the bloated inefficiency of Guangdong's existing tax-collection methods by implementing a system of checks and balances, and by creating agencies under the Ministry of Finance to collect the revenues directly at their source. By reducing the role of tax farmers and licensed intermediaries as much as possible, Soong removed much of the wealth that went into their pockets and placed it in government coffers instead. By April 1926, approximately 90 percent of all levies were collected by government tax agencies.[60] Although people were still paying from seventy to one-hundred-odd taxes, instead of increasing the existing mountain of levies and duties, revenue was increased through direct collection by government personnel.[61]

An example of this dynamic turnaround under Soong's leadership can be readily seen in Canton's rising income between 1924 and 1926. During 1924 the government earned a total of $7,986,000; for 1925 it rose to $19,015,801; but tax

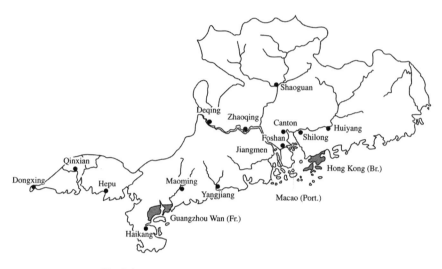

Map 5. Locations of Monopoly Sales Bureaus as of July 1926

receipts in 1926 jumped fourfold to $80,200,000.[62] By eliminating the most egregious practices such as tax farming in non-opium revenue collection, Soong put the Canton government on secure financial ground before the launching of the Northern Expedition in mid-1926. In stark contrast, however, owing to the decentralized nature of the opium trade, Soong reluctantly reinstituted traditional tax-farming arrangements with local opium merchants.

After Soong replaced the Opium Suppression Superintendent's Office with the Opium Suppression Office in late 1925, the system underwent further refining. Soong farmed out the opium monopoly to the Gongcheng Gongsi and divided profits with the firm. He established several *jianchasuo* (inspection posts) along the West River to interdict smuggling. As a consequence, the government's income from opium rose modestly to over $1 million for the five-month period from December 1925 to April 1926.[63]

In May 1926, Soong adopted the method of *guandu shangban* (government supervision, merchant operation), which permitted the Xingyuan Gongsi to transport and sell opium under the Ministry of Finance's watchful eye. The Xingyuan Gongsi paid $350,000 a month to Canton and split any profit above that amount on a thirty-seventy basis. This arrangement lasted only two months and had little effect on Guangdong's omnipresent smuggling problem.

In July 1926, the Central Political Committee voted to expand the existing monopoly over opium paste sales to include the unregulated traffic in raw opium and to enter into tax-farming arrangements with other provincial opium merchants to accomplish that task.[64] Canton subsequently abolished the Opium Suppression Office and established the Zhuanmai Zongju (Monopoly Sales Bureau) with subbureaus throughout Guangdong. The Ministry of Finance contracted with several firms *(baoshang)*, granting them permission to sell opium and collect taxes at various levels of the trade in return for set monthly payments to Canton. The firms also assumed responsibility for transporting opium to Canton and other regions in Guangdong where the Monopoly Sales Bureau had branches. The bureaus were essentially licensed wholesale and transport companies operating on behalf of the Ministry of Finance. The *baoshang* subcontracted the collection of tax revenues on opium sales to other merchants *(zhaoshang)* at various levels of the retail trade. The fiscal benefit of this new system was revenue of $2,120,000 between May and September 1926; and Soong forecast that the implementation of additional antismuggling measures would push yearly revenues above $10 million, which occurred in 1928.[65] By the time of the Northern Expedition, there were over thirteen branch Monopoly Sales Bureaus and inspection posts scattered along important river routes, seaports, and cities in Guangdong (see Map 5).[66]

Opium Suppression during the Northern Expedition

One of the main concerns of Sun's successor, Chiang Kai-shek, was securing adequate funds to finance the Northern Expedition. As soon as the Beifa commenced in July 1926, it became clear that opium revenues were necessary to provision the ever-growing number of troops under the banner of the National Revolutionary Army. As the army marched northward through central and north China, its numbers grew from approximately one hundred thousand when the Northern Expedition began to over 1.6 million when it ended in June 1928.[67] The enormous appetite of the National Revolutionary Army could not be sated by revolutionary slogans alone. In fact, "opium suppression" during the Northern Expedition played a vital logistical role in the Guomindang's drive to unify China.

Opium Suppression from Canton to Wuhan

As the National Revolutionary Army fought its way from Guangdong to the strategically important cities of Wuhan, Nanjing, and Shanghai on the middle and lower Yangtze, and then on to Beijing, the task of provisioning the army became a logistical nightmare. Before the army captured a city, the retreating enemy carried off vast sums of money from banks and other businesses, thereby denying them to the Guomindang.[68] In addition to the usual costs of war, the army so often used "silver bullets" (i.e., silver dollars) to buy the defection of commanders in opposing armies that the practice also became a drain on finances. One solution to the chronic shortage of funds was that in the wake of the advancing troops opium suppression offices mushroomed everywhere.[69]

The alacrity with which the National Revolutionary Army moved northward was remarkable. By mid-September 1926, it had taken the strategic Yangtze tri-city area known as Wuhan (Wuchang, Hankou, and Hanyang). When the army captured Wuhan, one of the chief sources of income for the armies remaining behind was the so-called special tax (teshui) on opium.[70] While Wu Peifu's armies still controlled Wuhan, the revenues from this tax in Hankou alone had ranged between $2 and $4 million a month.[71] By the time Wu's forces had withdrawn from the region, they had bled local businessmen dry. However, because the Northern Expedition had little effect on the opium trade, the Guomindang continued to tap this rich source at Hankou to cover its ever-growing military expenditures.[72] When the Nationalists moved their seat of government from Canton to Wuhan in late 1926, Soong rationalized Wuhan's taxation system based on his success in Canton. In other words, he established an opium suppression office at Hankou in the spring of 1927.[73]

By that time, Nationalist troops had seized control of the provinces of Hunan, Hubei, Jiangxi, and Fujian, while retaining their base area of Guangdong and Guangxi. In a recent interview, Zhou Yongneng recounted the difficulties he experienced provisioning Chiang Kai-shek's army at this time. Zhou had been working in Jiujiang for the Northern Jiangxi Office of Finance when Chiang Kai-shek summoned him to Nanchang. On arrival there, he learned that Chiang Kai-shek had already appointed him director of the Provincial Department of Finance because of his outstanding record in raising money. When Zhou met with Chiang, he protested. "When I was working in the Northern Jiangxi Financial Office," he told Chiang, "I raised over $2 million, and most of this was borrowed from the rich. But now, owing to the devastation wrought by warfare, this whole region [i.e., Jiangxi] is destitute and it would be very difficult to raise money. You want me to be director of the Department of Finance, but I'm afraid that I won't do a good job." Chiang insisted. "Now is the opportunity for members of the Revolutionary Party [Gemingdang, i.e., the Guomindang] to make a contribution to their nation," he told Zhou. Zhou's first act in his new position was to extend the deadlines for paying other taxes to the new government. But more important, he set up opium suppression offices throughout the province to finance the National Revolutionary Army.[74]

Opium Suppression in Nanjing and Shanghai

After Chiang Kai-shek split with the Communist-influenced Wuhan government in April 1927, he established a rival regime at Nanjing. The Nanjing government's first pronouncements on opium suppression came several months later. Because Shanghai was the largest opium market in the world, the government expected to raise "special taxes" to expedite the completion of the Northern Expedition. At the time, Chiang required $20 million a month to keep his armies active.[75] On 13 June, the Guomindang's Central Political Council voted to suppress opium within three years, but it did not announce its policies to the public until the following September. In the interim, Nanjing created under the Ministry of Finance a Weijin Wupin Chajichu (Contraband Substances Inspection Office) in Shanghai with branch inspection offices in Wusong, Pudong, Zhabei, Nanshi, Minhang, and Liuhe.[76] It also opened another Opium Suppression Office in Nanjing, with Li Jihong as director.

The new three-year plan stipulated that the Guomindang would completely suppress opium use and trafficking by July 1930. In Zhejiang and Jiangsu provinces, the government farmed out monopolies for the sale of "opium-cure medicine." At the beginning of the second year, Nanjing intended to take over the trade and reduce the volume annually until all trafficking was terminated in July 1930.[77]

Before implementing the new policy, Nanjing replaced the Contraband Substances Inspection Office with the Shanghai Opium Suppression Bureau, and made the latter agency directly responsible for opium affairs in Zhejiang and Jiangsu.[78] The suppression bureau was a part of the Shanghai Public Security Bureau and took over the branch offices of the defunct inspection office. The Shanghai Opium Suppression Bureau monopoly was farmed out to the Xinyuan Gongsi for $15,400,000 a year, to be paid in eight installments. The Xinyuan Gongsi, in turn, subcontracted the monopoly for Zhejiang to the Zhongxing Gongsi and farmed out the retail trade in Shanghai to the Dazheng Gongsi.[79]

The tax farmers assessed a plethora of taxes on the shipping, sale, and smoking of opium-cure medicine in the two provinces. To sell the drug legally, retailers (i.e., opium dens) were required to purchase licenses from the suppression bureau at a cost of between $500 and $3,000 a month. Retail shops could only buy opium stamped by the bureau, and the contract encouraged them to sell as much of the narcotic as possible. Similarly, opium smokers over the age of twenty-five had to have permits to inhale the drug legally. The smoker's permits cost $3 a month for merchants, gentry, and women, and $1 a month for members of poorer classes, while travelers could purchase temporary permits for 30 cents a day.[80]

The three-year plan developed glitches from the start. For example, the Shanghai Opium Suppression Bureau began to act arbitrarily in enforcing the monopoly. There were reports that officers of the agency were conducting illegal searches of residences and shops, destroying private property in the pursuit of nonmonopoly opium. When illegal opium was actually discovered, bureau officials levied heavy fines. When the searches proved fruitless, they took valuables instead. Alarmingly, the bureau started blackmailing wealthy opium smokers who did not want their habit to become public knowledge.[81]

The biggest problem for the monopoly holders was competition from the Green Gang, which continued to operate from its headquarters in the French Concession.[82] Even though Nanjing assured the Xinyuan Company that its monopoly was safe, Chinese military and naval interests long involved in Shanghai's opium trafficking were unwilling to give up their remunerative sideline occupations. Shipments of nonmonopoly opium therefore continued to reach the French Concession. In November 1927, for instance, the Shanghai Opium Suppression Bureau seized a shipment of between four hundred and five hundred cases of Persian opium, worth perhaps $2,500,000, on the Chinese section of the waterfront consigned to the Three Prosperities Company. Du Yuesheng prevailed upon Bai Chongxi—head of the Guomindang military in Shanghai—to release it, and Bai permitted its delivery to the French Concession.[83] This official complicity in the nonmonopoly trade and competition from the Green Gang caused the Xinyuan and Zhongxing companies—and ultimately the Nanjing government—to lose money.

On 16 November, T. V. Soong canceled the contracts with the Xinyuan and Zhongxing firms. Apparently, the Xinyuan Company, $180,000 behind in its payments to the government, had tried to bribe Soong and the head of the Shanghai Opium Suppression Bureau and when that failed threatened Nanjing officials with assassination if they canceled the monopoly. The Zhongxing Gongsi also had its contract terminated, and Nanjing confiscated the company's $420,000 deposit.[84]

After this debacle, Nanjing made substantive changes to its opium policy in the lower Yangtze. The Shanghai Opium Suppression Bureau was abolished and replaced by Zhejiang and Jiangsu opium suppression bureaus. Each bureau had numerous branches in various counties. But in Shanghai, the Zixin Gongsi—a subsidiary of the Three Prosperities Company—received the monopoly from Jiangsu Opium Suppression Bureau.[85] The two provincial governments were thereafter responsible for suppression work under the jurisdiction of the Ministry of Finance.[86]

In other provinces controlled by the National Revolutionary Army in late 1927, the link between opium revenues and funding for the Guomindang's Northern Expedition was equally obvious. According to a 1927 survey by the National Anti-Opium Association, poppy cultivation increased when an area came under Guomindang control, with transportation and sales regulated by military officials.[87] After Nationalist armies took Hunan, levies on the opium trade reached $10 million, while opium revenues collected that year in Jiangxi, Guangxi, and Hubei were reported to have been $3 million, $7,558,300, and $10 to $20 million, respectively.[88] An observation by the International Anti-Opium Association was even more explicit:

> Millions have been raised out of opium for military operations and civil propaganda. Nationalist Government monopolies exist in every large center, and are so efficiently organized that enormous revenues result. And although the veil of the so-called "Opium Wars" has invariably been referred to on every Nationalist platform and in every proletarian demonstration, the Government is raising the very last cent out of the cultivation and use of opium.[89]

On 7 January 1928, Chiang Kai-shek emerged from "retirement" and took active responsibility for restarting the stalled engine of the Beifa war machine. The fuel for the armies directly under his command was derived primarily from the three provinces of Anhui, Jiangsu, and Zhejiang, these being the regions under firm control of the forces loyal to the government. According to Soong's calculations in January 1928, the monthly revenues received by the regime were $8,865,000, with $1 million, or 11 percent, of the total derived from opium taxes.[90]

As the Northern Expedition moved toward Beijing in the spring of 1928, Nanjing issued new regulations designed to standardize the cultivation, transportation, distribution, sale, and taxation of opium-cure medicines in the expanding areas under its jurisdiction.[91] The resulting streamlining of the collection process was largely the work of Soong, who became minister of finance once again when Chiang returned to power in January.[92]

The most significant of the new regulations were the Revised Opium Suppression Regulations promulgated in early April 1928. Although they still committed the government to the complete suppression of opium within three years, individuals under twenty-five years of age could now smoke opium with a doctor's permission. Smoking paraphernalia could no longer be manufactured, but a license to sell existing stocks was available for a fee.[93]

Another difference between the old and new regulations concerned opium cultivation. The old regulations forbade the planting of poppies, but the new ones designated regions in which the government would permit cultivation to fill "medicinal" needs. The new regulations thus reflected Nanjing's desire to integrate "opium suppression" vertically according to the levels of Republican political power—national, provincial, and local. In the Ministry of Finance at Nanjing, the Opium Suppression Office (Jinyanchu) was responsible for all opium affairs. Under its direction, each province was to establish an Opium Suppression Bureau (Jinyan Zongju) with branches in so-called vital municipalities. Every bureau was to have a warehouse (*gongzhan*) to store and protect the opium-cure medicine, and a medicinal manufacturing facility (*yanyaosuo*) to boil and distribute opium paste. Each bureau and branch was to establish an opium cure hospital (*jieyanyuan*) to assist addicts desirous of kicking the habit. Finally, each opium suppression bureau was to organize a *hujidui* (escort and arrest corps) to protect shipments, confiscate illegal opium, and arrest smugglers.[94]

Each "nonvital" city and county was to have a branch opium suppression department (*jinyan fensuo*). County magistrates would handle opium affairs at the *xian* (county) level, while agents from the county governments were to manage branches in "nonvital" cities. To consolidate tax collection, the Ministry of Finance set up monopoly transportation departments (*zhuanyunsuo*) in strategic places to collect the special taxes on shipments of monopoly opium.[95]

While Soong was fine-tuning Nanjing's monopoly, that same month (April 1928) the Guomindang's representative at the League of Nations Opium Advisory Committee, Zhao Quan, explained the Nationalists' policy in the most Bismarckian diplomatic language. He denied the existence of a monopoly in Nanjing under the Ministry of Finance's direction as well as the widespread cultivation of poppy in China. Regarding other opium affairs—perhaps with tongue in cheek—Zhao claimed: "Chinese opium, though good for the manufacture of morphine, is no good for smoking. So long as Indian opium is available, no addict will smoke Chinese opium. . . . So long as the Chinese Government maintains its opium prohibition policy and does its best to prevent violations of the Chinese anti-opium laws, it should not be blamed if such violations do take place."[96] Two months later, Beijing and Tianjin fell to the National Revolutionary Army forces, heralding both the successful end of the Guomindang's Northern Expedition and the dawn of a new era in China. As far as the relationship between opium and warlordism was concerned, however, the more things changed, the more they remained the same.

4 Nanjing's Response to Attacks on Opium Policy, 1924–1937

THE CAPTURE OF BEIJING BY the National Revolutionary Army in June 1928 heralded a new era in Chinese history. The Guomindang moved quickly to distance itself from the humiliations China had suffered for a century and more while Beijing was the national seat of power. The choice of Nanjing as the new capital was deliberate as well as symbolic. It was in 1842 in the "Southern Capital" that the Qing government signed the Treaty of Nanjing and in so doing initiated a process that would sign away the dignity and sovereignty of the nation to foreign imperialists by the end of the nineteenth century. Sun Yat-sen had wanted Nanjing to be capital of the new republic in 1911 but was thwarted by Yuan Shikai and other warlords for seventeen years. Now his heirs in the Guomindang had made the dream a reality.

Making Nanjing the national capital was not without its ironies and contradictions, however. The most significant—and obvious—of these was the Guomindang's use of opium revenues to sustain its political position in the place where a treaty ending the Opium War of 1839–1842 had begun the national humiliation. "In my opinion, the problem of opium suppression (*jinyan*) in China is synonymous with the problem of good government," Sun had stated in his "Judu yixun," "for traffic in opium cannot coexist with a National[ist] government deriving its power and authority from the people."[1] How could the Nationalists live with this contradiction after completing the Northern Expedition and positioning themselves to move from military to civilian rule?

Public opinion had been outspokenly critical of the Guomindang's use of "opium suppression fines" and similar *jinyan* double-talk to finance the

86

Northern Expedition. In addition, the fledgling government needed the support of foreign powers like the United States and Great Britain to fulfill its commitment to abolish the unequal treaties. A strong stance against opium could earn the Guomindang international as well as national goodwill and improve its prospects of leading China and the Chinese people into a new era of prosperity, stability, and security. In July 1928, the new government therefore announced a change in its opium policy from *yujin yuzheng* (suppression through taxation) to *juedui jinyan* (total, absolute, or complete prohibition).

Despite the new capital, the new government, and the new opium policy, the structures of Chinese politics and economics had not changed. On the contrary, after 1928 they seemed to become more entrenched. The production and use of opium and other narcotics was increasing; warlordism, including the Communist challenge to the Nationalists, continued in much of the country; and local governments depended on opium revenues for financial survival. What emerged out of this continued incipient chaos—as concerned opium policy—was the dichotomy of de jure prohibition and de facto monopoly.

The National Anti-Opium Association and the Guomindang's Policy of *Yujin yuzheng*

The ambiguity of Sun Yat-sen's 1924 "Anti-opium Will" at once justified Canton's policy of "suppression through taxation" while promising a policy of complete prohibition when the Guomindang had destroyed warlordism and established a national government. Opium revenue was an important key to the success of the Northern Expedition. Out of sheer logistical necessity, those in the Ministry of Finance—most notably T. V. Soong—promoted an opium policy that was identical to that of the warlords. To many Chinese, especially Christian organizations such as the National Christian Council or the National Anti-Opium Association, the ends did not justify the means.

Pursuant to Sun's death in 1925, anti-Christian agitation carried out by Communist workers in the Guomindang became more pronounced as the Northern Expedition approached Shanghai. Christian churches and mission property were targeted for looting or occupation by the National Revolutionary Army, and Chinese Christians were frequently threatened or punished unless they joined in pro-Nationalist demonstrations. With the winds of Chinese nationalism blowing increasingly from Canton, members of the National Christian Council began taking a more patriotic stance on issues such as the

May Thirtieth Incident and Guomindang attacks on the unequal treaties.[2] It is not surprising, therefore, that in 1926 the National Anti-Opium Association incorporated Sun Yat-sen's "Anti-opium Will" into its own antinarcotics program (see Figure 6).[3]

According to Joseph Fewsmith, when the "Thought of Sun Yat-sen" began to filter into the public mind during the Northern Expedition, the party's ability to control the interpretation of its professed ideology grew increasingly difficult. As a result, the Guomindang became vulnerable to criticism from critics quoting the words of its own founder.[4] In no way associated with the Guomindang, the National Anti-Opium Association used the words of Sun, which otherwise formed the basis of Guomindang claims to revolutionary legitimacy, to criticize the Nationalist policy of *yujin yuzheng*. As reports from both the national and international anti-opium associations confirmed that National Revolutionary Army troops were encouraging poppy production and establishing numerous suppression offices to collect opium taxes along their routes, the National Anti-Opium Association stepped up its criticisms and damaged the public's perception of the party during the drive for national unification.[5] Thus, when Guomindang troops entered Shanghai in late March 1927, the National Anti-Opium Association was a potent public force with which they had to reckon.

The first official contact between the National Anti-Opium Association and the Guomindang came in April 1927, when the association sent General Secretary Zhong Ketuo and his assistant Garfield Huang to Wuhan to meet with party leaders. Zhong and Huang's objective was to present the Guomindang with a petition titled "Eight Demands to the Government." The petitioners asked the Wuhan government to prohibit the cultivation of poppies in areas under its control, to set a date for ending the opium traffic, to establish opium treatment clinics, to dismiss any of its own officials found smoking or trafficking in opium, to halt the importation of foreign drugs, to require publishers to include anti-opium materials in textbooks for primary and middle schools, to protest to those nations that allowed trafficking in their Asian colonies, and to appoint an opium prohibition committee to implement the policies requested in the petition.[6] By presenting such a document to the Nationalists, the National Anti-Opium Association was making the first of many attempts to stake its claim to leadership, or at least coleadership, in the fight against drugs in China. It was apparent that the association's hierarchy envisioned an important role for itself in helping the Guomindang fulfill the second stage of Sun's "Judu yixun."

Figure 6. This National Anti-Opium Association poster shows the people of China following behind Sun Yat-Sen's "Anti-opium Will" and attacking the Black Demon of Opium and the White Demon of Morphine. The caption underneath reads "The Nation against the Scourge of Narcotics." Source: *Opium, A World Problem* 2.1 (Nov. 1928): 27.

In the aftermath of the Wuhan-Nanjing schism that brought about a sep-arate Nationalist government under Chiang Kai-shek in Nanjing, the Minis-try of Finance had established an opium monopoly in Shanghai and other lower Yangtze cities to fund the Northern Expedition through its completion. Accordingly, in June 1927 the association officially presented its "Eight Demands" to Nanjing, which responded by having the next (150th) meeting of the Central Political Council resolve that it would undertake a campaign to suppress opium use and trafficking within the next three years.[7]

These responses failed to satisfy the National Anti-Opium Association, for under the three-year plan an opium monopoly system continued in place. In August 1927, the association reacted by convening a "General Anti-Opium Conference." Representatives of some sixty leading public organizations in Shanghai attended the conference to hear Li Jihong, director of the Ministry of Finance's Opium Suppression Office, explain Nanjing's policy that legal-ized the trade for three years.[8] Outraged by the implications of the new policy, the National Anti-Opium Association launched an aggressive campaign against the monopoly, insisting that it contravened Sun's "Anti-opium Will."[9]

Maintaining the pressure on Nanjing through its publications, supportive Shanghai periodicals, and public rallies, on 24 November Sun Fo (Sun Ke), then minister of finance, telegrammed the National Anti-Opium Association asking that it dispatch a delegation to Nanjing to discuss opium policy.[10] Zhong Ketuo and Garfield Huang then carried a five-point proposal to Nan-jing on 6 December, urging the government to prohibit opium and other nar-cotics and to abolish opium taxes. Even Zheng Hongnian, vice-minister of finance, candidly admitted that Nanjing's current policy "does not prohibit opium, but actually allows people to indulge in drugs."[11]

The main source of contention between the National Anti-Opium Associ-ation and Nanjing was the former's insistence that opium prohibition could never mean anything more than a scheme to raise revenue as long as it re-mained under the jurisdiction of the Ministry of Finance. Consequently, the association began insisting that the government create an independent Na-tional Opium Prohibition Committee (Jinyan Weiyuanhui) to oversee anti-narcotics activities and convene a National Opium Prohibition Conference (Quanguo Jinyan Huiyi) to be attended by, among others, the government's leading military and political figures.[12] They also petitioned the Fourth Ple-nary of the Guomindang's Second National Party Congress (February 1928), urging Nanjing to change its opium policy; and in late March, the association sponsored mass meetings to push for real prohibition.[13]

Although the government announced another "revision" of its opium laws in April 1928, the basic policy remained unchanged. On 1 May, the National Anti-Opium Association condemned the revision with scathing criticism:

> As we look around at the conditions within China, opium is everywhere, how sickening! HOW SICKENING! We truly hope that the government authorities will comply with Sun Yat-sen's "Anti-opium Will" and implement the Guomindang party platform, address the suffering of the people, adopt the National Anti-Opium Association's proposals to completely prohibit opium, and earnestly eradicate it in order to save the tarnished reputation of our country and forever consolidate the foundation of this nation.[14]

In the summer of 1928, as the Nanjing government sought to make the transition from the "period of military rule" to the "period of political tutelage" in accordance with Sun's blueprint for national reconstruction, conditions were ripe for a change in policy. Garfield Huang ventured to Nanjing and conferred with Interior Minister Xue Dubi and Jiangsu governor Niu Yongjian, who informed Huang that the government had decided to prohibit opium and other drugs in accordance with the proposals made by the National Anti-Opium Association.[15] On 18 July, Nanjing announced the new policy of complete prohibition, and a week later it made public the composition of a newly created National Opium Prohibition Committee.[16]

The membership of the committee reflected not only the linkage between National Revolutionary Army military commanders and their interest in opium, but the impact of the National Anti-Opium Association's yearlong campaign to influence opium policy. Zhang Zhijiang, a Christian general who had an impressive antinarcotics record while serving under Feng Yuxiang, was named chairman.[17] Zhong Ketuo and Li Denghui—respectively the general secretary and the chairman of the National Anti-Opium Association— were appointed alongside Chiang Kai-shek, Feng Yuxiang, Li Zongren, He Yingqin, Li Liejun, Li Jichen, and Chen Shaokuan—the latter group well aware of the importance of opium revenue to military success.

The association's hard-fought victory against a Guomindang opium monopoly was codified into law with the Opium Prohibition Act (Jinyanfa) and Opium Prohibition Regulations (Jinyanfa Shixing Tiaoli) on 10 September 1928.[18] Nanjing subsequently convened the National Opium Prohibition Conference, which met during the first ten days of November. This conference climaxed the National Anti-Opium Association's crusade against the

Nationalists' policy of *yujin yuzheng*. Chairing the conference was Zhang Zhijiang, assisted by Li Denghui as vice-chairman.[19] Seventy delegates represented the Nanjing government, the National Revolutionary Army, the provinces, and nongovernment entities (including the National Anti-Opium Association).

The conference was notable not because of any actions it took or proposals it made, but because of the revelations it made concerning the centrality of opium and the opium trade in Chinese life. The delegates learned, for example, that the Nationalist government derived at least $40 million annually from assorted levies on the drug, which would presumably be lost if the prohibition policy succeeded. In addition, accusations of opium smoking and complicity in the trade were made against high-ranking military and government officials.[20] In light of such revelations, Chiang Kai-shek boldly pledged that "henceforth, the National[ist] government will absolutely not derive one copper from opium revenue. If anything of this sort is suspected and it is reported by this body, we could then regard this government as bankrupt and place no confidence in it."[21]

On the last day of the conference, participants signed the National Opium Prohibition Conference Anti-opium Oath:

> I hereby solemnly swear that I will abide, with absolute sincerity, by the "Anti-opium Will" of the late *zongli* Sun Yat-sen, the Guomindang's policy of complete prohibition, the Opium Prohibition Regulations of the National[ist] government, as well as the public opinion of the people to exterminate the evil of opium for the completion of the National[ist] revolution. In the event of my breaking this oath, I shall be prepared to accept the severest form of punishment that can be meted out by the party and the government.[22]

The Significance of the National Opium Prohibition Committee

Convening the opium conference, creating the National Opium Prohibition Committee, and passing prohibition laws marked the first phase of Guomindang efforts to reassert its leadership over national opium policy, which had been appropriated by the National Anti-Opium Association since 1924. The National Opium Prohibition Committee, an appendage of the Executive Yuan, contained two main departments (General Administration, and Inspection and Medical Analysis) and four subcommittees (International Phases of Opium Suppression, Examination of Prohibition Record, Investigation of Dangerous Drugs, and Examination of Addicted Officials).[23]

A significant function of the National Opium Prohibition Committee was formulating national prohibition laws and regulations for consideration by Nanjing. The committee formally convened in January 1929. One of its first acts was to establish 3 June as a national holiday in honor of Lin Zexu's burning of British opium on that day in 1839, an exploit that sparked the ensuing Opium War. Originally the brainchild of Wang Jingqi—National Anti-Opium Association executive committee member and concurrently Chinese representative to the League of Nations—the celebration of Jinyan Jinianri (Opium Prohibition Memorial Day) was the state's answer to the association's Anti-opium Week.[24] The National Opium Prohibition Committee was also empowered to oversee antinarcotics education in China. It issued the monthly Chinese-language magazine *Jinyan gongbao* (Opium Prohibition Bulletin; 1929–1930), which later became *Jinyan weiyuanhui gongbao* (National Opium Prohibition Committee Bulletin; 1931), and published anti-opium speeches and teachings of Sun Yat-sen and other Guomindang leaders, as well as various tracts, posters, and literature.[25]

The National Opium Prohibition Committee's most important tasks were collecting statistics and censuring Nanjing over shortcomings in prohibition enforcement. Each year the committee would compile data and publish an annual report in English to the League of Nations titled *Traffic in Opium and Other Dangerous Drugs*. With members of the National Anti-Opium Association such as Li Denghui and Zhong Ketuo serving on the committee, the National Opium Prohibition Committee was not afraid to embarrass the government publicly over flagrant violations of prohibition laws. For example, it petitioned the government to abolish the Qingli Lianghu Teshuichu (Hubei-Hunan Special Tax Clearance Office) and the Liangguang Yapian Zhuanmaiju (Guangdong-Guangxi Opium Monopoly Bureau), which continued to collect taxes on the drug in violation of national opium policy.[26] The National Anti-Opium Association joined in these attacks, alleging that the former agency had collected over $14 million for Nanjing during fiscal 1929.[27]

The National Opium Prohibition Committee was also given the authority to dismiss government employees who were discovered to be opium smokers. In early May 1930, thirty-four civil servants, most of them employed on the Shanghai-Nanjing and Shanghai-Hangzhou railways, were fired following medical examinations.[28] That same month, the committee passed a resolution designating Nanjing as a model area for prohibition. The Central Hospital in

China's new capital was to establish opium treatment facilities, with provincial and municipal governments following its lead.[29]

This National Anti-Opium Association–Guomindang alliance for prohibition provided tangible benefits for both sides. The association received the stamp of state legitimacy and enhanced the political influence of the organization and its leaders, while Guomindang opium policy obtained the moral legitimacy and public support previous "opium suppression" efforts had lacked. Coopting important leaders of the association, duplicating its function with a state bureaucracy, and muting public criticism were crucial first steps along the road to controlling the debate over national opium policy.

The *Jiang'an* and Gao Ying Scandals

Despite such attempts to convince the public of Nanjing's sincerity to implement Sun's "Anti-opium Will," from the closing ceremonies of the National Opium Prohibition Conference, it became apparent that the Guomindang's policy of complete prohibition was quixotic at best, hypocritical at worst. Within a fortnight of conference members taking the Anti-opium Oath, talk about opium centered on the *Jiang'an* scandal. On the night of 21 November 1928, a vessel in the fleet of the China Merchants Steam Navigation Company, the *Jiang'an*, arrived in Shanghai from Hankou. A detail of soldiers from the Wusong-Shanghai Garrison were unloading a large shipment of opium from the steamer when several policemen from the Shanghai Gonganju (Public Security Bureau) surprised them.[30] Outnumbering the policemen, the soldiers overcame them and took them into the French Concession. After the soldiers delivered the cargo to Green Gang associates, they released the policemen.[31]

When the incident became public, Nanjing directed Zhang Zhijiang and two officials from the Ministry of Justice to investigate it. The chairman of the National Opium Prohibition Committee took the investigation seriously, vowing to make it a litmus test for government prohibition efforts.[32] Zhang's inquest concluded in late December, placing blame for the incident on two officers—Fu Shaoxiang of the Wusong-Shanghai Garrison and Dai Shifu of the Shanghai Gonganju—who were dismissed for dereliction of duty. Moreover, it cost Zhang Dingfan his position as mayor of the Special Municipality of Shanghai and Wusong.[33] Zhang Zhijiang appears to have been deeply troubled by his findings. After turning in the report, he tendered his resignation as chairman of the National Opium Prohibition Committee. Nanjing refused his resignation, and Zhang remained head of the committee on paper until late 1930, when he was reassigned as superintendent of pacification (i.e., Communist eradication) in Jiangsu province.[34] Most likely, what prompted Zhang to tender his resignation was the identity of those in the Guomindang hierarchy who approved and protected the opium shipment to Shanghai. Although their identity is uncertain, contemporary rumors contained the names of Chiang Kai-shek, T. V. Soong, Feng Yuxiang, Bai Chongxi, Xiong Shihui, and Li Jichen.[35]

A second embarrassing blow to the policy of prohibition occurred on 5 July 1929. On that day in San Francisco a keen-eyed U.S. Customs officer inspecting trunks belonging to Gao Liaoshi, the wife of Chinese Vice-Consul Gao Ying, discovered 2,500 tins of opium with a street value of perhaps US$500,000. Also implicated in the attempted smuggling was Sun Yuan, former chancellor of the consulate.[36]

Gao Ying, his wife, and Sun Yuan were indicted on four counts of narcotics smuggling by a federal grand jury, but at the behest of C. C. Wu (Wu Chaoshu), the Chinese minister in Washington, D.C., the three were deported to China and tried in Nanjing. The resulting trial in October and November revealed a large-scale narcotics smuggling operation whose trans-Pacific route began in Shanghai, passed through Hong Kong and Honolulu, and terminated in San Francisco. Gao and his spouse were found guilty and sentenced to long prison terms of six years and four years, respectively, and heavy fines. Sun Yuan was initially found not guilty and the charges against him were dismissed, but at his retrial in 1931, Sun was similarly convicted and sentenced to five years' imprisonment.[37] The fact that high-level diplomats in the Nationalist government were engaged in international narcotics trafficking further undermined the public's faith in Nanjing's commitment to complete prohibition.

On the eve of 1931, there was little doubt that Nanjing's policy of complete prohibition was a total failure. Scandals involving Guomindang officials permeated the air, the National Opium Prohibition Committee was leaderless, and the National Opium Prohibition Conference—designated by law to meet annually—was repeatedly postponed and never convened again. With military expenditures spiraling beyond the means of legitimate revenue, Guomindang officials felt they had no choice but to align their official opium policy more closely with their unofficial policy.

Year twenty of the Republican calendar proved fateful for the Nationalist government. Man-made catastrophes included the Japanese invasion of Manchuria, a spreading Communist insurrection in central and southern China, intraparty strife, and increased residual warlord activity. The domestic economy and finances lost their immunity to the global economic crisis. As more industrially advanced nations abandoned the gold standard and erected trade barriers to protect their ailing economies, the value of silver rose, prices paid for domestically produced goods dropped, and export markets quickly evaporated.[38] Natural disasters included the flooding of the Yangtze and Huai rivers, affecting over twenty-five million people and causing approximately $2 billion in damage.[39] The cumulative effect of these misfortunes reduced the number of reliable income sources for Nanjing at a time when military expenditures were rising, thereby creating conditions that favored a reassessment of Guomindang opium policy.

Increased Tension between the National Anti-Opium Association and Nanjing

The first indication of a shift away from the policy of complete prohibition came with the appointment of Dr. Liu Ruiheng (J. Heng Liu) as chairman of the National Opium Prohibition Committee in December 1930. Liu was then the minister of public health and was soon to be director general of the National Health Administration. He had received his medical degree from Harvard University in 1913, conducted cancer research at the Rockefeller Institute, and performed the surgery on Sun Yat-sen in 1925 that discovered the *guofu*'s inoperable cancer.[40]

Immediately after his appointment, Liu asked F. W. Maze, inspector general of Maritime Customs, about opium policy. Maze suggested the best policy would be "to place the opium trade and cultivation of the poppy under strict Government control, with a view to eventually stopping smoking altogether. . . . In other words, the existing irregular trade in opium ought to be regularized and come under the authority of the Government."[41] It appears that Maze's suggestion was taken to heart by T. V. Soong and Chiang Kai-shek, for shortly thereafter Nanjing attempted to make an opium monopoly official policy.

In early January 1931, the National Anti-Opium Association queried Nanjing about a rumored change in opium policy, and Liu replied that no change was in the works.[42] Nonetheless, on 9 February, the government announced a reorganization of the National Opium Prohibition Committee that included three high-ranking members of the National Anti-Opium Association, namely, Zhong Ketuo, Wu Liande, and R. Y. Lo.[43] Nanjing subsequently dispatched another member of the committee, Li Jihong, to Taiwan to study the Japanese opium monopoly there.[44] A day after the reorganization, the *Shanghai Evening Post and Mercury* reprinted an article by Wu Liande titled "Opium Problem Reaches Acute Stage—Case for International Cooperation and Control," which had received little attention when it had first appeared two weeks earlier in *The Chinese Nation*. According to Wu, China had produced almost 12,000 tons of opium in 1930, and the Nationalist government had lost between $50 and $100 million by failing to tax it effectively because of the policy of prohibition. Wu then laid out a new policy that would abandon prohibition and, implicitly at least, give Nanjing a monopoly on the regulation and taxation of the drug.[45]

Wu's test balloon ignited a firestorm of protest from the National Anti-Opium Association. Feeling betrayed by Wu Liande, the association proposed that it no longer permit any of its executive members to serve concurrently on the National Opium Prohibition Committee. A few days later (on 19 February), Garfield Huang and Wang Jingqi brought together two hundred representatives from leading public bodies in Shanghai, who issued a "call to arms" to the people of China to oppose every effort to return to the monopoly system.[46] For weeks, arguments over that system raged in the press, soon degenerating into a nasty personal battle between Wu Liande and Garfield Huang. Once the dust had settled, though, the National Anti-Opium Association had again forced Nanjing to back down on opium policy by rallying public opinion and using its organizational skills.

In a confidential message to the U.S. consulate in Shanghai, the association later charged that the proposed monopoly scheme was part of Nanjing's efforts to secure a large loan from a "certain European power," evidently Great Britain. The message further charged that Wu Liande and Liu Ruiheng had hatched the scheme with the backing of the League of Nations officials sent to China in late 1930. The basis for the latter charge concerned experts dispatched by the League to recommend ways for Nanjing to finance its pressing programs of national reconstruction in the midst of a global economic depression. The impetus for such recommendations was China's agreement to abolish the *lijin* and native customs (junk-borne trade) taxes in 1931 and the resulting annual losses of $100 million in revenues to central and local governments.[47]

The National Anti-Opium Association had what it considered to be reliable information that one of the experts, Dr. Ludwig Rajchman of the League's health section, had proposed a loan from Britain that Nanjing could secure only through revenues generated by a government opium monopoly. Rajchman was to assist Nanjing in getting League support for a monopoly similar to the ones operating in the Asian colonies of the imperial powers.[48] If the report is correct, it helps explain the Guomindang's move to change its opium policy at that time.

It seems more likely, however, that Chiang and Soong had already committed themselves to establishing a state monopoly based on their experience with the Special Tax Clearance Office system already functioning in Hunan and Hubei (to be discussed in Chapter 5). But if the National Anti-Opium Association charge was true, the Rajchman proposal may have offered Chiang and Soong a timely opportunity to test public reaction before changing the policy.

Despite the apparent victory by the association, records from the Ministry of Finance suggest that Nanjing proceeded as it intended to proceed. Sometime after 10 January 1931, Nanjing dispatched Li Muqing, director of the Hankou Main Office of the Hubei-Hunan Special Tax Clearance Office, to Henan province with orders to establish an opium taxation system there.[49] Henan had been the scene of bloody fighting between Chiang's armies and those of the Yan-Feng confederacy in mid-1930. As soon as the province came under Nanjing's control later that year, the Nationalist government set about erecting there the kind of financial structure already in place in Hunan and Hubei, which centered on an unofficial opium nonopoly as the chief source of provincial revenue.

In this structure, as Li Muqing explained to Soong in February 1931, there were yet no set rules for collecting special taxes in Henan. Li therefore drew up a set of rules *"fangzhao Lianghu banfa"* (based on the Hubei-Hunan regulations).[50] The main office in Henan was located at Zhengzhou, inside the Salt Inspectorate, with a branch at Lingbao near the Shaanxi border. As in Hunan and Hubei, the Henan Special Tax Clearance Office had a series of sub-bureaus, twenty-one to be exact, located in cities along important river and rail routes.[51] Thus, while the Shanghai press was debating the question of prohibition, a Guomindang monopoly was already a fait accompli in Hubei, Hunan, and Henan provinces.

To legitimize the monopoly system, the Nationalist government had to overcome public opposition to it. The leading force of public opposition was the National Anti-Opium Association and more specifically, its general secretary Garfield Huang. Beginning in March 1931, Huang became the target of a concerted effort by Nanjing to undermine public support for the association as a means of undercutting public opposition to the monopoly policy.

This second phase of Guomindang attempts to control the opium dialogue eschewed any hint of the cooperation that characterized the earlier phase. In mid-March 1931, Huang and his wife May Pai (Bai Zhiying), a Shanghai physician, traveled to Taiwan to study the Japanese monopoly, following in Li Jihong's footsteps.[53] While they were in Taiwan, a report in both Chinese- and English-language newspapers in Shanghai alleged that Maritime Customs inspectors had once found opium in Mrs. Huang's luggage, while another version said that the drug was morphine and not opium and that Hong Kong Customs had found it. The *China Critic* also ran a story headlined "Mrs. Garfield Huang and Mrs. Kao Ying," which unfavorably compared May Pai to the wife of the San Francisco consul involved in the notorious 1930 smuggling case.[53]

By late spring, it had become evident that the charges against Huang and his wife were false and that the source of the allegations was someone high at the National Opium Prohibition Committee. According to Huang, the source was "a high official connected with the Central Opium Suppression Committee at Nanking," the man who "was the chief sponsor of the legalization scheme . . . as a prelude of an extensive plot aiming at the total collapse of our labor."[54] The reference was obviously to Wu Liande.

As these events unfolded, Huang and his wife were involved in a bitter lawsuit with Cheong Eng-sun of Xiamen over the sale of property belonging to May Pai's mother. Cheong, a dentist, was a trustee of the property in question, and Huang had falsely accused him in a National Anti-Opium Association publication of smuggling cocaine. The press reports also revealed that Huang had abused his position at the association by attacking Cheong and had even placed a bounty on the dentist's head![55] Needless to say, these revelations tarnished the reputation of the National Anti-Opium Association as well as of Garfield Huang and thus played into the hands of the opium monopolists in Nanjing.

The Opium Smuggling Prevention Department and the Soong Assassination Attempt

In the spring of 1931, Chiang Kai-shek was also busy with the Hu Hanmin controversy concerning a provisional constitution for the Nationalist government. The National People's Conference met in May to address this issue among other things, including the question of opium policy. Delegates considered four proposals on the subject, including one calling for the complete prohibition of the drug trade within six years.[56] Internationally renown anti-opium activists such as Ellen La Motte and Pope Pius XI telegrammed the conference to reject proposals favoring a government monopoly.[57] The delegates took no definitive action on the subject, adopting instead a resolution put forth by Generalissimo Chiang declaring Nanjing's intention to use a "scientific method" to solve the opium problem.[58]

Chiang's "scientific method" translated into a second failed attempt to establish an opium monopoly as national policy. In June, the Fifth Plenary of the Third Central Executive Committee adopted a "Resolution for the Complete Prohibition of Opium within Six Years" *(Liunian jinjue yapian zhi jueyian)*. The resolution stipulated that the government confiscate and destroy all opium and other narcotics without legitimate medical use.[59]

To achieve the stated goals of the resolution adopted by the Fifth Plenary, Nanjing quickly created the Jinyan Chajichu (Opium Smuggling Prevention Department) under the direction of Li Jihong in late June. Li in turn announced the establishment of a string of branch departments in Hubei, Hunan, Jiangxi, Anhui, Zhejiang, Jiangsu, and Fujian, with their headquarters in Hankou.[60] After the Opium Smuggling Prevention Department was in place, it was apparent that it was in fact a government monopoly. In Anhui, to illustrate, the department set uniform tax rates on the cultivation and sale of opium, and charged monthly permit fees for opium smokers.[61] Overall, Nanjing expected this system to produce between $100 million and $200 million a year in revenue.[62] But despite the ambitiousness of the system, public opposition led by the National Anti-Opium Association made it short-lived, and on 8 July the Executive Yuan abolished the plan (see Figure 7).[63]

On 23 July, unknown assailants set off several bombs and unleashed a hail of bullets in the North Shanghai Railway Station. Their target was Nanjing's minister of finance, T. V. Soong. Although Soong emerged from this life-threatening melee unhurt, seven others were wounded by ricocheting bullets, three of whom died immediately or later in local hospitals.[64] In the weeks following the assassination attempt, rumors circulated in Shanghai periodicals that Du Yuesheng had masterminded the plot and that it was connected to the failed Opium Smuggling Prevention Department venture. One version claimed that Du had paid the government $6 million as part of a tax-farming agreement with Soong's Ministry of Finance. When the scheme fell through, Du demanded a cash refund but received worthless government bonds

Figure 7. Navy blue flag of the ill-fated Opium Smuggling Prevention Department, to be flown by steamers shipping opium. Source: Number Two Historical Archives, Quanzonghao 3, No. 1121, Li Muqing to T. V. Soong (7/1/31).

instead, and thus the ambush was meant to send Soong a strong message.[65] Another version was that the Shanghai Opium Smuggling Prevention Department–during its very brief incarnation—had confiscated over $1 million in opium belonging to Du's Three Prosperities Company.[66] Although these rumors were false, they provided more ammunition for the critics of Nanjing's dichotomous opium policy.[67]

Undeterred, the monopolists renewed their attacks on the National Anti-Opium Association, specifically targeting its finances. The association's main sources of income were the American Boxer Indemnity Remissions Fund, advertisements in its monthly publication *Judu yuekan*, and private contributions.[68] Back in 1927, the China Foundation, which oversaw allocations of the Boxer Fund, agreed to provide the National Anti-Opium Association $30,000 a year for four years. In the summer of 1931, when the time came to renew this allocation in the aftermath of two failed attempts to legalize the opium trade, Nanjing used its influence to deny the renewal.[69] This move effectively crippled the organization, for more than half of its revenues came from this single source.[70]

Nanjing's Responses to Criticism

The hypocrisy inherent in Nanjing's policy of de jure prohibition/de facto monopoly continued to draw fire from sources within the party and government, and externally from the National Anti-Opium Association and the press. In November 1931, at the Guomindang Fourth Party Congress, a resolution titled "Zongli yixun lijin yapianan" (Resolution on the Strict Prohibition of Opium in Accordance with Sun Yat-sen's Anti-opium Will) was adopted. It severely criticized the party's failures to date and outlined a four-year, three-stage method for achieving the complete prohibition of opium in China.[71]

On 3 May 1932, Gao Yutang, a member of the Control Yuan in Nanjing, publicly called for the impeachment of Liu Ruiheng, chairman of the National Opium Prohibition Committee. Gao accused Liu, among other things, of encouraging the cultivation, transportation, and sale of opium to line his own pockets, and blamed him for the failed efforts to bring about a government monopoly in 1931.[72]

In early June on the fourth commemoration of Opium Prohibition Memorial Day, an editorial that appeared in *Xinhankou ribao* (New Hankou Daily News) captured the cynicism this situation fostered among the masses:

> What could be worse? In the country all that one can see is poppy growing everywhere, in the cities there are opium dens along every street, government offices openly collect taxes on opium, and citizens openly smoke it. . . . As a result, the whole of China depends upon opium for its revenues, and entire communities depend upon it for life. This condition is much more ludicrous and lamentable than the Opium Prohibition Memorial Day. . . . Although Mr. Lin [Zexu] in Heaven is not pleased with the publication of this news item, yet the collectors of the opium tax on Earth will smile with their hands on their beards. This is our opium prohibition memorial, and it is also the proper way to commemorate opium prohibition.[73]

In an effort to calm growing public apprehension over rumors of an imminent legalization of the trade, on 20 June the Guomindang issued still another restatement of its official policy from the temporary seat of the central government in Luoyang, Henan (owing to the Japanese attack on Shanghai in early 1932). Known as the "Luoyang Mandate," it read

> It is hereby ordered that all the responsible local officials must hereafter obey and faithfully execute the various laws and regulations concerning opium prohibition. . . . Any official found guilty of negligence in the enforcement of such laws, thereby adversely affecting the welfare of the people, will be punished to the fullest extent of the laws.[74]

Despite the crumbling facade of a virtuous commitment to prohibition, the government continued to attack its critics. By late 1932, leading businesses in Shanghai that had previously advertised in *Judu yuekan*, such as the Bank of China and the Bank of Communications, quit doing so for fear of antagonizing Nanjing.[75] Similar apprehensions likely explain why the National Anti-Opium Association moved its offices out of the Shanghai Bankers Association building in 1933.[76] Public contributions also declined as a result of government pressure, especially by Wu Liande, whose importuning proved very effective.[77] This rather unflattering image of Wu Liande is noteworthy because of the high regard most historians have for a man who probably contributed more to modernizing Chinese medicine than anyone else in the twentieth century. It is also interesting that, in his autobiography, Wu makes no mention whatsoever of his work with either the National Anti-Opium Association or the National Opium Prohibition Committee, and was wholly unimpressed with Nationalist antinarcotics efforts.[78]

Another tactic employed by the Guomindang was intimidation. When Garfield Huang returned to Xiamen from Taiwan in 1931, men identified as "gangsters" boarded the Dutch steamer he was traveling on and attempted to kidnap him before he disembarked.[79] Also, when the association attempted to publish information on the government's opium monopoly in 1932, Nationalist censors prohibited the publication in various periodicals, including *Shenbao* and *Xinwenbao*. Soon afterwards, on 25 November, someone planted a bomb in Garfield Huang's home with a letter warning him to discontinue his efforts against the unofficial monopoly. Similarly, unknown individuals frequented his home and his office threatening to kill Huang shoud they find him in residence.[80] By the spring of 1933, Garfield Huang announced that the National Anti-Opium Association was experiencing financial difficulties that severely handicapped its antinarcotics activities, while the association guarded

Huang's movements from the public eye.[81] Nanjing, it seems, would have its way on opium policy.

Chiang Kai-shek Unveils the Six-Year Plan

Before the summer of 1932, either party or central government agencies such as the National Opium Prohibition Committee issued official proclamations concerning opium policy. By this time, Generalissimo Chiang had come to realize the indispensability of opium revenues to his anti-Communist campaigns in central China. Furthermore, his government had gained an unfavorable reputation at home and abroad in the arena of narcotics suppression, a casualty of China's realpolitik. As chairman of the Military Affairs Commission that was supervising "Communist bandit suppression" in the provinces of Anhui, Hubei, and Henan, Chiang had his field headquarters in Hankou enact martial law, thus gaining complete civil authority over these so-called bandit suppression zones (*jiaofei shengfen*). Therefore, he began issuing antidrug directives from his field headquarters, which in turn initiated a process that gradually resulted in the militarization of Guomindang opium policy.

On 28 August 1932, Chiang issued a directive from Hankou stipulating that all party, government, and military personnel in addition to all students in the provinces of Anhui, Henan, and Hubei who smoked opium or used other drugs had two weeks to report to local authorities and pledge to rid themselves of the habit within thirty to forty-five days. Anyone who failed to report and was later discovered to be an addict would face a military firing squad.[82]

Over the course of the last few months of 1932, Generalissimo Chiang issued further directives and regulations ordering military and civil officials in the ten provinces of Hunan, Hubei, Jiangxi, Jiangsu, Anhui, Henan, Zhejiang, Fujian, Gansu, and Shaanxi to eliminate poppy cultivation; and he even appointed and dispatched special commissioners to supervise eradication work in those regions.[83] In 1933, new regulations were promulgated from the Military Affairs Commission that set a six-year timetable for the eradication of the poppy in Nationalist-controlled areas of China. Chiang demarcated ten "interior" provinces (the provinces listed above with Shanxi and Shandong added to the list and Gansu and Shaanxi removed) where poppy growing was completely illegal and declared the "frontier" provinces of Sichuan, Yunnan, Guizhou, Shaanxi, and Gansu to be regions where cultivation would be gradually reduced within the span of six years. In addition, the transportation, wholesale, and resale of opium in these regions would be centrally controlled by the Military Affairs Commission, and all opium users would be required to purchase a smoker's permit to indulge their habit legally.[84]

By 1934, the expanding unofficial monopoly and the generalissimo's control over it had to be reconciled with the Guomindang's official policy of complete prohibition. Chiang was well aware of the political repercussions that such a change in national opium policy would entail. In order to mute public criticisms over the de facto legalization of the trade, he presented it under the guise of a military-supervised antinarcotics campaign called the Six-Year Opium Suppression Plan (Liunian Jinyan Jihua). On 23 June 1934, Chiang issued a circular order declaring that the cultivation, transportation, use, and sale of opium would be completely suppressed within six years:

> In accordance with the resolution adopted at the National People's Conference in 1931 for the complete prohibition of opium within six years using scientific methods, first we must issue various kinds of laws covering the cultivation, transportation, smoking, and sale of opium to strictly increase government management and control. Therefore, by following a step-by-step method for gradually reducing opium each year, we will correct failed policies of the past with the goal of thoroughly eradicating this evil once and for all.[85]

Although Chiang Kai-shek had enacted military jurisdiction over opium suppression work in the bandit suppression zones since 1932 and was judging offenders under military law, legally speaking, control of narcotics affairs remained under the jurisdiction of the central government's National Opium Prohibition Committee. This division of authority set the stage for a showdown between Chiang and the committee. Just before Chiang's announcement of the six-year plan, there had been criticism of the National Opium Prohibition Committee in the Legislative Yuan for spending millions of dollars with nothing to show for it.[86] Immediately following Chiang's circular order of 23 June, the committee asked the central government to transfer authority over drug-related matters in the bandit suppression zones to Chiang's military command. On 12 July, the government completed the transfer, which also extended Chiang's jurisdiction to the municipalities of Nanjing and Shanghai.[87]

The six-year plan, which included draconian measures against the use of opium derivatives such as morphine and heroin, earned the generalissimo substantial approbation both domestically and internationally.[88] Even Garfield

Huang of the National Anti-Opium Association praised Chiang's stance on the morphine and heroin problem. Nevertheless, Huang was dubious of the motives behind poppy eradication in the bandit suppression zones. He said:

> So far there has been no step taken to suppress the cultivation of the poppy in the provinces of Sichuan, Yunnan, and Guizhou, the chief producing centers and the source of supply of the government opium now being distributed through the monopoly organs. . . . Unless poppy cultivation is prohibited in these three provinces, the suppression of opium enforced by the government will amount to nothing more than *the suppression of the competition.*"[89]

The New Life Movement and the Six-Year Plan

An interesting relationship evolved between Chiang's six-year plan and the New Life Movement in Nanjing.[90] Chiang Kai-shek needed a moral pretext for his drug policy, since it was apparent that the six-year plan was no more than camouflage for his military monopoly. The generalissimo's twin endeavor transformed Nanjing into a drug-free zone and a showcase for the public purposes of these two campaigns.

In February 1934, Chiang launched the New Life Movement (Xinshenghuo Yundong) in a speech given in Nanchang, Jiangxi. The ideological tenets of the movement were centered on an eclectic mix of Confucianism, Christianity, Fascism, and martial values.[91] For the average citizen, the New Life Movement targeted corruption, "face," extravagant spending, or unsavory traditional social customs such as spitting or urinating in public that were seen by Chiang as hinderances to progress and modernization. In other words, as James C. Thomson put it, the movement "relied entirely on a psychological remolding through the reform of personal habits."[92] Smoking opium was viewed through the same prism, in spite of its fiscally imperative role in the generalissimo's state-building goals.

Subsequent to the inauguration of the New Life Movement in mid-February 1934, the impact of the resulting crusade was most evident in Nanjing. The impetus for launching the movement there came from Wang Jingwei, president of the Executive Yuan.[93] On 16 March, Wang and others in the capital established the New Life Movement Promotional Association (Xinshenghuo Yundong Cujinhui). Wang, in addition to Chen Lifu, Ye Chucang, and Luo Jialun were among the prominent leaders of the New Life Movement Promotional

Association. Also on that day, the Nanjing municipal government opened its long-awaited Opium Treatment Hospital.[94]

In early April, the promotional association announced a program to improve life in Nanjing. Everyone was to get out of bed before 7:00 A.M., wear clean clothing, walk on the right side of the street, refrain from smoking on the street, and be punctual, frugal, and orderly. All told, there were some ninety-six rules of conduct for the masses to follow prescribed by Chiang Kai-shek.[95] To support such practices, Mayor Shi Ying promised to "thoroughly eliminate evil habits" in the capital and sponsored a Qingjie Yundong (Cleanliness Movement) that culminated on 1 May with a Cleanliness Movement Parade.[96]

It was at this parade that anti-opium propaganda first appeared in conjunction with New Life Movement activities. According to *Zhongyang ribao* (Central Daily News), among the pamphlets handed out at the parade, two dealt solely with eradicating opium and other drugs.[97] Three days later, Mayor Shi Ying launched the Suqing Yanduchang Sanhai Yundong (Exterminate the Three Evils of Opium, Gambling, and Prostitution Movement). Shi had claimed that the Japanese were flooding China with opium, heroin, and morphine as part of a diabolical plot to destroy the Chinese race.[98]

During each night of the weeklong observance of the "Three Evils" campaign (4–11 May), an important government leader gave a radio address or speech to an assembled audience against the use of narcotics.[99] A fortnight later, another weeklong event called the Suqing Yanduchang Lianhe Xuanchuan Dahui (Exterminate the Three Evils of Opium, Gambling, and Prostitution Joint Educational Conference) addressed these issues and how to educate the public not to engage in social vices. The event culminated in a commemoration of Opium Prohibition Memorial Day (3 June), notable for the public burnings of confiscated drugs and assorted paraphernalia.[100]

After a six-month period of relative inactivity, in early December Chiang ordered the Nanjing police to arrest all opium smokers in the city. Within three days, the police rounded up more than 1,500 offenders, so many in fact that municipal officials had to meet in an emergency conference to discuss how to deal with them.[101] The result of these officials' deliberations was the Shoudu Suqing Yandu Weiyuanhui (Capital Exterminate Opium and Dangerous Drugs Committee) and a new offensive against narcotics in Nanjing.

The Capital Exterminate Opium and Dangerous Drugs Committee designated Nanjing a *juedui jinyan qucheng* (drug-free zone). Unlike other parts of China where opium smoking was quasi-legal with a permit, in Nanjing it was strictly forbidden.[102] The committee was also responsible for a change in the method of prosecuting drug offenders in the municipality. Convicted heroin and morphine felons were executed by firing squads, in public areas with full press coverage, but opium smokers underwent mandatory detoxification. To accommodate the number of smokers needing treatment, officials requisitioned emergency facilities across the city, including health clinics, Confucian temples, and even an elementary school.[103]

Before the end of the twenty-third year of the republic, the Capital Exterminate Opium and Dangerous Drugs Committee and the New Life Movement Promotional Association cosponsored "Exterminate Opium and Dangerous Drugs Education Week" on 17 to 23 December.[104] This event climaxed a year in which Nanjing evolved as the national model for opium addiction treatment, became a drug-free zone that executed morphine and heroin offenders, and linked the espoused goals of Chiang's six-year plan and New Life Movement in the public's mind.

The Six-Year Plan Becomes Official Policy

In 1935, as his armies pushed the Communists to Yan'an and faced increasing pressure from the Japanese in the north, Chiang forged ahead with what Hu Shize (Victor Hu)—Nanjing's representative to the League of Nations— called a "military period of campaign against narcotics."[105] He continued the aggressive drive to eliminate poppy production in the hinterland regions, to end heroin and morphine use, and to register opium smokers. A genuine effort was also made to open addiction treatment centers throughout regions south of the Great Wall. Then, in the summer of 1935, Chiang took the next logical step; he abandoned the farce of prohibition and firmly established a government opium monopoly as official Guomindang policy.

While in Guiyang, the provincial capital of Guizhou, Chiang established a temporary headquarters in the midst of chasing the Communists through southwest China on their historic "Long March." In early April, he issued directives modifying his six-year plan into a six-year/two-year plan. The Jinyan Shishi Banfa (Regulations for the Enforcement of Opium Suppression) and the Jindu Shishi Banfa (Regulations for the Enforcement of Narcotics Suppession) replaced the ineffective Opium Prohibition Act and Regulations of 1929. The Jindu Shishi Banfa stipulated that "dangerous narcotics" such as morphine and heroin must be eliminated within two years, while the Jinyan Shishi Banfa reiterated that opium would be more gradually suppressed within six years.[106]

These new directives read like a dreary recitation of previously enacted and failed policies. What distinguished these new directives as far as dangerous narcotics were concerned was the death sentence for anyone convicted of manufacturing, transporting, or selling heroin or morphine, and long, mandatory prison terms and confiscations of property for their accomplices. Those addicted to dangerous narcotics had eight months to enter treatment facilities voluntarily, while those arrested underwent forced detoxification. Beginning in 1936, convicted addicts would receive statutory imprisonment of five years or longer; after 1937, however, it was the death penalty or lifelong incarceration.[107] Perhaps in Generalissimo Chiang's mind, those who trafficked in or used harder drugs were aiding and abetting the Japanese and could thus be viewed as traitors to the nation. It appears that the uncompromising two-year plan for heroin and morphine offenders made the sale of opium to his fellow countrymen more palatable.

A strange convergence of events occurred in the two weeks surrounding 3 June 1935. It was during that auspicious fortnight that the League of Nations Opium Advisory Committee passed a resolution praising Chiang Kai-shek for his efforts to suppress opium in China; the generalissimo officially announced a change in Guomindang policy from complete prohibition to suppression through taxation; and the Nationalist government observed—with much fanfare—Opium Prohibition Memorial Day.

In Geneva, the League of Nations Opium Advisory Committee was convening its twentieth session (20 May–5 June). The Chinese representative Hu Shize leaked a report from Nanjing showing the preliminary results of Chiang's efforts to combat narcotics under the six-year plan. From May to December 1934, the government had established 597 opium treatment hospitals and clinics in fifteen provinces and five municipalities, had successfully treated 81,344 opium addicts, and had executed 257 people for heroin or morphine offenses. The report also reviewed the antinarcotics propaganda and educational work of the Guomindang and its efforts to eradicate poppy cultivation.[108] Based on the news reports reaching China from Geneva, it was clear that members of the League were impressed with Chiang Kai-shek's war on drugs. It was no surprise, then, when on 24 May the League's Anti-Opium Information Bureau issued a statement lauding Chiang and his government for the "unmistakable progress" they were making against the scourge of narcotics.[109]

In the afterglow of League approbation, on 29 May the Central Political Council appointed Chiang Kai-shek *jinyan zongjian* (director general for opium suppression) and abolished the National Opium Prohibition Committee.[110] Thereafter, all drug-related matters were Chiang's responsibility, not only as chief of the suppression effort, but as chairman of the Military Affairs Commission. This development signaled an end to the policy of complete prohibition and a victory for the proponents of *yujin yuzheng*, which ironically was the internationally sanctioned method for dealing with the opium problem embodied in the Geneva Opium Accord of 1925 that China had refused to sign. Article 3 of the accord stipulated that signatory nations had agreed to end their monopolies within fifteen years.[111] Coincidentally, that was the same year (1940) the six-year plan was scheduled for completion.

In celebration of Opium Prohibition Memorial Day on 3 June, Liu Ruiheng, who had just lost his post as chairman of the National Opium Prohibition Committee, praised Chiang's anti-opium efforts in Nanjing. China had entered a new era of opium suppression, Liu proclaimed, and before long the Republic of China would be rid of the dreaded narcotics evil once and for all.[112] Following his appointment as *jinyan zongjian*, Chiang issued still another set of directives to bring opium policy and the agencies concerned with its oversight and enforcement into line with his new authority.[113] No longer bothered by the National Opium Prohibition Committee, to say nothing of the National Anti-Opium Association, and his position buttressed by his military authority, Chiang was now in a position to exert unprecedented control over opium policy.

Du Yuesheng and the Shanghai Municipal Opium Suppression Committee

Following the dissolution of the National Opium Prohibition Committee, on 15 June Generalissimo Chiang created the Jinyan Weiyuanhui Zonghui (General Commission for Opium Suppression) within his Military Affairs Commission's field headquarters. For all intents and purposes, the General Commission for Opium Suppression performed essentially the same tasks as the defunct committee, such as the collection of statistics on suppression work, antinarcotics propaganda, formulating laws for the director general, and coordinating all efforts with various provincial, municipal, and county-level governments.[114] With his hand-picked cronies such as Li Jihong and Huang Weicai on the commission to ensure compliance with his suppression agenda (i.e., to raise revenue), Chiang Kai-shek was free to act accordingly.[115]

This fact might explain one of Chiang's unexpected actions, the appointment of Du Yuesheng to the newly created Shanghai Municipal Opium Suppression Committee on 1 July 1935.[116] Western scholars have viewed Chiang's relationship with the Green Gang as "the politics of gangsterism" or "criminalizing the government" and cite Du's appointment to the Shanghai committee as proof positive.[117] The appointment is best understood, however, in the context of Chiang's state-building goals, one of which was to increase his control over the opium trade through the monopoly system. From Chiang's perspective, one obvious way to advance his purposes was to appoint China's most successful smuggler to the Shanghai Municipal Opium Suppression Committee.

As will be described in Chapter 5 in more detail, Du Yuesheng had been a tax farmer for Nanjing since the government established its Special Tax Clearance Office monopoly in 1929. By the time of the appointment, Du Yuesheng was president of the Shanghai Special Business Association (Shanghai Teye Gonghui), an opium merchant guild that replaced the Special Business Clearance Association when the Opium Suppression Supervisory Bureaus were created in 1934.[118] Du's knowledge of the opium trade, including the illicit trade, as well as his access to local and national political leaders made him, in Chiang's eyes, an ideal choice for the Shanghai Municipal Opium Suppression Committee.

Du Yuesheng was also a recovered opium addict. According to Zhang Jungu, Du's effective treatment was the result of a joint effort in 1928 by T. V. Soong and Liu Ruiheng, the latter of whom personally assisted Du through a month of painful withdrawal.[119] Since one of the duties of the Shanghai Municipal Opium Suppression Committee was to supervise the treatment of addicts, Du's own experience may have enhanced his effectiveness as a member. Assuredly, those who heard Du speak before the Municipal Board of Education in 1935 on "The Problem of Opium Suppression in Shanghai" were hearing from a man who knew his subject matter.[120] Perhaps it is best to say that Du's appointment to the Shanghai Municipal Opium Suppression Committee reflected nothing more unusual than the continued links among opium, warlords, and the underworld organizations that had been forged in Shanghai during the late 1910s.

The Central Commission for Opium Suppression and Praise from the League of Nations

As his control over the opium trade and special taxes increased in tandem with the success of his armies across south and central China, Chiang Kai-shek made no significant changes in his opium policy during the last eighteen months before the Marco Polo Bridge Incident of 7 July 1937. As director general for opium suppression, Chiang's primary concern was extending the opium monopoly into the growing number of provinces coming under his control and devising methods of increasing revenue from it. The eighteen law codes produced during that span of time bear witness to that effort.[121]

In early February 1936, Chiang chaired the first meeting of the Zhongyang Jinyan Weiyuanhui (Central Commission for Opium Suppression), originally known as the General Commission for Opium Suppression, in Nanjing.[122] At the First Plenary of the Central Commission for Opium Suppression, the generalissimo explained why his government had never dealt successfully with the opium problem. One reason, he said, was the widely held misconception that opium suppression was an impossible task, which encouraged defeatism. Another misconception was that Japanese aggression was a greater threat to China than opium. But, said Chiang, if China could solve the opium problem, fending off a military aggressor would be easy. Therefore, the opium suppression effort was a supreme national test, and he called on the Chinese people and their leaders at all levels to eradicate poppy cultivation and the opium trade everywhere. Chiang then reaffirmed his commitment to eliminating opium and other narcotics, declaring that his government would never alter its six-year timetable for the sake of revenue.[123]

Meanwhile, Nanjing's war on drugs continued to earn the praise of European nations that had previously ridiculed Chinese antinarcotics efforts. Members of the League of Nations Opium Advisory Committee in the summer of 1936 echoed the plaudits they had made a year earlier. The new target of international criticism was Japan. Condemnation from all quarters focused on that nation's role in turning Manchuria and Rehe into huge poppy fields and in flooding northern China and Fujian with opium, heroin, and morphine.[124] In contrast, Europeans were so swayed by the initial achievements of Chiang's six-year plan that even Madame Tussaud's Wax Museum in London removed its Chinese opium den exhibit, a featured attraction there for decades.[125]

In this new atmosphere, Hu Shize signed the 1925 Geneva Opium Accord on behalf of Nanjing.[126] Internationally, this action signified China's dedication to opium suppression by means of the monopoly system, known in China as *yujin yuzheng* and recognized by League members as the most "modern" method for dealing with the problem. At least on this level, China had finally achieved parity with the imperial powers.

The End of the National Anti-Opium Association

Following the announcement of the six-year plan, Garfield Huang lamented that "the legalization of the opium trade and opium smoking by the Central government has proved a sad and retrogressive step in the morals of this modern government."[127] Even after fellow Christian Chiang Kai-shek was appointed *jinyan zongjian*, dissolved the National Opium Prohibition Committee, and assumed total control over Guomindang opium policy, the National Anti-Opium Association never wavered from its stance that revenue derived by the state from opium sales was morally reprehensible and unacceptable under any circumstances.

Crippled by financial problems and bereft of the public support it engendered during the 1920s and early 1930s, the National Anti-Opium Association continued its lonely crusade against a state monopoly. Sensing the weakness of the association, the Guomindang launched its final attack on the organization. Chiang Kai-shek, supported by Chinese and foreign Christians whom he increasingly relied on to resurrect the dying New Life Movement,[128] endeavored to force the association to adopt a new policy and program that were more sympathetic to the six-year plan. In early May 1937, for example, Shanghai missionaries supportive of the generalissimo's policies attempted to seize control of the organization. However, Li Denghui and other members of the executive committee rallied behind Huang, declaring that the National Anti-Opium Association would rather suspend its work than compromise is long-held position against legalization of opium and would never hand the association over to any party—including the missionaries.[129]

Several weeks later, an informal discussion was held between members of the National Anti-Opium Association executive committee and several missionaries and leaders of the New Life Movement who were close to Chiang Kai-shek. Paul Yen (Yan Baohang), a member of the National Christian Council and long associated with the New Life Movement hierarchy, was the generalissimo's point man. At this meeting, the Nanjing group offered to fund the association indefinitely, with Garfield Huang as general secretary, so long as Huang and the association did not criticize the six-year plan until after 1940. The modified program of the association would be limited to antinarcotics education and exposés on Japanese drug trafficking in China for international and domestic purposes. The Nanjing group also offered "to clear up General Chiang's misunderstandings regarding Mr. Garfield Huang's strong anti-government and anti-monopoly activities of the past" if Huang consented to the proposal.[130]

While the National Anti-Opium Association was mulling over the government's offer, on 3 June 1937 (Opium Prohibition Memorial Day), the director general of opium suppression reviewed the initial results of his six-year plan at a public gathering to celebrate the national holiday in Nanjing. Chiang claimed that opium cultivation had been eliminated in twelve provinces and reduced in several others, that over 3.6 million smokers had registered with the government, and that facilities for treating addicts had opened in 970 locations.[131] But, Chiang continued, several hundred thousand people still depended on the opium trade for their livelihood and would attempt to impede the government's work. The key to success in the suppression effort, Chiang emphasized, lay in the New Life Movement:

> The suppression of opium and other narcotics is the most important foundation of this New Life Movement. The movement places special emphasis on the virtues of orderliness, cleanliness, punctuality and diligence, which are directly opposed to the laziness and slovenliness of opium addicts. . . . While we ourselves should lead a new life, we must also use our utmost influence with a view to delivering the opium addicts from the Valley of Death. Only thus can we fulfill the responsibility imposed by the New Life Movement.[132]

In closing his speech, Chiang then invoked the spirit of Lin Zexu to energize the Chinese people with the power to overcome all obstacles in their path.

Fusing together biblical imagery, the New Life Movement, and the six-year plan, and even conjuring up the ghost of Lin Zexu, Chiang Kai-shek had seized the moral high ground in his military campaign against narcotics. Backed by legions of statistics to justify his policy of *yujin yuzheng*, the generalissimo's drug war had impressed many Chinese and foreigners alike. Several weeks after Chiang's anti-opium sermon, Garfield Huang and the National Anti-Opium Association executive committee decided to refuse Nanjing's offer. On 28 June 1937, the Zhonghua Guomin Juduhui formally announced its dissolution, fulfilling a 1934 prophecy to American consular officials that it would "rather die as a martyr than to live an easy life."[133]

5 *Practical Determinants of Guomindang Opium Policy*

WHY DID THE GUOMINDANG'S EFFORTS to prohibit opium fail so spectacularly? There were two basic reasons for the perpetuation of the warlord system and its addiction to the poppy. During the Northern Expedition, the National Revolutionary Army incorporated militarists and armies it could not control and then exacerbated the situation by appointing many of these warlords and their military commanders to important positions in the party and in national and local governments.[1] Nor did the climax of the Northern Expedition end the high level of military expenditures. Despite two Military Reorganization and Disbandment conferences held in Nanjing in 1929, warlords refused to surrender their only source of political power.[2] Beginning that same year, Li Zongren and Bai Chongxi (the Guangxi Clique), Zhang Fakui, and Tang Shengzhi in succession rebelled against the central government, prompting an immediate military response. Yan Xishan and Feng Yuxiang led an anti-Chiang movement the following year, plunging north China into six months of bloody warfare resulting in 250,000 casualties.[3] Meanwhile, the Communists took advantage of the unremitting internal strife to establish soviets in Jiangxi, Hunan, Hubei, Henan, and Anhui provinces, motivating Chiang Kai-shek to launch the first of five anti-Communist campaigns in December 1930.[4]

The second reason was the failure, or inability, to reform the structure of local as opposed to national finances. Nanjing sponsored the National Economic Conference and the National Financial Conference in June and July 1928 to facilitate its access to the resources vital for Guomindang state building.

While the central government delimited Maritime Customs, salt, and consolidated taxes as national revenues, it left local governments to fend for themselves. This meant that local governments were still dependent on land, *lijin*, opium, and a burdensome array of levies for their survival.[5] Therefore, nothing changed in 1928 and immediately thereafter to alter the structural relationship between warlord politics on the one hand and opium on the other. Following the abolition of *lijin* and native customs duties in 1931, this relationship only intensified.

Creation of the Qingli Lianghu Teshuichu

The revolt of the Guangxi Clique in the central Yangtze region between March and May 1929 enabled Chiang Kai-shek and his followers to gain control of the strategic provinces of Hubei and Hunan. After Hankou fell to Chiang's armies in April, T. V. Soong arrived in the city to reorganize provincial finances once again. His stated tasks were to delineate between national and local sources of revenue, to ascertain the amount of debt incurred by public entities in the region, and to open a Hankou branch of the Nanjing-operated Central Bank of China to expedite solutions to the other two tasks.[6] While he was in Hankou, Soong also oversaw the creation of the Qingli Lianghu Teshuichu (Hubei-Hunan Special Tax Clearance Office). Ironically, he completed this last task on 17 April 1929, three days after the National Opium Prohibition Committee had publicly denounced the Wuhan Branch Political Council for continuing to collect opium taxes at Hankou in violation of prohibition.[7]

Ostensibly, Soong established the Special Tax Clearance Office to enable local opium merchants to *qingli* (clear out or liquidate) their existing stocks of opium within a three-month period (April–July). However, the three months passed, and Nanjing repeatedly extended the deadline, permitting the opium merchants to sell their merchandise and the local government to collect desperately needed revenue therefrom.[8] The Special Tax Clearance Office had quickly become a permanent, invaluable tax-collecting agency for the provincial governments of Hubei and Hunan, not to mention the central government. Shen Gongli, director of the Hankou Main Office in early 1930, best explained the rationale for extending the life span of the agency. In a letter to T. V. Soong, Shen argued that without government protection of the "special business merchants" *(teye shangren),* it would be impossible to put the finances of Hubei and Hunan in order. The opium trade was so deeply intertwined with the local economy that provincial finances had become severely addicted to the drug.[9] To illustrate the lucrative nature of the commerce in Hankou, in August 1932—during a slack business year—the Chinese periodical *New China Daily News* estimated Hankou's daily opium transactions at $70,000, or $25,550,000 annually.[10]

By late 1930, as the need for revenues by the provincial governments of Hubei and Hunan escalated, this single office in Hankou spawned numerous offspring. Important Lianghu market cities along river and rail routes became the sites of branch special tax clearance offices (see Map 6). In Hubei, Hankou maintained its leading position as the nexus of the narco-economy in central China. The main office *(zongchu)* of the clearance office monopoly in Hankou was responsible for overseeing all special tax matters in Lianghu. Under the jurisdiction of Nanjing's Ministry of Finance, the Hankou Main Office supervised branch offices *(fenchu)* situated in Yichang and Xiangfan, agencies *(banshichu)* located in Huayuan and Laohekou, and an inspection post at Shashi.[11] Hunan's main office was located in the provincial capital of Changsha, with an agency in Hongjiang, in addition to five inspection posts situated in Baoqing, Changde, Jinshi, Rucheng, and Mayang.[12]

The Special Tax Clearance Office monopoly, although functioning in direct violation of the policy of complete prohibition, was the Guomindang's first attempt since the end of the Northern Expedition to regulate the unruly Yangtze commerce. Besides managing the day-to-day affairs of special tax collection, the Hankou Main Office operated several steamships that made the Yichang-Hankou-Shanghai runs, although during the monopoly's early years private vessels also transported cargoes downriver.[13] An executive body that oversaw the Hankou Main Office called the Jiandu Weiyuanhui (Supervisory Committee) was composed of Hubei's military and civil leaders. It originally had eight members but was expanded to nine in March 1931 to accommodate Liu Xiang's attaché stationed in Wuhan at the behest of Chiang Kai-shek.[14] Within the main office was the Jianguansuo (Inspection and Management Department), wherein "special goods" *(tehuo)*—as the opium was officially described—were inspected and weighed, and taxes assayed. Afterwards, the transport and wholesale/warehouse merchants (i.e., tax farmers and brokers) moved the opium into their own godowns for storage until their clients paid off their debts within a specified period of time.[15]

Prominent transport and wholesale firms in Hankou, which had organized an opium *fatuan* in 1922, simply renamed themselves the Teye Qinglihui (Special Business Clearance Association) and adapted their practices

Map 6. The Lianghu Special Tax Clearance Office System, 1930

accordingly.[16] In the markets with main and branch special tax clearance offices, transport and wholesale merchants established *teye gongsi* (special business companies). The *teye gongsi* performed the following tasks on behalf of the clearance offices: purchasing and importing special goods from other provinces for sale locally, exporting opium produced locally or in other provinces to destinations downstream, storing special goods for *keshang* (out-oftown merchants), reporting and collecting taxes on behalf of the clearance offices, affixing revenue stamps and sealing strips *(fengtiao)* to monopoly opium, and wholesaling and retailing the drug.[17]

All special business companies (which were joint-stock ventures) had to have sufficient capital before the special tax clearance offices granted licenses for operation. For example, Hankou capitalization was set at $100,000, while the *teye gongsi* in Yichang required $50,000.[18] Those meeting that criterion paid a yearly "special license fee" *(texu zhengfei)* and a monthly "business fee" *(yingyefei)* to the local special tax clearance office. Although *teye gongsi* merchants collected and paid taxes to the clearance offices, they were entitled to a "procedural fee" *(shouxufei)* on every *dan* of opium taxed, plus a "sales commission" *(yongjin)* for each ounce bought and sold, as compensation for their services rendered to the state.[19] The *teye gongsi* entrepreneurs were explicitly forbidden from buying and selling smuggled (i.e., nonmonopoly) opium but frequently ignored such restrictions.

Retail sales were regulated through the *tehuo fashousuo* (special goods sales departments). There was a hierarchy of special goods sales departments throughout a given province. A main department *(zongsuo),* servicing either one or several counties, was required to sell a stipulated amount of opium each month and paid a security deposit on every *dan* it received from the *teye gongsi* plus quarterly license and monthly business fees to the special business companies. Branch departments *(fensuo)*—actually opium dens—paid special license fees too, but monthly business fees were divided into three classes based on volume of sales.[20]

Special business clearance associations and members of their executive committees performed invaluable services for the clearance offices. In Hankou, for instance, the Special Tax Clearance Office main office farmed out collection of the *teye gongsi* license fees and stamp taxes to the Hankou Special Business Clearance Association. The Hankou Special Business Clearance Association warehoused monopoly opium on behalf of other merchants; informed the Ministry of Finance of market conditions, illegal confiscations, or harmful taxes that affected the trade; was responsible for debts owed by the *teye gongsi* to the Special Tax Clearance Office; and even lent money to the clearance office to cover its monthly subsidies to the Hubei provincial government in lean months.[21] Additionally, as managers of the *teye gongsi* and quasi–clearance office functionaries, Special Business Clearance Association leaders calculated and collected various taxes for the government.

This new tax collection arrangement between the Guomindang and opium merchants was almost identical to those used in Guangdong or during the Northern Expedition. For all intents and purposes, it was still *guandu shang-ban*. Nevertheless, the Special Tax Clearance Office monopoly would provide irreplaceable financial benefits locally and nationally, and a means for Nanjing to extend its influence into central and southern China, where recalcitrant warlords maintained their independence by encouraging the trade.

Special Taxes and Local Government Finances

The indispensability of special tax revenues in central China for both local and national governments was fueled by constantly rising military costs inflated by the bandit suppression campaigns. A considerable sum of capital was remitted to the National Treasury by the Hankou Main Office between April 1929 and June 1931. According to a document prepared by Minister of Finance H. H. Kung (Kong Xiangxi) for Generalissimo Chiang in 1934, the Lianghu Special Tax Clearance Office paid into Nanjing's coffers a total of $32,209,028.77 for that period.[22] For fiscal years 1930 and 1931, opium receipts were the Nationalist government's fifth largest source of nonborrowed income but did not appear in its published budgets.[23]

In absolute terms, it was at the provincial and municipal levels that the value of opium tax dollars was unmatched by more legitimate sources. He Chengjun, chairman of the Hubei provincial government and commander of the Third Bandit Suppression Army, stated that of all the revenues collected at Hankou before late 1931, half went to Nanjing, 30 percent to the Hubei treasury, and the remainder to Liu Xiang in Chongqing as compensation for military escorts of opium shipments from Sichuan to Hankou.[24] By early 1932, the share allocated to Hubei was augmented to 40 percent.[25] The Hankou Main Office made monthly payments to the Hubei provincial government and the Hankou municipal government under the heading of "central government subsidies." For example, in the months of May and September 1930, disbursements to the Hubei treasury amounted to $5,450,000 and $7 million, respectively.[26]

Payments to the Hankou municipal government were quantitatively smaller but qualitatively more substantial. By May 1930, one-third of all municipal revenue was obtained from special tax receipts.[27] In September 1930, Li Muqing (director of the Hankou Main Office) wrote to T. V. Soong concerning the need to disburse special tax funds to repair the roads and wharves in Hankou and to expand the military garrisons. Since keeping the docks and wharves in good condition was essential to the economic life of the city, Li asked Soong to authorize $11,000 a month for these purposes.[28]

To keep pace with escalating demands for military funds to fight the communists, Shen Gongli (director of the Hankou Main Office before Li) had imposed an amalgamated surtax of $150 on each *dan* of special goods, raising the total transit duties from $600 to $750.[29] In Yichang, an itemization of the surtax included $60 for police and education, $30 for dike construction, $30 for military disbandment, $15 for warehousing fees, $5 for revenue stamps, and $5 for public welfare.[30] Although each additional levy was earmarked for a specific local outlay, the dragon's share poured back into the black hole of provincial military expenditures.

The Special Tax Clearance Office System and "Poppy Politics"

The Ministry of Finance records reveal how Chiang Kai-shek and T. V. Soong systematically manipulated the Yangtze opium traffic to facilitate the expansion of Guomindang political power not only into areas where Communists were present, but into outlying provinces as well. The ability of Sichuan, Yunnan, Guizhou, Guangxi, and Guangdong to resist Chiang's centralization efforts was bolstered by the fact that they were either regions of heavy cultivation or major conduits and markets for the opium trade.

The resulting "poppy politics" as practiced by Nanjing in 1930 had four basic features. It involved a concerted attempt to monopolize the opium traffic along the Yangtze River from Chongqing to Shanghai by unifying tax collection procedures and by providing safe passage for ships and their cargoes downriver. The immediate objective was to generate more capital to offset rising costs associated with bandit suppression. The effort also sought to manipulate the trade routes for opium produced in Yunnan and Guizhou so as to bypass the Guangxi Corridor and thus deprive the Guangxi Clique and later anti-Chiang elements in Guangdong of this revenue. Generalissimo Chiang furthermore sought to use the trade as a means of improving Nanjing's estranged relations with the autonomous provincial governments of Yunnan, Guizhou, and Sichuan. Finally, at the terminus of the Yangtze commerce, the Ministry of Finance and Du Yuesheng secretly concluded a revenue-sharing agreement to dispose of Special Tax Clearance Office product. Thus, what began with the creation of the Lianghu Special Tax Clearance Office in 1929 became part of a grander strategy for extending political power into central, south, and southwest China.

In January or February 1930, Nanjing dispatched Chen Shaogui, its special finance commissioner for Hubei and Hunan, to Sichuan.[31] The purpose of Chen's mission was to work out a deal with "residual warlord" Liu Xiang. Nanjing needed Liu's cooperation to rationalize the collection of transit duties in Hubei and eastern Sichuan, to reduce smuggling and tax evasion, and to provide armed escorts for opium shipments from Chongqing to Hankou. What resulted from Chen's negotiations was the Chuan-E Lianyun Banfa (Sichuan-Hubei Joint-Transport Method).

The agreement stipulated that Liu's Caizheng Tongchouchu (Consolidated Finances Office) would collect taxes in Chongqing, while the Wanxian Chajichu (Wanxian Opium Smuggling Prevention Department) repeated that task near the Sichuan-Hubei border. After shippers had paid their taxes, Sichuanese officials would weigh the goods, attach revenue stamps to the cargo, and seal it with *fengtiao*. A passport would be provided, indicating the weight and destination of the goods under the code name of *yaopin* (medicines). The merchants and bureau personnel in Sichuan would fill out a *liandan*, also called a *shuidan* (tax receipt), indicating the weight, type of opium, amount of taxes paid at that location, number of packing crates, its destination, and a stipulated period of time for which the receipt was valid. Copies of the tax receipt would be forwarded to Yichang and Hankou to guard against fraud. Shipments were then escorted out of Sichuan by a detachment of twenty to thirty soldiers. Once the cargoes reached Yichang and Hankou, opium from Sichuan with the *liandan* received a 16.7 percent discount on the official rate per *dan* ($500 instead of $600) but paid surtaxes ($150) according to the nondiscounted rate. Cargoes without documentation (*liandan*) paid the higher official rates and surtaxes plus a *buzheng chuanshui* (compensatory tax for not paying duties in Sichuan).[32]

Special goods from Guizhou and Yunnan also received preferential rates to induce shippers in those provinces to shift from their customary routes through the Guangxi Corridor to new ones through Hunan or Sichuan to Hankou. Shen Gongli referred to this enterprise as the Chuan-Qian-E Lianyun Banfa (Sichuan-Guizhou-Hubei Joint-Transport Method), an expansion of the previous agreement between Nanjing and Liu Xiang.[33] To entice shippers in Guizhou to accommodate accordingly, *qiantu* was assessed a discounted tax rate of only $400 per *dan* with no surtaxes. The chairmen of the Yunnan (Long Yun) and Guizhou (Mao Guangxiang) provincial governments agreed to encourage the new system by increasing levies on all opium exports to Guangxi.[34]

Shen Gongli discussed the political ramifications of these arrangements with the Ministry of Finance. "In recent years," Shen wrote Soong in March 1930,

> a large amount of Guizhou goods have changed their route through southern Guizhou, passing through Liuzhou and Qunzhou [Guangxi] in order to be sold in Wuzhou and Canton. This is the largest source of military funds for Guangxi province. . . . Guangxi is the place that the rebels occupy, our government cannot indifferently watch the special goods going south to the advantage of the rebels. . . . The goods that normally would flow through Guangxi but are now coming into Sichuan [from Guizhou] are a way for the government to cut off this source of military funds for our enemy [Guangxi] and increase our own revenues.[35]

Again in May, Shen informed Soong, "According to the agent [Chen Shaogui] who explained this in person, the change in the route for goods to Hankou is related to Guizhou and Sichuan's wholehearted support for the central government to cut off the flow of military funds to the Guangxi Clique."[36]

Another feature of poppy politics was the issuance of *yuzhengjuan* (advance tax payment vouchers) by the Hankou Main Office. The *yuzhengjuan* were a lucrative means of raising capital in the short run while rewarding opium merchants who used the Special Tax Clearance Office monopoly. The Hankou Main Office sold the vouchers to opium merchants who used them to pay transit levies at Yichang, for which they received a 33 percent discount off of the official rate of $600 per *dan* ($400 with vouchers) but not the surtaxes. As a consequence of the savings involved, there was a strong demand for the vouchers, which circulated as highly valued currency in Hubei and Sichuan (see Figure 8).

While Chen Shaogui was in Sichuan discussing the Joint-Transport Method, he and Liu Xiang agreed to the issuance of $5 million in *yuzhengjuan*, with 60 percent going to Nanjing and 40 percent to Sichuan to "rescue Liu Xiang's finances."[37] However, for some reason that is not clear from the surviving documents, the vouchers were never issued to Liu. By June 1930, Liu Xiang on several occasions queried He Chengjun, chairman of the Hubei provincial government, about the delay. He Chengjun then asked T. V. Soong:

> I truly do not know what the complications are. Within the last year, the Guangxi Clique, Feng Yuxiang, Tang Shengzhi, and Yan Xishan have continuously wreaked havoc. All of them have collaborated with Deng Xihou and Tian Songyao in Sichuan, who have also sent people out to collaborate with them. . . . Only the attitude of Liu Xiang has been loyal to the central

Figure 8. A sample one-hundred dollar *yuzhengjuan* [advance tax payment voucher] issued by the Ministry of Finance for the Hubei-Hunan Special Tax Clearance Office. It was used by opium merchants when paying "special taxes" at the Yichang branch office. Source: Number Two Historical Archives, Quanzonghao 3, No. 1023, Li Muqing to T. V. Soong (8/19/30).

government in comparison with the others [warlords in Sichuan]. Liu Xiang forced Liu Wenhui to support the central government for the sake of our Gonggu Xi'nanji (Plan to Secure the Southwest).[38]

Finally, in August the Hankou Main Office dispatched $2 million in *yuzhengjuan* to Liu to "be used for military allocations."[39] British consular reports claimed that this $5 million deal was not only a way for Sichuan and Nanjing to raise capital quickly, but also a means for Liu Xiang to purchase arms and ammunition sent by Chiang Kai-shek.[40]

At the other end of the Yangtze, Nanjing reached an understanding with Du Yuesheng to sell Special Tax Clearance Office opium in Shanghai. Du Yuesheng's name is mentioned in a document from Chen Shaogui to T. V. Soong dated 10 June 1930 regarding the transport of special goods from Hankou to Shanghai.[41] A British consular report from that same month claims that Soong and Du had also agreed to split the profits from a shipment of two thousand cases of Persian opium arriving from Bushire. Military protection was provided by Xiong Shihui, defense commissioner for the Shanghai-Wusong Municipality.[42] Another Ministry of Finance document lists ten shipments from the Hankou Main Office to Shanghai for the period from July to November 1931.[43] Although the details of the agreement and the mechanics of the Shanghai operation are hazy, hard archival evidence for collusion between Du Yuesheng and the Ministry of Finance in the Special Tax Clearance Office monopoly is overwhelming.

Smuggling, Corruption, and Predation

Nanjing experienced countless difficulties in the Special Tax Clearance Office monopoly within a year of its conception. Smuggling, corruption, fickle allegiance from warlords in south and southwest China, natural disasters, and a lack of adequate silver specie along the upper Yangtze negatively affected Nanjing's opium enterprise.

An example of smuggling's effect on the markets from Shanghai to Chongqing occurred in April 1930. Guo Rudong, commander of the Sichuanese Twentieth Army, was ordered by Nanjing to move his twenty thousand troops from the Sichuan border area to Huangzhou in eastern Hubei. Guo and his soldiers used the massive redeployment to conceal the shipment of several thousand *dan* of opium through Yichang and Hankou without paying any taxes en route.

Once the duty-free shipments flooded the markets of Hankou and Shanghai, they severely crippled the sales of Special Tax Clearance Office products.

According to Director Shen Gongli in Hankou, the price of special goods in Shanghai and Hankou dropped several times owing to this deluge of lower-priced merchandise on the market. The result was that in Yichang the selling price for Sichuan opium was $1.70 per *liang*; at Hankou and Shanghai it was only $1.80 or less. For the Hankou Main Office to turn a profit, transit duties at Yichang and Hankou increased the selling price downriver. Normally, *chuantu* retailed in Hankou for $2 to $2.20 per ounce and for $2.30 to $2.50 in Shanghai. Because of the depressed value of opium available on the black market, merchants were not purchasing their goods from the Hankou Main Office's Inspection and Management Department. Unclaimed stocks of Special Tax Clearance Office product jumped from 2,000 to 4,000 *dan* in one month. This increase in turn affected the cash flow of financial institutions in Yichang and Chongqing, because monopoly merchants were unable to find buyers for their higher-priced goods in Hankou and Shanghai. All that the Hankou Main Office could do was wait until stocks of the smuggled product were depleted and the laws of supply and demand brought the value of opium in the middle and lower Yangtze markets back to normal levels.[44]

Another incident involved predatory attacks on Special Tax Clearance Office shipments by Nationalist troops and local militia in Jiangsu province. From the spring of 1930 to January 1931, central government troops stationed at the Nanjing and Zhenjiang garrisons, abetted by the Zhenjiang Baoandui (Zhenjiang Peace Preservation Corps), had confiscated shipments of special goods en route to Shanghai from Hankou. A total of eighteen illegal confiscations had taken place during this ten-month feeding frenzy, costing Hankou special business merchants over $5 million to $6 million in losses. In early January 1931, representatives from the Hankou Special Business Clearance Association traveled to Nanjing and held face-to-face discussions with Soong and Generalissimo Chiang. As a result of these talks, special troops from the generalissimo's field headquarters were dispatched to escort subsequent Special Tax Clearance Office cargo shipments along the Yangtze from Hankou to Shanghai.[45]

A final affair revolved around a steamship called the *Yuchuan*. On 26 May 1930, the *Yuchuan* arrived in Hankou from Yichang carrying 316 cases (30.5 tons) of Yunnan and Guizhou opium worth approximately $2 million. Without warning, troops from the Wuhan Garrison surrounded the vessel, arrested the escort party, and confiscated the opium, because it lacked the official revenue stamps from Yichang. Shen Gongli thereupon wired T. V. Soong, and Chiang Kai-shek ordered Garrison Commander Xia Douyin to release the special goods immediately to the Hankou Main Office.[46]

Director Shen insisted that the confiscated shipment was not smuggled opium but part of the Joint-Transport Method. Even special business merchants from Sichuan, Guizhou, and Yunnan residing in Yichang sent a radiogram to Soong supporting Shen's position.[47] With so many irregularities surrounding the incident, He Yingqin ordered an investigation that eventually implicated Shen Gongli and Chen Shaogui in various acts of corruption. The outcome of the investigation was the dismissal of Shen Gongli as director of the Hankou Main Office and the recall of Chen Shaogui to Nanjing.[48]

Yunnan and Guizhou Pull Out of the Special Tax Clearance Office Monopoly

Back in early 1931, Yang Tong of the Hankou Main Office wired T. V. Soong about the revival of opium shipments through the Guangxi Corridor. Yang reported that Guangxi authorities were luring Guizhou and Yunnan merchants and their cargoes by reducing transit duties at the same time Hunan provincial chairman He Jian had increased rates from $450 to $700 per *dan* on Guizhou opium moving through his province, despite requests from Hankou that Hunan lower its duties.[49]

A few months later, Soong sent identical orders to Long Yun and his counterpart in Guizhou, Mao Guangxiang, to stop the flow of native product into rebellious Guangxi and Guangdong. The new route would follow Special Tax Clearance Office monopoly thoroughfares stipulated under the Joint-Transport agreements. To persuade Long and Mao, Soong sweetened the offer. "The central government has approved the dispensing of subsidies [to your province] for the period of one year, effective 6/1/31 to 5/31/32."[50] Nanjing's minister of finance also promised that Guizhou and Yunnan authorities would be compensated $180 for every *dan* of opium they sent through Special Tax Clearance Office arteries above the 10,000 *dan* expected from each province, and enclosed $1 million in *yuzhengjuan* to both Long and Mao "to help your province during this financial crisis."[51]

Soong's generosity notwithstanding, the responses from Yunnan and Guizhou were less than enthusiastic. Long Yun told Soong that because of Cantonese investments in his province, the most economic route for *yuntu* was through Guangxi to Guangdong. The roads through Sichuan and Hunan, he noted, traversed difficult terrain and accrued higher taxes. Thus, merchants naturally preferred to use the easier and tax-friendlier route through Guangxi. If his government ordered merchants to stop sending opium through Guangxi and Guangdong, he continued, they would be impoverished, and Yunnan's finances would end up in worse shape then they were already. Long Yun therefore told Soong he could not carry out his order.[52] Ma Kongfan of the Guizhou Department of Finance described to Soong essentially the same plight and also refused to implement Nanjing's directive. Adding insult to injury, in 1932 Guizhou signed an economic cooperation treaty with Guangdong and Guangxi to facilitate the flow of opium among the three provinces.[53] Viewing Chiang's growing power as a threat to their own autonomy, southwestern warlords—along with the opium produced in their provinces—sought out the path of least resistance.

Besides the political factors reducing the volume of monopoly opium, the Yangtze River flood of 1931, which had peaked in July, left Hankou under four to eight feet of water for almost a month and impaired maritime communications for several months thereafter. By the time river traffic was back to normal in early 1932, the Japanese unexpectedly attacked Shanghai. As a consequence, Special Tax Clearance Office shipments were once again curtailed until the crisis passed.[54]

Hubei was especially hard hit by these events, as Xiong Zijia related to Soong:

> After the abolition of the *lijin* tax, our provincial finances have further suffered from the Yangtze flood, and we are in desperate straits. All military, police, government administrative, and educational expenses were completely reliant on central government subsidies and special tax assistance monies for their maintenance.... During the last days of January, the Shanghai Incident unexpectedly occurred. Merchant transports [from Sichuan and Yichang] abruptly halted because they have adopted a wait and see attitude. It is because of this that the reported number of goods taxed in February was barely over 1,300 *dan*.[55]

Xiong added that he had been forced to borrow money from whatever source he could, including the Central Bank and the Hankou Special Business Clearance Association.

Yang Tong and He Baohua's Proposals

When Li Muqing was ordered to organize the Henan Special Tax Clearance Office in early 1931, Yang Tong and He Baohua replaced Li as codirectors of the Hankou Main Office. In May, they wrote a letter to T. V. Soong outlining a course of action to reinvigorate the floundering monopoly at the key entrepôts of Yichang and Hankou. Five reasons were given for the recent decline in tax revenues: (1) the market value of monopoly opium was low; (2) Special Tax Clearance Office taxes were stifling; (3) the *huishui* (remissions fee) charged by local banks was extortionate in Yichang and eastern Sichuan; (4) the cash flow in these regions was stagnant; and (5) smuggling was ubiquitous along the Sichuan-Hubei border. Yang and Bao's a priori reasoning assumed that the root of all problems started with excessive Special Tax Clearance Office levies that drove up the banks' remissions fees and rates for loans and mortgages. These two factors encouraged rampant smuggling, which in turn drove down the market price for opium. Consequently, the higher-priced monopoly products accumulated at the Yichang and Hankou Special Tax Clearance Office Jianguansuo, thereby decreasing state tax receipts.[56]

The codirectors outlined five measures for improving the situation. First, surtaxes would be reduced. By eliminating the $50 per *dan* military affairs surtax at Hankou and decreasing the $60 dike construction surtax by $10, collections would increase. Moreover, if Liu Xiang could be convinced to lower official rates by $30 to $50 per *dan*, then the total savings for merchants shipping goods from Chongqing or Wanxian to Hankou would be around $100 per *dan*. Second, monetary incentives would encourage larger shipments to Yichang. Yang and Bao proposed standardizing the weights for all shipping containers at 2 *dan* or 2,000 ounces (at the time, weights varied between 1,000 and 1,800 ounces), and rewarding merchants with gratuities at set rates of $2 for fifty-plus crates, $3 for one-hundred-plus crates, $10 for three-hundred-plus crates, and so forth. In this way, there would be a greater incentive for transport merchants to ship their goods through the monopoly.

The third idea related to addressing the financial doldrums experienced in Yichang and eastern Sichuan. High interest rates on short-term loans and mortgages in addition to outrageous fees attached to remissions transactions were exacerbated by a lack of silver specie. To remedy the problem, the codirectors proposed opening branches of the Central Bank in Yichang and Chongqing. Yichang was given a higher priority, because a Central Bank could provide enough capital and low-interest loans to opium merchants to energize commerce in the city. Not only would a Central Bank stimulate the opium trade, but it would promote the use of central government currency in a region still awash in a sea of lower-valued Sichuan, Guizhou, and Yunnan scrip.

Smuggling of nonmonopoly opium was most serious along the Sichuan-

Hubei border. Steamers bound from the Sichuan ports of Wanxian and Chonqing would use devious techniques to decrease their tax burden at Yichang. The favored method was the use of *Ba-Zi yundan* (transport manifests to the ports of Badong and Zigui in western Hubei) issued by the Wanxian Chajichu. The manifests permitted vessels to sell their goods at the small-time upper Yangtze markets of Badong and Zigui. However, the crews would enter Hubei from Sichuan and either off-load the goods to smaller craft that sailed alongside the ships or pack opium in oilskin bags and toss them overboard, where they would float several feet below the surface, to be retrieved later by accomplices. The opium would then be taken overland to points below Yichang, thereby evading taxation. When ships arrived in Yichang with much less opium than was indicated on the manifest from Sichuan, merchants would claim to have sold it in Badong or Zigui, although tax officials knew better. To rectify this situation, Yang and Bao proposed abolishing the *Ba-Zi yundan* altogether, having the maritime licenses confiscated from ships known to engage in this practice and adding crippling fines for the ship owners.

The final suggestion emphasized more stringent inspection at the Special Tax Clearance Office agencies and greater incentive for clearance office inspectors, local military, and police to report smuggled shipments. More lucrative rewards were needed to induce a more vigilant attitude among inspection personnel. Instead of the current reward of 30 percent of the opium's total value, a 50 percent bounty would ensure more thorough inspections and stricter enforcement.[57]

The Military Affairs Commission Field Headquarters Absorbs the Monopoly

By the summer of 1932, there were many difficulties confronting Chiang Kai-shek. The most significant in terms of opium policy was a growing rift between the generalissimo and T. V. Soong. Two weeks before the landmark Lushan Bandit Suppression Conference of 16–17 June to discuss anti-Communist strategy, Soong temporarily resigned as minister of finance. Soong's action was attributed to his displeasure with Chiang's policy of appeasing Japanese aggression and the generalissimo's demand for additional funds for the planned Fourth Bandit Suppression Campaign, the latter of which threatened to undermine Soong's policy of fiscal conservancy. A compromise was reached whereby Soong resumed his duties in early July, after it was agreed that no new bonds would be issued to finance Chiang's latest anti-Communist campaign but that the funds to cover increased military expenses would be supplemented by increased salt and other taxes.[58]

The issue of opium taxation was reported to have played an important role in the controversy.[59] From archival materials reflecting the status of the Special Tax Clearance Office system before and after the Lushan Bandit Suppression Conference, it appears that Chiang Kai-shek and Soong consented not only to extend the Special Tax Clearance Office system into Jiangxi, Anhui, and Jiangsu, but to disengage the Ministry of Finance and the Central Bank from the opium monopoly.[60] By the end of 1932, Chiang Kai-shek would place all matters pertaining to the unofficial monopoly under the jurisdiction of his Military Affairs Commission.

The change was precipitated by the cumulative maladies plaguing the Special Tax Clearance Office system. The amount of opium that passed through Hankou reflected the monopoly's dire circumstances. According to the National Anti-Opium Association, the quantity of special goods taxed annually by the Main Office in 1929 was 100,000 *dan* and in 1930, 117,000 *dan,* only to decline steadily to 70,020 *dan* in 1931 and 59,860 in 1932.[61] The effect of decreased opium revenues was an increased burden on an already cash-strapped central government. The Hankou Main Office started borrowing large amounts from the Central Bank in July 1931, chiefly to pay subsidies to Hubei. Five months later, the Main Office owed $3 million in principal and interest.[62] By April 1932, the situation was reaching critical mass, because the Special Tax Clearance Office was unable to meet its payments to the Hankou Branch Central Bank. During that month, an official of the Central Bank's main office in Shanghai underscored the chronic failure of the Hankou Main Office to meet its loan repayments on schedule, accusing Special Tax Clearance Office officials of acting in bad faith and requesting Soong to order them to pay the arrears. "Henceforth," the official ended his memorandum on a note of urgency, "repayments must be made according to schedule in order to safeguard the bank's assets and maintain public confidence in our solvency."[63] The accumulating Special Tax Clearance Office debts with the Central Bank and the anemic monopoly under the ministry's direction played important roles in the Soong resignation drama.

Before disengaging his ministry from the monopoly, Soong ordered the expansion of Special Tax Clearance Office agencies in other provinces along the lower Yangtze as a method to revive slumping sales. By July, in the provincial capital of Zhenjiang, the Jiangsu Quansheng Teshuiju (Jiangsu Provincial Special Tax Bureau) was established as the center of Jiangsu operations.[64] Two months later, Director of the Hankou Main Office Huang Zhenxing noted that "in Shanghai, Jiangxi, and Anhui, the *gongyun* (government transport) method has been implemented," meaning no private vessels could transport special goods from Yichang to Shanghai.[65] Du Yuesheng, who had been unceremoniously forced out of the French Concession to the Chinese-administered district of Nanshi (Nandao) in summer 1932, reopened for business. With the assistance of Yang Hu, commander of the Special Services Department of the Shanghai Peace Preservation Corps, Du disposed of the opium in return for a $3 million monthly payment to Nanjing.[66]

It appears that Chiang Kai-shek had begun to address many of the monopoly's troubles highlighted by Yang Tong and He Baohua a year earlier. In October 1932, Chiang ordered from his Military Affairs Commission field headquarters that in the near future an "agricultural bank" be organized to assist impoverished farmers in regions liberated from the Communists.[67] Also during this period, the generalissimo ordered the creation of an Escort and Smuggling Prevention Corps (Hujidui) to combat rising illegal shipments of opium along the Yangtze. To accelerate the work of the Hujidui, his field headquarters supplied the corps with military hardware.[68] Chiang also dispatched an agent to the Shanghai Maritime Customs Office to coordinate antismuggling work between the two agencies. Additional personnel were later dispatched to other key cities in which the opium monopoly was operational.[69]

The climax to these activities was when Chiang Kai-shek officially assumed control of the Special Tax Clearance Office monopoly. Beginning in October 1932, the Hankou Main Office remitted all revenues to the Military Affairs Commission field headquarters for disbursement at the generalissimo's discretion. Examples of allocations included $500,000 a month for *fuzhuangfei* (military uniforms expenditure), $2,325,000 between September and December 1932 for "Hubei provincial government subsidies," and various amounts for dike construction, subsidies to the Yichang and Yidu municipal governments, and the Jiangsu provincial government.[70]

When the Military Affairs Commission field headquarters absorbed the Special Tax Clearance Office system between October and December 1932, Chiang completely severed ties linking the Ministry of Finance with the agencies involved in the monopoly.[71] Perhaps to conceal any irregularities committed by Ministry of Finance personnel, a mysterious fire erupted in the ministry's storage room where all the special tax documents were located, damaging a large number of them.[72]

Improving the Monopoly

After Chiang Kai-shek placed the Hubei Special Tax Clearance Office under military control in late 1932, he began addressing the problems of the opium monopoly. One of the pressing issues was a lack of capital and credit for opium merchants in central China. Yang Tong and He Baohua had earlier recommended opening branches of the Central Bank in Yichang and Chong-qing to alleviate the problem of high interest rates on short-term loans and mortgages, and extortionate fees attached to remissions transactions resulting from the lack of silver reserves.[73] However, since Chiang and Soong had agreed to disengage the Central Bank from the trade in mid-1932, this was not an option.

Chiang's response was the Four Provinces Agricultural Bank to implement what the codirectors had suggested to Soong earlier, but on a much grander scale. In the spring of 1933, the Four Provinces Agricultural Bank (Yu-E-Wan-Gan Sisheng Nongmin Yinhang) was formed with a capitalization of $10,000,000 derived equally from national and provincial governments, on the one hand, and the sale of stock to opium merchant investors, on the other.[74] The announced purpose of the bank was to assist farmers, especially those in areas liberated from the Red Army, by providing them with low-interest loans to purchase livestock, seed, and farm implements as a step toward rehabilitating the rural economy by improving agricultural production.

In lieu of its professed intentions, when the Four Provinces Agricultural Bank opened for business in April 1933, it became a clearinghouse for tax receipts collected by the opium monopoly, with Chiang's field headquarters controlling allocations of those receipts. Wherever Special Tax Clearance Office agencies were located, branch banks were established.[75] Thereafter, bank personnel collected taxes on behalf of the Special Tax Clearance Office, not the opium merchants or their clearing office compatriots.

In late 1933, Zhou Lisheng, a member of the Control Yuan, made a tour of Hubei province and later reported his findings in Nanjing. Zhou's report called for the impeachment of Huang Zhenxing (director of the Hankou Main Office) and was equally critical of the generalissimo's new bank. "Even the Four Provinces Agricultural Bank," Zhou wrote, "which is announced as

existing to afford relief to the peasants, has forgotten its task of extending relief to the peasants and has used the money intended for farm-relief to make
loans with opium as security, thereby injuring the peasantry."[76]

Government Warehouses as Another Means to Augment Control

In order to establish the government warehouses required to manage the supply and movement of opium at Hankou and other key markets, Chiang had to
weaken the power of independent merchants. Previously, the opium monopoly
at Hankou and other cities under the Special Tax Clearance Office system was
run by local opium merchants who reported and collected taxes for the Special
Tax Clearance Office and managed the transport, purchase, and sale of government opium.[77] To increase state regulation, Chiang needed to weaken the
power of the so-called Forty-eight Houses (sishiba jia), transport and wholesale
merchants who controlled the trade in central China's largest opium market
through the Special Business Clearance Association. Their cozy relations with
Special Tax Clearance Office officials and entrenched positions in the monopoly bureaucracy led to many abuses amply chronicled in the Ministry of Finance records.[78]

Before Chiang issued the regulations for a government warehouse scheme,
transport and wholesale companies could purchase smuggled opium on the
black market and sell it from their own warehouses for larger profit margins.
They also stored Special Tax Clearance Office opium for the monopoly, charging storage fees for providing such services because the agency's Jianguansuo
proved too confining for the task. Under Chiang's improved system, teye gongsi
vending illegal goods would be subject to heavy fines or even seizures of their
property and assets, and the burdensome storage costs could be eliminated. Because the government warehouse project threatened those practices, it was understandable that Special Business Clearance Association merchants refused to
contribute the $3 million Chiang had requested of them for the venture.[79] Several
opium merchants who broke ranks and supported the generalissimo's venture
were murdered, it appears, by persons associated with the Forty-eight Houses.[80]

Undaunted, Chiang turned to other sources, and his Hankou Warehouse
(located in a converted godown of the China Merchants Steam Navigation
Company) opened for business in early May, followed by another in Zhengzhou, Henan, five months later. To further standardize business practices in
Wuhan, an Opium Exchange (Pingjia Weiyuanhui) was established inside

the Hankou Warehouse, where merchants set prices "for the improvement of revenue collection, convenience of merchants, and the stabilization of opium prices."[81] Formerly, this had been done at the headquarters of the Special Business Clearance Association.

The Four Provinces Agricultural Bank and the Special Tax Clearance Office warehouse system further reduced the role of Special Business Clearance Association merchants in the revenue extraction machinery. Previously, clearance association merchants working for the Special Tax Clearance Office Jianguansuo had filled out the *shuidan* for other merchants and collected a rather steep $10 to $15 "procedural fee" *(shouxufei)* on each *dan* of special goods taxed.[82] Henceforth, officials from the Four Provinces Agricultural Bank would handle all matters relating to taxation, charging a lower procedural fee of $2 per *dan*.[83] Also in accordance with the new policy, *teye gongsi* would be jointly responsible for bank notes used by opium merchants to purchase monopoly products as a measure to guard against insolvency.[84] The regulations forced most merchants to seek credit from the Four Provinces Agricultural Bank, increasing its profitability and significance in financing the generalissimo's war on drugs.

Chiang took other steps in late 1933 to augment the flow of goods passing through Special Tax Clearance Office agencies by reducing local taxes on opium traversing provinces where the monopoly operated. In October, he issued a directive forbidding local governments from collecting surtaxes on opium shipments. Since special taxes were now considered "*guojia zhongyao zhi xiangyuan*" (important sources of the nation's military funds), all taxes had to be officially collected and legitimately used. Local governments, warlords, and corrupt officials had been collecting surtaxes and pocketing much of the money; the new policy, however, was to "*huasi weigong*" (transform private [exactions] into public [revenue]).[85] One result of this change was a dramatic reduction in tax rates at Yichang and Hankou.[86] Another effect was a substantial increase in the quantity of opium taxed by the Hankou Main Office. According to the National Anti-Opium Association, the amount of "black rice" taxed at Hankou in 1933 was 71,760 *dan*, compared to 59,860 the preceding year.[87]

Creation of the Opium Suppression Supervisory Bureau

International and domestic conditions affecting China's economy were an additional impetus for Nanjing to use opium as a panacea for its mounting financial difficulties. The global economic depression had already weakened China's agricultural, industrial, and financial productivity when Japanese and American policies exacerbated the crisis. Following in the wake of Japanese encroachment in north China and Inner Mongolia, the Kwantung Army launched an economic invasion to undermine Nanjing's largest source of non-borrowed income, Maritime Customs. From 1934 to 1937, the Kwantung Army aided and abetted the smuggling of Japanese-manufactured goods into north China from Manchuria. Artificial silk, sugar, and kerosene were among dozens of products entering Nanjing-controlled areas duty-free. Based on contemporary estimates, annual losses in Maritime Customs receipts were $26 million in 1934 and 1935, $59 million in 1936, and $87 million in 1937, or approximately $200 million combined.[88]

The U.S. Congress passed the Silver Purchase Act in June 1934. In the midst of the Great Depression in America, representatives from western mining states railroaded through both houses a massive federal government purchase of silver at inflated prices to revive the economies of their home districts. Ironically, one of the arguments for raising the price of silver was that it would increase buying power in China.[89] The effects, however, were devastating. A mass exodus of silver from China (primarily Shanghai) ensued, moving across the Pacific to banks in the United States. Conditions for producers deteriorated because prices for agricultural and industrial commodities dropped at home, while making Chinese exports more expensive.[90]

Besides aggravating domestic economic troubles, the U.S. policy struck at one of the pillars of Nanjing's finances—government bonds. Following H. H. Kung's appointment as minister of finance in 1933, he commenced the large-scale issuance of Nanjing securities to cover Chiang's mounting military expenditures. By mid-1934, about one-third or more of the income-earning assets of Chinese banks in Shanghai were tied up in government bonds. After the Silver Purchase Act catalyzed the outflow of silver from Shanghai, Nanjing's finances were seriously jeopardized, because over 20 percent of all central government income was generated by the sales of bonds to and the granting of loans from Shanghai banks.[91] It was in this stifling economic and financial climate that Chiang Kai-shek's monopoly was reorganized and expanded.

By early 1934, the Hubei Special Tax Clearance Office in Hankou had been under the jurisdiction of Chiang Kai-shek's Military Affairs Commission field headquarters for over a year.[92] While the generalissimo was preoccupied supervising a fifth campaign against the Communists in Jiangxi, his underlings continued to run things in the old way. In mid-March, Chiang learned that the director of the Hankou Main Office, Huang Zhenxing, and his brother Huang Yaoting, in collusion with perhaps a hundred other civil and military officials (including Yang Yongtai), had embezzled more than $8 million in tax receipts earmarked for bandit suppression.[93]

To remedy the situation, Chiang brought in his trusted opium expert Li Jihong to reorganize and expand the special tax system in late March. On 1 April 1934, Li created the Shisheng Jinyan Duchachu (Opium Suppression Supervisory Bureau for the Ten Provinces) to oversee the monopoly in the bandit suppression zones.[94] This agency was crucial to the espoused goal of the six-year plan to control the trade in order gradually to eliminate it. The main bureau of the Opium Suppression Supervisory Bureau, like its predecessor, was situated in Hankou. Twenty-nine branch bureaus were established in the nine provinces of Jiangsu, Anhui, Jiangxi, Hubei, Hunan, Sichuan, Henan, Shaanxi, and Fujian by 31 December 1934.[95] Each province had a branch bureau supported by several agencies and general affairs departments. By July 1937, the Opium Suppression Supervisory Bureau system encompassed at least sixty-one bureaus and subbureaus, with the provinces of Guangdong, Guangxi, Gansu, and Guizhou added to the nine listed above (see Map 7).[96] Although Zhejiang was originally included as one of the ten provinces, when it received the drug-free zone designation in late 1934, the monopoly there was abolished.

To reduce the wanton corruption and administrative malpractice that plagued the former Special Tax Clearance Office system, under the Opium Suppression Supervisory Bureaus further bureaucratization and rationalization occurred. Li divided the main bureau in Hankou into seven offices: Supervised Transport, Accounting, Warehousing, Smuggling Prevention, the Office of the Superintendent, the Office of the Director, and the Secretarial Office.[97] The Office of the Superintendent was created to supervise the directors of the provincial bureaus and subbureaus, since two of the previous Hankou Main Office directors—Huang Zhenxing and Shen Gongli—had been caught in various acts of corruption between 1930 and 1934. The superintendent was directly appointed by Chiang to guard against the ingrained concept of *shengguan facai* (becoming a government official in order to get rich).[98] A more direct method was to shoot Opium Suppression Supervisory Bureau officials charged with misappropriating special tax revenues, as was ordered by Chiang Kai-shek in November 1934.[99]

Another bureaucratic innovation was the tax receipts issued by Opium Suppression Supervisory Bureau personnel. Under the Special Tax Clearance

Map 7. Locations of Opium Suppression Supervisory Bureaus, July 1937

Office monopoly's *liandan* (or *shuidan*) method, only two pieces of paper, called the *huodan* (invoice) and the *tidan* (bill of lading), were issued. The *huodan* was wired ahead to the next Special Tax Clearance Office to verify the consignment's total weight and accumulated duties up to that point. The merchants who purchased the opium were not given a copy of the paperwork until they arrived at the Special Tax Clearance Office Jianguansuo to pay their bill of lading. Because *teye gongsi* merchants filled out all tax forms for the actual consignees and stored the monopoly opium in their own warehouses, only the name of the special business company that brokered the deal on their behalf appeared on the bill of lading. Thus, legal ownership of the goods was transferred to the tax brokerage houses.[100] In other words, the procedures did not protect the commodity rights *(wuquan)* of the purchaser, because his name did not appear on the official documents.

Under the Opium Suppression Supervisory Bureau monopoly, a new paper trail called the *"siliandan"* (four-part tax receipt) was implemented. The *siliandan* included the *cungen* (ticket stub), which was inscribed by officials in the issuing bureau's Supervised Transport Department and kept on file by its Accounting Office. A *duikan* (verification slip) was mailed by one supervisory bureau to the other, containing the type of opium, its weight, the total amount of taxes and surtaxes, and so forth. The third part of this receipt was the *tidan* given to the actual buyer by Opium Suppression Supervisory Bureau personnel at the time of purchase. The *jiaohe* (final tally) was calculated by Supervised Transport Department personnel at the supervisory bureau where the goods were purchased and sent to the Accounting Office of the Opium Suppression Supervisory Bureau main office in Hankou and kept on file. When the *duikan* arrived at the final destination, the local supervisory bureau's accounting office personnel would walk the receipt over to the nearest branch Farmers Bank. The Farmers Bank was entrusted to collect the monies owed by the purchasing merchants, comparing the *duikan* with the merchant's *tidan* when he was ready to pay his bill.[101] In this manner, several layers of safeguards were built into the new system to protect both purchasing merchants and state revenues.

The generalissimo's Opium Suppression Supervisory Bureau dominated the traffic at a level unmatched by previous warlord or Guomindang agencies. Appendix Table 18 reveals the profitable impact the aforementioned reforms had on Chiang's Opium Suppression Supervisory Bureau monopoly in comparison to the Special Tax Clearance Office.

The Farmers Bank as a Microcosm of Warlord Financing

Any study of Chiang's six-year plan must take note of the familiar link between the Farmers Bank (Nongmin Yinhang), originally the Four Provinces Agricultural Bank created in 1933, and the monopoly he managed under the Military Affairs Commission. As the military monopoly spread, the Farmers Bank became the fourth largest financial institution in China at a time when other banks were suffering from the effects of the global economic depression and appreciation of silver prices. The success of the Farmers Bank and Chiang's expanding monopoly were clearly interrelated.

When the bank opened for business in 1933, its branches were located in the cities where Special Tax Clearance Office agencies collected transit duties in Hubei, Henan, Anhui, and Jiangxi.[102] After Chiang inaugurated the Opium Suppression Supervisory Bureau monopoly in April 1934 under the six-year plan, the bank established branches beyond the four provinces it was ostensibly created to serve. By December 1937, the bank had ninety-six branches, subbranches, and loan posts in fourteen provinces (see Map 8).[103] The Farmers Bank collected transit duties, shipping costs, and insurance fees on on behalf of the Opium Suppression Supervisory Bureau along with making loans to and providing mortgages for opium merchants.[104]

The regulations governing Fujianese opium merchants traveling to Hankou to purchase monopoly opium clearly illustrate the ties that bound the two agencies together: "The accountants at the Fuzhou Branch Opium Sup-

⊙   Farmers Bank and Opium Suppression Supervisory Bureau in the same city

Map 8. Locations of the Farmers Bank, 1937

pression Supervisory Bureau will collect the tax receipt from the government transport and will then take the tax receipt to the Farmers Branch Bank at Fuzhou and entrust the bank to collect the monies owed on behalf of the Fuzhou Branch Opium Suppression Supervisory Bureau."[105] Similarly, the Guizhou Branch Opium Suppression Supervisory Bureau in Guiyang instructed merchants on its tax collection procedures: "If merchants do not have enough capital on hand, then 30 percent can be collected in cash, the remaining 70 percent in the form of loans or mortgages [based on the value of the opium] from the Farmers Bank."[106]

The growth of the Farmers Bank was not solely the result of its involvement in the opium trade, but that involvement was certainly a dominant factor. In early 1935, Minister of Finance H. H. Kung became chairman of the board for the financial institution, and shortly thereafter the Farmers Bank received authorization to issue up to $100 million in circulating notes.[107] Stuart J. Fuller, U.S. delegate to the League of Nations, remarked that the authorization "indicates that the opium trade has been a profitable one for the past three years and that some confidence in its future is felt."[108]

After the Currency Reform of November 1935 was enacted, the right to issue circulating notes was restricted to three government-controlled banks: Central Bank, Bank of China, and Bank of Communications. A several-month grace period was permitted for other paper notes and silver to be exchanged for the new scrip. If the notes of the Farmers Bank could not circulate as legal currency, the public would have no confidence in them, and the bank's ability to finance the opium trade would be compromised. In early February 1936, Nanjing granted the Farmers Bank the right to monopolize the issuance of *fabi* (legal tender) in conjunction with the three other government banks.[109] The Farmers Bank's new-found power in Republican financial circles was underscored by the relocation of its headquarters from Hankou to Shanghai in April 1937.[110]

The Currency Reform of 1935 was another example of the connection between Guomindang opium policy and state building. By controlling the right to issue notes through the four government-operated banks, the unification of China's anarchic currency system was well under way by 1937. The Farmers Bank accelerated this process, because its branches were located in regions awash in a multitude of devalued paper scrip and silver coins, especially rural market towns where no other government banks existed. Consequently, the Farmers Bank was able to funnel *fabi* into circulation and to integrate provincial economies more closely with Nanjing by using a standardized medium of exchange, while simultaneously absorbing the silver needed to stabilize exchange rates and increase foreign currency reserves.[111] As a symbol of Nanjing's authority, the use of *fabi* in provinces such as Guangdong, Guangxi, Sichuan, and Shanxi was a strong indicator of the central government's strenghtening influence before the Marco Polo Bridge Incident.

Furthermore, the bank's board of directors exemplified the close personal links between political and economic leadership and the opium trade in Nationalist China. In addition to Chiang's brother-in-law H. H. Kung serving as chairman of the board, other directors were prominent Shanghai bankers and men related to the Opium Suppression Supervisory Bureau monopoly, such as Wen Qun, Li Jihong, and Wang Chengying.[112] Wen Qun and Li Jihong were members of the Central Commission for Opium Suppression, and Li especially had a long history of involvement in Guomindang monopolies. Wang Chengying was director of the Guizhou Provincial Opium Suppression Supervisory Bureau in Guiyang.[113]

The Farmers Bank prospered as its involvement in the opium trade escalated after 1934. Between 1933 and 1936, deposits in the bank jumped from $8.3 million to $155.4 milion, while loans rose from $6.2 million to $78.2 million, and notes in circulation exploded from $2 million to $208 million for the 1933–1937 period. Meanwhile, the bank's assets skyrocketed from $26 million in 1934 to $349 million at the end of 1936 (see Appendix tables 19 and 20).

Guizhou as the Key to Liangguang

In 1935, Chiang Kai-shek took advantage of an unstable situation in Guizhou to settle an embarrasing political problem with the fractious provinces of Guangdong and Guangxi (Liangguang). The governments of these anti-Chiang provinces were reliant on opium revenues to maintain their independence. In 1930, Chen Shaogui had negotiated with Guizhou and Yunnan to divert their opium from the Guangxi Corridor as part of a "Plan to Secure the Southwest." At the time, Nanjing controlled only the lower Yangtze region and had to rely on favorable tax rates to induce opium merchants, civil officials, and military officials in these two provinces to ensure compliance. Following Hu Hanmin's arrest in early 1931, the formerly pro-Nanjing governments of Yunnan, Guizhou, and Guangdong sided with the Guangxi Clique and commenced funneling their opium through the Guangxi Corridor, with negative repercussions for the Special Tax Clearance Office monopoly.

Before Chiang's armies entered Guizhou, the province was weak, impoverished, and politically divided. When Wang Jialie seized power there in 1932, he was the fourth warlord in ten years to claim nominal authority of the province.[114] The martial quality of Guizhou soldiers was not very high, owing to their fondness for the native product, earning them the nickname of *"shuanqiangbing."* As Red Army troops on the Long March poured across the border from Guangxi and threatened the provincial capital of Guiyang in the winter of 1934–1935, warlord Wang Jialie reluctantly welcomed Chiang's military assistance. When his army was there in full force, Chiang took full advantage of the situation to bring the province under his control. On 6 April 1935, the former provincial government "resigned" and Chiang appointed trusted subordinates to key positions, among them Wu Zhongxin as chairman of the Guizhou provincial government and Li Zhonggong as director of provincial finances. Li Zhonggong, it should be pointed out, was also a member of the Central Commission for Opium Suppression.[115]

In Guizhou, Chiang also attended to the opium situation. He told a correspondent from the *North China Herald* on 1 April 1935, "It would be a crime suddenly to order [poppy] suppression without doing something to help the farmers with other crops and assist the victims to be cured of the evil."[116] A few days later, the generalissimo prohibited the collection of "poppy fines," a euphemism for poppy-sprout taxes.[117] Under the six-year plan, Guizhou was designated a gradual reduction zone, so by incorporating Guizhou into his military monopoly, Chiang was taking over one of the most productive centers of poppy cultivation in China.

In late September 1935, the Guizhou Branch Opium Suppression Supervisory Bureau was created in Guiyang to oversee this trade and collect the lucrative revenues generated from it (see Map 9).[118] According to Xiao Juetian, director of the Guizhou branch, farmers in the province produced some 61 to 81 million *liang* of raw opium annually, roughly the equivalent of 2,300 to 3,000 tons.[119] In addition to the Opium Suppression Supervisory Bureau agencies, two brigades of *jisibing* (smuggling prevention soldiers) were formed to patrol the Guizhou-Guangxi and Guizhou-Hunan borders to interdict the flow of nontaxed goods.[120] Thus, the generalissimo's monopoly had fully integrated Guizhou into its expanding scope of operations.

Previous works have stated that all trade among Guizhou, Guangxi, and Guangdong was stymied after Chiang's reorganization of the provincial government.[121] However, this was not entirely the case. What transpired was a precipitous decrease in the volume of trade after June 1935, resulting from

Map 9. The Guizhou Opium Suppression Supervisory Bureau System, 1935–1937

higher duties placed on *qiantu* by the Guizhou Opium Suppression Supervisory Bureau. Before the Tongzhi Guizhousheng Jinzheng Banfa (Regulations for Controlling the Administration of Opium Suppression in Guizhou) came into effect on 1 October, the price per *dan* of Guizhou opium, including taxes, was very cheap, selling for about $200. After the regulations were implemented, special goods shipped to Guangxi paid a total of $470 in local levies, surtaxes, and export fees, which drove the price up to $670 per *dan* before they left the province.[122]

Therefore, *qiantu* shipped to Guangxi after the tax increase was more expensive and thus more prohibitive to Cantonese and Guangxi merchants. Guizhou Opium Suppression Supervisory Bureau records show that between November 1935 and March 1936 only ten purchases of monopoly opium amounting to just over 1,000 *dan* were shipped to Guangxi from Guizhou, a precipitous drop from the normal annual average of 10,000 *dan*.[123] American consular reports described a growing anxiety in Liangguang over the price increases, which was aggravated by the diversion of Yunnan opium away from the Guangxi Corridor to the newly built roads used by the Guizhou Opium

Suppression Supervisory Bureau.[124] In Guangxi, which normally raised $14 million to $18 million a year in transit taxes alone—constituting 35 to 50 percent of provincial revenues—the situation was particularly acute. The Guangxi Clique encouraged large-scale poppy planting in 1936 to supplement this lost revenue, although before that time the province had been relatively poppy-free.[125]

When Guangdong and Guangxi initiated their abortive offensive against Nanjing in early June 1936—resulting shortly thereafter in Chiang's control of Guangdong and a more accommodating Guangxi—Western media in Shanghai immediately reported a linkage between the crisis and the opium trade.[126] What had precipitated the crisis, as Opium Suppression Supervisory Bureau documents and other sources revealed, was the economic impact of Chiang's control of Guizhou's opium traffic and the massive road-building program linking the frontier provinces of Sichuan, Yunnan, and Guizhou with the areas in central China firmly under Nanjing's thumb. The road construction, in turn, expedited the flow of opium from these regions into the Opium Suppression Supervisory Bureau monopoly and away from the Liangguang region.[127] The cumulative effect of these policies was amplified by the 1935 Currency Reform and Hu Hanmin's death shortly before the revolt, both of which hastened the desperate actions of Liangguang warlords in June and July 1936.[128]

Such developments did not go unnoticed by the American military advisor "Vinegar" Joseph Stilwell, who informed Washington in March 1935:

> By means of secure domination of the opium traffic [Chiang Kai-shek hopes] to increase the political power of the National Government over provinces whose allegiance is doubtful. . . . Opium is the chief military prop of all power in China, both civil and military. No local government can exist without a share of the opium revenues. If the central government can control the opium supply of a province, that province can never hope to revolt successfully.[129]

After the Southwest Political Council was defeated in mid-1936, the Opium Suppression Supervisory Bureau monopoly was extended into Guangdong and Guangxi. T. L. Soong (Song Ziliang) was dispatched to Guangdong in August 1936 to serve concurrently as Nanjing's special commissioner of finance and director of the newly established Guangdong Branch Opium Suppression Supervisory Bureau in Canton, along with Li Jihong as resident supervisor of the Guangdong Opium Suppression Committee.[130] In

Guangxi, a Guangxi Branch Opium Suppression Supervisory Bureau was set up in Wuzhou, with subbureaus in Nanning, Guilin, Bose, and Liuzhai.[131] These measures were no doubt intended to solidify Nanjing's influence in the recalcitrant south, as Stilwell's remarks indicate.

The Last Days of the Opium Monopoly

Under the six-year plan, the raison d'être of the Opium Suppression Supervisory Bureau monopoly was to decrease the volume of the opium trade via state regulation. When the Nationalist government initialed the 1925 Geneva Opium Accord in the summer of 1936, it committed itself to a specified method and deadline that were admittedly difficult to execute given the existing circumstances in China. The majority of opium monopolies in the Asian colonies had their own manufacturing facilities for boiling raw opium to ensure the quality and purity of the finished product and, more important, to control the quantity of *regao* reaching the colonial smoking population. Nanjing became interested in the rationalization of opium paste manufacturing only after the publication of a report in December 1936 by A. E. Blanco, director of the League of Nations Anti-Opium Information Bureau. In the report, Blanco suggested that without effective government regulation of *regao* manufacturing, China would never be able to suppress opium use completely in six years.[132]

In early 1937, Director General Chiang ordered a feasibility study of a state monopoly on opium paste manufacturing. The study group dispatched a mission to several of the Asian colonies that had such a system, including Taiwan, Hong Kong, Macao, the Straits Settlements, and the Netherlands East Indies. Owing to the outbreak of war with Japan in July, however, the mission returned after visiting only Batavia and Singapore. On the basis of this truncated trip, the group recommended implementing a manufacturing monopoly.[133]

Under a manufacturing monopoly, the opium merchants, who had already lost their control over tax collection, transportation, and warehousing monopoly opium, would lose this business as well. Currently, wholesale and retail merchants who manufactured opium paste for the Opium Suppression Supervisory Bureau often mixed raw smuggled and monopoly opium when manufacturing their *regao*. According to Opium Suppression Supervisory Bureau documents from 1936, in 1935 Japanese opium smuggled in from the north was encroaching on bureau markets in Anhui, Henan, Jiangxi, and

Jiangsu provinces, and retailers were purchasing the lower-priced nonmonopoly goods and selling them to their customers mixed with Opium Suppression Supervisory Bureau product.[134] A manufacturing monopoly would help to curtail such abuses, because the Opium Suppression Supervisory Bureau system to date monopolized only the transportation and sales of raw opium. Although the boiled-opium monopoly was not implemented owing to the war with Japan, it does appear that the Nationalists were taking the logical steps toward a more complete domination of the opium trade and the goals of the six-year plan.

Opium Revenue in the Context of Total Revenue

During the thirty-eight months that the Opium Suppression Supervisory Bureau monopoly functioned before 7 July 1937, it generated substantial income for Chiang Kai-shek's Military Affairs Commission. Zhong Ketuo, longtime member of the National Anti-Opium Association who also served on the central government's National Opium Prohibition Committee, General Commission for Opium Suppression, and Central Commission for Opium Suppression from 1929 to 1937, told an American consular official in June 1937 that "about half of the national opium revenues are returned to the provincial governments as subsidy, the remainder being placed in a special military fund in Chongqing under the control of He Guoguang, the Director of the Generalissimo's office [field headquarters] there."[135]

Nanjing did release data concerning the amount of income received from the Opium Suppression Supervisory Bureau monopoly—albeit sanitized first by the Military Affairs Commission, the General Commission for Opium Suppression, or the Central Commission for Opium Suppression—officially through the League of Nations or unofficially through Zhong Ketuo. The amounts acknowledged through these methods for the years from 1934 to 1937 were $26 million, $35 million, $32.9 million, and $30 million, respectively.[136] Such low figures must be taken lightly, because data published by central government agencies were less than truthful. In contrast, the amounts estimated by Garfield Huang were more believable. Huang stated that Nanjing earned $100 million, $103 million, and $112 million yearly from 1934 to 1936.[137] Moreover, Frederick T. Merrill estimated that net profits from the monopoly "must have been well over five hundred million dollars" for 1934 to 1937.[138] Merrill consulted with highly reliable sources such as Stuart J.

Fuller, Harry Anslinger (commissioner of narcotics, U.S. Department of Treasury), Leon Steinig (a member of the League's Opium Section), and M. S. Bates (vice-president of Nanjing University).

Using Huang's estimates for 1934 to 1936 as a basis of comparison with the official published budgets from that period provides an educated guess—admittedly imperfect—of opium's fiscal proportions in the context of Guomindang finances. Total revenues those years were tallied at $896 million, $1,031 million, and $1,182 million, respectively. Provided that opium revenues were concealed within the published budgets, for each of the years above they would have accounted for 11.2 percent, 10 percent, and 9.5 percent of the total and ranked third in nonborrowed income behind customs and salt revenues.[139]

Chiang Kai-shek understood opium as a key to power in the warlord system. By controlling the trade under his Military Affairs Commission, he deprived regional warlords of the source of their independence, while supplying his armies in central and southern China with the means to eliminate the Red Army as well as pacifying the rebellious provinces of Guangdong and Guangxi. In other words, "opium suppression" as practiced by the Guomindang was synonymous with control of the opium trade as a means to solve the Guomindang's political and financial difficulties, to the extent that it did solve them. In light of the evidence at hand, perhaps Mao's dictum that "political power grows out of the barrel of a gun" is only half correct, because political power in prewar Republican China also sprouted from the seeds of the poppy.

Conclusion

THERE WERE MYRIAD SOCIOLOGICAL, physiological, economic, and political land mines in China's road to complete prohibition, particularly in the Nanjing Decade, when Nationalist leaders were expected to achieve a goal that had eluded Chinese governments since the early 1700s. The difficulties they encountered were evident in a dynamic opium policy that vacillated from one side of the issue to the other and for a time even straddled the fence in between. Based on the evidence presented in this volume, one might jump to the conclusion that Guomindang anti-opium campaigns were merely an exercise in deception. Nanjing prioritized raising revenue and dominating the opium traffic to achieve purely political objectives. Any party that got in its way, the National Anti-Opium Association, for example, would suffer the consequences.

Nevertheless, such a facile judgment would prove myopic with respect to the six-year plan. Its monopolistic intentions notwithstanding, poppy eradication and the treatment of opiate addiction were key military targets in Chiang Kai-shek's war on drugs. Examining the results of the six-year plan in these two areas as well as China's post-1937 struggle with narcotics will provide a more balanced evaluation of Guomindang successes and failures.

Poppy Eradication

When Generalissimo Chiang commenced issuing directives from his Military Affairs Commission field headquarters in 1932, his strategy to suppress poppy cultivation entailed a classic divide and conquer approach. Provinces in southeast and northwest China were designated *fenqi jinzhong shengfen* (gradual reduction zones), while those regions to the east were *juedui jinzhong shengfen* (poppy-free zones). In its 1935 report to the League of Nations, the General Commission for Opium Suppression claimed that the ten provinces of Henan, Hebei, Hubei, Anhui, Jiangsu, Jiangxi, Zhejiang, Fujian, Shandong, and Shanxi had been declared "entirely free from poppy cultivation."[1] When Director General Chiang gave his anti-opium sermon on 3 June 1937, Chaha'er and Hunan were added to the list, raising the total number of provinces purportedly cleansed of poppies to twelve.[2]

How did peasants respond to the forced change in their planting habits, given that opium was China's leading cash crop? What crops were substituted by farmers following strict enforcement of the laws? Most important, was poppy eradication as successful as Nanjing asserted?

Expectedly, there were reports of peasant resistance to the six-year plan. In April 1934, for instance, farmers in Jiangsu's Siyang county armed themselves with rifles and iron bars to prevent provincial troops from uprooting their poppy sprouts and seriously injured the county magistrate's secretary. Angry peasants were quoted as saying, "We would rather die than to see our poppies destroyed." A similar reaction took place in Chaoxian, Anhui, where peasants organized Red Spears societies for the explicit purpose of safeguarding their poppy fields.[3]

Although armed resistance was reported in the poppy-free zones, it comprised isolated episodes in counties of weak government control, and it decreased annually. With the creation of opium suppression committees at provincial, municipal, and county levels in conjunction with resident commissioners appointed by Chiang and stationed in each provincial capital to supervise poppy eradication work, the state's ability to enforce anti-poppy laws in the poppy-free zones strengthened accordingly. This phenomenon was accelerated by the success of the fifth "bandit suppression" campaign against the Communists in southern and central China during 1934–1935.

Crop substitution is a vital component of any strategy to curtail the production of narcotics. Whether it be poppies in China in the 1930s or coca and poppies today in South America, finding a surrogate crop that is remunerative enough for impoverished peasants to cultivate willingly is no small task. This paradox is particularly acute in countries where agricultural production dominates the national economy, as was the case in Republican China. According to published reports from the era, the crops most substituted for the poppy were cotton, tea, corn, peas, sorghum, wheat, soybean, and tung trees.[4] In Hubei, cotton, tung, and tea were popular replacements, while in Gansu and Shaanxi, cotton, sorghum, and wheat were preferred surrogates.

Eyewitness accounts from foreigners and nongovernmental Chinese sources confirm Guomindang claims of successful crop substitution in several poppy-free zones. *Dagongbao*, which for years had virulently condemned Nanjing's opium policy, reported in late April 1935 that poppy production had been markedly curtailed in western Hubei, resulting in large increases for cotton.[5] Information collected from a wide variety of sources by the League of Nations likewise corroborates a high level of success in the poppy-free zones, even in difficult provinces such as Fujian.[6]

Guomindang boasts of astronomical decreases in opium production in the gradual reduction zones of Sichuan, Yunnan, Guizhou, Shaanxi, Gansu, Suiyuan, and Ningxia, however, are misleading. Little confidence should be placed in the data released for public consumption, particularly for Sichuan, Guizhou, and Yunnan. According to Central Commission for Opium Suppression data for the years 1934 to 1937, the total amount of raw opium produced in the seven gradual reduction zones was 5,571 tons in 1934, 3,673 in 1935, 1,583 in 1936, and 873 in 1937.[7] In contrast, U.S. consular estimates suggest that in 1935 China produced 12,000 to 18,000 metric tons, accounting for over 90 percent of world production.[8] Obviously, a great disparity exists between these two sets of data.

Data from the Opium Suppression Supervisory Bureau and foreign sources paint quite a different picture than the sanitized data from the Central Commission for Opium Suppression. In late 1935, director of the Guizhou Branch Opium Suppression Supervisory Bureau Xiao Juetian informed his main office that provincial output that year ranged between 2,275 and 2,976 tons, while for the same year the Central Commission for Opium Suppression reported production levels at 690 tons.[9] Similarly, U.S. consulates estimated Yunnan's 1934 crop at 4,446 tons, while the Central Commission for Opium Suppression stated it was 573 tons. Sichuan, the leading producer in China, was only permitted to grow poppies in ten counties. In 1937, the Central Commission for Opium Suppression claimed that only 332 tons was produced. In a letter from Chiang Kai-shek to Liu Xiang dated from July that year, however, the generalissimo accused Liu Xiang of permitting secret cultivation of at least 3,000 tons.[10]

Although these disparities are alarming, they do not necessarily mean that real decreases in gradual reduction zone poppy cultivation did not take place.

For example, Stuart J. Fuller stated before the twenty-second session (24 May to 12 June 1937) of the League's Opium Advisory Committee that U.S. consuls had estimated a 50 percent reduction in cultivation for the provinces of Sichuan, Yunnan, and Guizhou since 1934.[11] Generally speaking, it would be safe to assume that the six-year plan was reaping tangible results in regions south of the Great Wall. In contrast, areas occupied by Japanese troops—most notably Manchuria and Rehe—were increasing productive capacity. In 1937, it was estimated that Manchuria and Rehe combined had produced 2,364 tons of raw opium, minimizing the impact of generalissimo's antipoppy endeavor.[12]

Treatment of Opium Addiction

Another rationale for an opium monopoly under the six-year plan was a methodical, "scientific" approach to the problem. The state would undertake the establishment of opium detoxification centers to treat younger and less dependent smokers first, while showing compassion to the elderly and chronically ill users, who were granted more time to curb their craving for the pipe. By 31 December 1940, all smokers were to have been completely "cured" of their addiction. Theoretically speaking, in order to provide addicts and other smokers with the medicine they required, the Guomindang sought to control the production, distribution, and sales of opium as the means to reduce supplies to zero at the end of six years. All smokers, moreover, were required by law to purchase a smoker's permit to indulge the habit legally, enabling the government to monitor and quantify its performance in meeting the goals of the Six-Year Opium Suppression Plan.

Regions under Guomindang control were divided into drug-free zones, where smoking was completely prohibited, and gradual reduction zones, where it was conditionally permitted. The drug-free zones included the provinces of Zhejiang, Shandong, and Qinghai, seven counties in Jiangxi, and one (Zhongshan—named after Sun Yat-sen) in Guangdong, in addition to the municipalities of Nanjing, Qingdao, and Weihaiwei. Except for these areas, the provinces of Jiangsu, Hebei, Henan, Hubei, Hunan, Anhui, Jiangxi, Fujian, Guangdong, Guangxi, Sichuan, Guizhou, Yunnan, Gansu, Chaha'er, Suiyuan, and Ningxia fell within the scope of the data regarding opium smoker registration.

Before the Marco Polo Bridge Incident, three different registration periods were held annually from 1935 to 1937. The number of addicts registered by local governments in 1935 was 1,665,209; in 1936, 3,628,162; and in 1937, 4,160,285.[13]

Local governments faced many obstacles inducing addicts to register and purchase smoker's permits. According to Central Commission for Opium Suppression statements in 1936, the four most prevalent ones were that elderly people were terrified by the registration process, wealthy individuals and government officials feared "losing face" by the public spectacle, migratory laborers refused to use the permits, and smuggled opium (much of it funneled in from Japanese-controlled areas) was widely available, thereby making government registration unnecessary.[14]

Addiction treatment hospitals and clinics were another important yardstick for measuring government progress. Before 1934, little action was taken by Nanjing to unravel the Gordian knot of opium addiction. After the six-year plan was adopted, the number of detoxification facilities founded and operating in regions under Guomindang control from 1934 to 1937 was reported as 597, 1,263, 1,499, and 1,160, respectively.[15] Central Commission for Opium Suppression bureaucrats recorded the number of addicts successfully treated by such facilities as follows: 1934, 81,344; 1935, 339,198; 1936, 339,046; and 1937, 319,024; for a total of 1,076,612.[16] Although there were probably fifty million smokers at the time, perhaps ten million of whom could be classified as addicts, no previous Republican government could make or empirically substantiate a comparable achievement.

The big problem with Central Commission for Opium Suppression data, however, is the nondifferentiation among patients treated for opium, heroin, and morphine addiction. Moreover, the data did not distinguish between first-time and repeat patients. In Nanjing, for instance, from February 1934 to December 1936, the Capital Opium Treatment Hospital claimed to have "cured" 24,379 smokers.[17] Dr. Wang Zuxiang, who supervised the treatment of Nanjing's opium addicts, estimated that over 20 percent of that number could be classified as recidivist.[18] In other facilities where treatment procedures were not as rigidly enforced, rates of opium recidivism were undoubtedly higher.

Given the enormity and intractability of an opium conundrum exacerbated by a weak central government, extraterritoriality, "residual warlordism," Japanese interference, and a global economic depression, Guomindang achievements were impressive, to say the least. In the poppy-free zones, the ability of the state to enforce its regulations at the village level indicated a degree of influence higher than at any other time since the 1911 Revolution. Even in the gradual reduction zones beyond Nanjing's control, production levels were declining. Furthermore, the fact that for each year from 1934 to 1937 a rising number of addicts were corralled by the state to procure a smoker's permit underscores the strengthening bonds between national laws and local enforcement. Despite some missteps, it would be sheer folly to ignore the significant progress the Nationalist government was making against the production and use of opium between 1934 and 1937.

China from 1937 to 1998

Following the Marco Polo Bridge Incident, the rapid loss of territory to Japanese troops effectively aborted the generalissimo's military campaign against narcotics. Chiang relinquished his position as director general of opium suppression in early 1938, and the responsibilities for fulfilling the targets of the six-year plan devolved onto the Ministry of Finance and the Ministry of the Interior. Although the central government was forcibly relocated to Chongqing as a result of wartime contingencies, in December 1940 it announced the successful conclusion of the six-year plan and vowed to continue the struggle against narcotics despite the war with Japan.[19]

Throughout the war and the civil war with the Communists that followed it, opium continued to play an important fiscal role for both the Guomindang and the Chinese Communist Party. But the Japanese military and the puppet regimes it created—such as the one under Wang Jingwei in Nanjing—were just as fiscally addicted, if not more so. What differentiated this activity from the Guomindang and Communist monopolies was the widespread support and encouragement of morphine and heroin peddling by the Japanese military, perhaps as a method to control Chinese populations in occupied territories.[20]

When the Communists loyal to Mao straggled into Shaanxi at the end of the Long March in 1935, they found themselves in a province notorious for poppy cultivation. Recent studies by Chen Yongfa reveal that at least during the 1941–1943 period Mao's government encouraged the cultivation and sale of opium to compensate for the loss of Nationalist subsidies.[21] However, following their victory over the Guomindang and the inauguration of the People's Republic of China, the Communists launched successful antidrug campaigns from 1949 to 1952 laced with heavy doses of nationalistic propaganda at mass rallies. But arguably more persuasive were the arrests and "reeducation" of numerous drug offenders, accentuated by public trials and executions of addicts, poppy growers, and opium merchants.[22]

In stark contrast to the Communists' domestic antinarcotics campaign, there is evidence that the People's Republic for years exported opium and heroin as a means of earning foreign currency and perhaps also as a weapon against the "decadent" West. In 1955, Premier Zhou Enlai reportedly informed Egyptian president Nasser that the People's Republic would use drugs to destroy the morale of American military forces in Asia.[23] Thus, narcotics became another weapon in the cold war arsenal.

Despite the Communists' impressive domestic record against narcotics for over two decades, following Mao's death in 1976 the problem resurfaced. Increasing prosperity resulting from the economic reforms of Deng Xiaoping coupled with the recrudescence of poppy cultivation in the southwest facilitated the swift return of the drug plague to China. In Yunnan and Guangdong, the situation has become particularly acute, with the arrests of traffickers rising rapidly in unison with growing levels of addiction. Yunnan authorities in 1994 alone executed some four hundred narcotics traffickers, and two years later Beijing designated 16 June as National Antidrugs Day, commemorating the event by executing at least 260 people for drug-related offenses.[24] On the eve of Hong Kong's return to China in June 1997, Lin Zexu—once vilified as an "agent of feudalism" during the Cultural Revolution—was rehabilitated by the state. On 4 June, Cantonese officials burned in public 300 kilograms of heroin and 200 kilograms of methamphetamine in honor of Lin Zexu's actions 158 years earlier.[25] Facing a narcotics crisis approaching the severity of that of the 1930s, it is not surprising that the Communists are now borrowing a page from the Guomindang's antidrug manual.

Since China's drug problem has come full circle, it is not so easy to paint the Guomindang effort in broadly negative strokes. Set against the mise-en-scène of domestic political turmoil and a hostile international climate, the Nationalists' attempts to formulate an effective drug strategy in the 1920s and 1930s faced a menacing array of stumbling blocks. Several factors directly or indirectly influenced Guomindang opium policy. Ideology, public opinion, and traditional and Western values and mores were significant, but economic and political considerations were dominant. It was the symbiotic relationship that had developed between the narco-economy and warlord politics more than anything else that shaped the Guomindang's vacillating—and sometimes hypocritical—response to China's narcotics nightmare.

For Chiang Kai-shek and the party-government to survive and finish the uncompleted task that began with the Northern Expedition, adopting a policy of complete prohibition under prevailing political and economic conditions was neither realistic nor desirable. It was tantamount to suicide. In order to pacify residual warlords and deal with a mounting Communist threat, covertly trafficking in opium in violation of national prohibition laws was an expedient method to generate desperately needed revenue. Jettisoning the farce of prohibition and legalizing the opium trade in 1934–1935 under a state monopoly, furthermore, was sound strategy. These decisions were continually reinforced by a global economic depression, unrelenting Japanese aggression, and ever-rising military expenditures. In a chaotic world where brute force was the ultimate arbitrator, to fulfill Sun Yat-sen's grand vision for a democratic and modern China, the Nationalists adopted a policy that was at once morally abhorrent and fiscally imperative. Even Sun himself was reconciled to that unpalatable reality in Canton. One cannot take aim at Generalissimo Chiang without hitting his mentor.

Are there any lessons to be gleaned from the Guomindang's experiences with narcotic drugs that have practical application today? The short answer is yes. Historically speaking, a policy of complete prohibition has never proven to be a guaranteed long-term solution. In many cases, the anticipated results are just the opposite. Prohibition, as the United States discovered with alcohol in the 1920s and 1930s, enables undesirable social elements to prosper and expand the scope and organization of their activities, while making "harder" drugs more attractive. In other words, it constitutes a greater threat to both the general welfare and the state than the situation before a policy of zero tolerance.

The state, therefore, has several alternatives to a policy of absolute prohibition. The first would entail the legalization of all designated "illicit" narcotics. This strategy is a bitter pill to swallow for politicians whose public image and support depends on the perception of moral legitimacy. A second option is to recognize that some drugs are not as dangerous as others and to sanction the former group's decriminalization or its legalization under a state-run monopoly. If the state decides to establish a monopoly, monies derived under such a program not only could fund antinarcotics education and addiction treatment clinics, but also could be dispensed at the state's discretion for a wide variety of non-drug-related expenditures. Dollars that previously supported criminal elements or insurgencies could be used constructively for the benefit of both state and society. Provided that the state's ultimate objective is to reduce the social, economic, and political threat of recreational drug use to the lowest levels possible, some sort of regulatory system must be implemented to achieve that goal.

The Guomindang opted for the second approach, categorizing opium as less harmful to the public welfare than heroin or morphine. State control over production, distribution, and sales reaped enormous benefits for the Nationalists. Opium tax revenues were used to weaken the avowed enemies of the state (both the warlords and the Communists), in addition to subsidizing much-needed treatment facilities for opium, heroin, and morphine addicts. The fight against harder drugs was intensified, although these efforts were relentlessly undermined by the Japanese. In the final analysis, to condemn the Guomindang blanketly for its compromises, failures, and ethical shortcomings under prevailing conditions is at once overly simplistic and unreasonable. Even the United States today, in spite of its technological prowess and billions spent annually on interdiction, education, and enforcement, is far from winning its own "war on drugs."

The complex issue of recreational drug use and state responses to it remains highly resistant to procrustean, unrealistic, and historically ineffective solutions. All modern states, especially the wealthy democratic polities of the West, must face the reality that they cannot completely control the lives of their citizens or prevent them from using or abusing so-called illicit drugs. The enormous demand for such recreational substances coupled with the lucrative narco-economy they generate and sustain are indomitable forces that cannot be legislated or adjudicated into abeyance. The failure of prohibition is laid bare in the United States by providing full press coverage for the occasional drug bust, filling prisons above capacity with users of illegal substances, and depriving citizens of their constitutional rights by employing double jeopardy when prosecuting and sentencing drug offenders. In China, it is revealed by executing addicts and traffickers, and even invoking the ghost of Lin Zexu. Such actions may serve well for propaganda purposes, but they do little to slow the accelerating narcotics juggernaut.

Appendix

Table 1

National Anti-Opium Association Survey of Poppy Cultivation in China,
1930: Results from Thirty Counties in Twelve Provinces for the Year 1929

Province and County	Poppy Acreage in *Mu*	Percentage of Field Area	+/- vs. 1928	Voluntary or Forced	Tax per *Mu* (C$)
Shandong					
Yidu	—	0.1	(-)	V	—
Pingdu	560	30.0	(+)	V	—
Shaanxi					
Jiakou	7,000	—		V	13
Yangxian	5,000	6.0	(-)	V	10
Henan					
Guanghe	5,000	0.1	(-)	V	8
Shangcai	—	2.0	(+)	V	8
Miyang	3,000	—	(+)	F	8
Luoyang	—	25.0	(+)	V	14
Luoning	—	20.0	(+)	V	12
Dengxian	10,000	2.0	(+)	V	15
Anyang	—	—		F	8
Luoshan	187	2.0	(-)	V	—
Fujian					
Pinghe	10	0.5	(-)	V	—
Qingliu	300	10.0	Same	V	6
Hubei					
Baokang	300	20.0	(+)	V	—
Enshi	—	—	(+)	V	4
Zaoyang	3,000	1.0	(+)		6

Province and County	Poppy Acreage in *Mu*	Percentage of Field Area	+/- vs. 1928	Voluntary or Forced	Tax per *Mu* (C$)
Anhui					
Chaoxian	750	15.0	(+)	V	—
Xixian	—	2.0		V	3
Huaiyuan	—	—		V	10
Guangdong					
Gaoming	—	—		V	7
Huaxian	40	—	(-)	V	—
Sichuan					
Kuifu	870	3.0			—
Yunnan					
Wuding	416	50.0		V	8
Weining	—	2.0	(+)	V	—
Jiangcheng	237	2.0		V	2
Guizhou					
Songtao	1,400	20.0	(-)	V	1
Yongcheng	—	8.0		V	—
Liaoning					
Yixian	1,900	0.3	(+)	F	9
Jilin					
Dunhua	70,000	7.0	(+)	Both	—

Source: Judu yuekan (Opium, A National Issue) *(JDYK),* 47 (March 1931): 2–5.

Table 2

Estimated Production of Opium in China, 1924–1937
(unit: long tons, 1:2, 240 lbs.)

Year	High Estimate	Low Estimate
1924	15,000+[a]	7,500+[b]
1927	—	7,255+[c]
1930	11,875+[d]	—
1934	—	*5,751[e]
1935	12,067+[f]	*3,763[g]
1936	—	*1,583[h]
1937	—	*875[i]

Note: *means excludes Manchuria and Rehe; + denotes at least this amount.

[a]*Opium Cultivation and Traffic in China (OCTC)*, 5.3 (May 1925): 1.

[b]*China Christian Yearbook*, 1926, 326.

[c]*JDYK* 23 (July 1928): 9.

[d]*China Weekly Review (CWR)*, 28 Feb. 1931, 445.

[e]League of Nations, *League of Nations Documents and Publications, 1919–1946*, Category XI: Traffic in Opium and Other Dangerous Drugs *(LON)*, C.218.M.146.1939.XI, 58–59.

[f]*LON*, C.278.M.168.1936.XI, 8.

[g]*LON*, C.218.M.146.1939.XI, 58–59.

[h]Ibid.

[i]Ibid.

Table 3

Estimated Production of Important Crops in China, 1931–1937
(unit: long tons)

Crop	NARB[a]	Perkins[b]
Rice	45,169,769	68,321,946
Wheat	21,935,154	23,129,464
Millet	8,020,706	13,592,857
Sorghum	6,768,339	12,119,643
Corn	6,057,501	10,037,500
Barley	7,722,773	9,546,429
Soybeans	6,183,265	8,279,464
Field peas	3,115,234	
Broad beans	2,927,694	
Peanuts	2,762,326	
Rapeseed	2,258,069	
Sesame	889,453	
Cotton	763,088	927,143
Tobacco	604,901	898,661

[a]National Agricultural Research Bureau (NARB) data span the years 1931–1934 and apply only to the twenty provinces of Chaha'er, Suiyuan, Ningxia, Gansu, Shaanxi, Shanxi, Hebei, Henan, Shandong, Jiangsu, Anhui, Hubei, Hunan, Sichuan, Yunnan, Guizhou, Jiangxi, Zhejiang, Fujian, and Guangdong. See *Crop Reports* 3.8 (Aug. 1935): 166–171.

[b]Perkins' data are for the years 1931–1937 and include all of China. See Dwight H. Perkins, *Agricultural Development in China, 1368–1968,* pp. 267–287.

Table 4

Estimated Acreage of Important Crops in China, 1931–1937
(unit: *mu*, 1:0.16 acres)

Crop	N.A.R.B.[a]	Perkins[b]
Wheat	298,068,000	405,289,000
Rice	275,388,250	391,796,000
Millet	105,238,000	172,960,000
Barley	98,596,000	129,570,000
Soybeans	79,287,500	160,570,000
Sorghum	78,544,250	145,070,000
Corn	67,201,000	104,020,000
Rapeseed	55,882,750	78,200,000
Cotton	54,443,750	70,030,000
Field peas	52,088,000	
Broad beans	39,684,000	
Sesame	22,515,500	23,210,000
Peanuts	22,465,000	30,890,000
Oats	14,573,000	
Tobacco	7,883,500	11,350,000
Opium		6,400,000*

*The figure cited for opium is based on 12,000 long tons per year, divided by the average yield per *mu* of 50 *liang* (4.2 lbs.).

[a]*Crop Reports* 3.8 (Aug. 1935): 160–165.

[b]Perkins, *Agricultural Development in China*, pp. 248–265.

Table 5

Average Yield per *Mu* of Important Crops in China, 1931–1937
(unit: lbs.)

Crop	NARB[a]	Perkins[b]	Average
Rice	353.9	376.2	365.1
Peanuts	275.6	275.0	275.3
Corn	201.3	212.3	206.8
Sorghum	193.2	187.0	190.1
Soybeans	174.6	178.2	176.4
Millet	165.8	176.0	170.8
Barley	174.6	165.0	169.8
Tobacco	171.6	165.0	168.3
Broad beans	165.0		165.0
Wheat	164.7	125.4	145.1
Field peas	134.2	N/A	134.2
Oats	130.9	N/A	130.9
Rapeseed	93.2	95.7	94.5
Sesame	89.1	85.8	87.5
Cotton	31.6	31.4	31.5
Opium	—	—	4.2*

*The figure for opium is based on the average of 50 *liang* per *mu*.
[a]*Crop Reports* 3.8 (Aug. 1935): 172–177.
[b]Perkins, *Agricultural Development in China*, 267–287.

Table 6

Average Investment Cost, Yield, Gross Value, and Net Profit
for Opium in 1929 (unit: Chinese dollars, 1:0.41 U.S.)

Province and County	Investment per *Mu**	Yield per *Mu* (*liang*)	Gross Value	Net Profit
Shandong				
Yidu	50.0	32	100	50.0
Pingdu	10.0	50	200	190.0
Shaanxi				
Yangxian	22.0	100	60	38.0
Henan				
Tanghe	15.5	90	80	64.5
Shangcai	24.0	50	40	16.0
Luoyang	26.0	40	40	14.0
Luoning	50.0	100	100	50.0
Dengxian	30.0	50	60	30.0
Anyang	30.0	50	100	70.0
Fujian				
Qingliu	38.0	12	50	12.0
Hubei				
Baokang	8.0	30	48	40.0
Enshi	10.0	40	40	30.0
Baokang	10.0	100	80	70.0
Zaoyang	8.0	50	30	22.0
Anhui				
Chaoxian	10.3	24	38	28.0
Xixian	20.0	40	50	30.0
Huaiyuan	35.0	60	60	25.0
Guangdong				
Gaoming	27.0	20	48	21.0
Huaxian	35.0	60	120	85.0
Yunnan				
Jiangcheng	10.0	20	10	0.0
Wuding	11.0	30	27	16.0
Guizhou				
Yongcheng	10.0	100	30	20.0
Songtao	7.4	30	11	4.0
Liaoning				
Yixian	42.0	20	40	-2.0
Totals	539.2	1198	1462	923.5
Average	22.5	49.9	60.9	38.5

Source: JDYK 47 (March 1931): 6.

*Investment costs include fertilizer and seed.

Table 7

Adjusted Farm Prices for Agricultural Products, 1929
(unit: Chinese dollars, 1:0.41 U.S.)

Crop	Price/Pound
Sorghum	0.028
Corn	0.029
Cotton	0.032
Rice	0.036
Millet	0.037
Barley	0.040
Soybeans	0.040
Wheat	0.046
Peanuts	0.053
Rapeseed	0.061
Sesame	0.082
Tobacco	0.175
Opium	**14.523**

Source: Perkins, *Agricultural Development in China*, p. 288; John L. Buck, *Land Utilization in China: A Study of 16,786 Farms in 168 Localities, and 38,256 Farm Families in Twenty-two Provinces in China, 1929–1933*, p. 319. Opium price from *JDYK* 47 (March 1931): 6.

Table 8

Estimated Gross Value per *Mu* of Important Crops in 1929
(Based on Tables 5 and 7)

Crop	Averge Yield per *Mu* (lb.)	Price per Pound	Gross Value (Chinese dollars)
Cotton	31.5	0.032	1.01
Sorghum	190.1	0.028	5.32
Rapeseed	94.5	0.061	5.76
Corn	206.8	0.029	6.00
Millet	170.8	0.037	6.32
Wheat	145.1	0.046	6.67
Barley	169.8	0.040	6.79
Soybeans	176.4	0.040	7.06
Sesame	87.5	0.082	7.18
Rice	365.1	0.036	13.14
Peanuts	275.3	0.053	14.59
Tobacco	168.3	0.175	29.45
Opium	**4.2**	**14.523**	**60.99**

Table 9

China's Average Annual Food Grain Imports and Exports, 1867–1940
(unit: metric tons, 1:2,200 lb.)

Years	Imports	Exports	Net Imports	Net Exports
1867–1870	19,375	—	19,375	—
1871–1875	21,540	—	21,540	—
1876–1880	22,030	—	22,030	—
1881–1885	11,530	—	11,530	—
1886–1890	214,340	—	214,340	—
1891–1895	346,450	—	346,450	—
1896–1900	297,360	—	297,360	—
1901–1905	251,750	—	251,750	—
1906–1910	465,010	—	465,010	—
1911–1915	390,770	139,590	251,180	—
1916–1920	328,670	355,560	—	26,890
1921–1925	1,070,170	262,830	807,340	—
1926–1930	1,295,560	356,730	938,830	—
1931–1935	2,142,205	133,040	2,009,165	—
1936–1940	628,581	70,220	558,361	—

Note: Food grain imports include rice, wheat, and wheat flour; food grain exports include sorghum, millet, wheat, and wheat flour. See Ramon S. Myers, "The Agrarian System," in John K. Fairbank and Albert Feuerwerker, eds., *The Cambridge History of China*, vol. 13, p. 258.

Table 10

Typology of 176 Opium Sellers in China, 1929

Description	Number	Percentage of Total
Type 1	42	23.8
Wicked merchant	34	19.3
Opium merchant	8	4.5
Type 2	11	6.2
Policeman	6	3.4
Government personnel	5	2.8
Type 3	23	13.1
Soldier	16	9.1
Retired soldier	7	4.0
Type 4	46	26.2
Bandit	2	1.1
Gangster	27	15.3
Local thug	10	5.8
Red or Green Gang member	7	4.0
Type 5	16	9.1
Local bullies and evil gentry	16	9.1
Type 6	38	21.6
Refugee	20	11.4
Opium smoker	4	2.3
Sailor	5	2.8
Woman	5	2.8
Child	2	1.1
Farmer	1	.6
Muslim	1	.6

Source: JDYK 47 (March 1931): 22.

Table 11

1929 National Anti-Opium Association Typology of Opium Smokers

Occupation	Percentage	Age	Percentage
Laborer	27	Under 30	28
Merchant	24		
Government worker	21	30–49	40
Military	17	Over 50	32
Student	11		

Source: JDYK 47 (March 1931): 37. I have recalculated the averages given by the National Anti-Opium Association.

Table 12

Nationalist Government Data Regarding the Ages of
27,435 Opium Offenders in 1931

Age	Male	Female	Percentage of Total
13–15	36	0	0.13
16–20	108	58	0.61
21–30	6,927	449	26.89
31–40	6,806	451	26.45
41–50	7,800	740	31.13
51–60	3,342	423	13.72
61–70	564	95	2.40
71–80	33	20	0.19
Over 81	9	0	0.03
Unknown	170	144	1.14

Source: Guomin zhengfu zhujichu tongjiju, ed., *Zhonghua minguo tongji tiyao* (Statistical Abstract for the Republic of China) (Nanjing, 1935), pp. 164–168.

Table 13

Nationalist Government Data Regarding the Occupations of
27,435 Opium Offenders in 1931

Occupation	Male	Female	Percentage of Total
Farmer*	4,532	48	16.69
Laborer	5,057	70	18.69
Merchant	5,023	188	18.99
Shipping/transport	2,232	51	8.32
Government employee	448	0	1.63
Self-employed	1,171	18	4.33
Service personnel	1,921	182	7.67
Unemployed+	966	1,207	7.92
Unknown	3,705	616	13.50

Source: Zhonghua minguo tongji tiyao, pp. 164–168.
*Includes agriculture, animal husbandry, fishing, and hunting.
+Includes students, loafers, those engaged in illegal professions, prisoners, and those too old or
too handicapped to work.

Table 14

Nationalist Government Data Regarding the Lifestyles
of 27,435 Opium Offenders in 1931

Lifestyle	Male	Female	Percentage of Total
Wealthy	328	61	1.42
Average	6,366	297	24.29
Spartan	8,063	686	31.89
Impoverished	8,093	968	33.03
Unknown	2,205	368	9.38

Source: Zhonghua minguo tongji tiyao, pp. 169–171.

Table 15

Nationalist Government Data Regarding the Educational Levels of 27,335 Opium Offenders in 1931

Level of Education	Male	Female	Percentage of Total
High	30	0	0.11
Average	1,206	8	4.43
Literate	7,648	25	28.33
Illiterate	14,938	1,845	61.17
Unknown	1,233	402	5.96

Source: Zhonghua minguo tongji tiyao, pp. 169–171.

Table 16

Estimated Number of Chinese Soldiers and Military Expenditures (Chinese dollars)

Year	Number of Soldiers	Total Expenditures
1916	500,000	$153,000,000
1918	1,000,000	$203,000,000
1924	1,500,000	—
1925	1,500,000	$600,000,000
1927	—	$700,000,000
1928	2,200,000	$800,000,000
1931	—	$1,335,000,000
1937	2,233,000	—

Source: Li Wenzhi and Zhang Youyi, comps., *Zhongguo jindai nongyeshi ziliao* (Source Materials on Modern China's Agricultural History), vol. 2, pp. 607–608; Thomas Rawski, *Economic Growth in Prewar China,* p. 35; F. F. Liu, *A Military History of Modern China: 1924–1949,* pp. 72–73.

Table 17

Estimated Opium Revenues for Fourteen Provinces, 1923–1928
(in million Chinese dollars)

Province	1923	1924	1925	1926	1927	1928
Fujian	$15	$20	—	—	$10–30	—
Henan	—	$12	—	—	$3	—
Hebei	—	—	—	—	$60	—
Hunan	—	—	—	—	$10	—
Hubei	$5–20	$15–30	$20	$20	$10–20	$27–28
Jiangxi	—	$5	—	—	$3	—
Shaanxi	$15	$10–24	—	—	—	—
Gansu	—	$20	$20	—	$5–20	—
Sichuan	$30	$30	$30	$30	$30	$30
Yunnan	—	$5	—	—	$50	—
Guizhou	—	$4	—	—	$6	—
Guangxi	—	—	—	$10	$7–10	$10
Jiangsu	—	—	$5–30	—	$6–15	—
Anhui	$5	$3	$3–6	$4+	—	—

Source: Great Britain, Foreign Office, British Foreign Office File 415: Confidential Print, "Opium," vol. 5, F 1249/238/87, F 82/82/87; United States, Department of State, *Records Relating to the Internal Affairs of China, 1910–1929,* 893.00/6030, 893.114/547, 893.00/5347, 893.114/522, 893.51/4848, 893.114, Narcotic Laws/6, 893.00/6161; *North China Herald,* 6 Dec. 1924, 397; *CWR,* 27 June 1925; *China Year Book,* 1926 623–633; *China Year Book,* 1928, 525–532; *OCTC* 4.2 (May 1924): 9, 15; 5.3 (May 1925): 8, 16, 18; *IAOA Annual Report* 4.1 (May 1924): 1; *Chinese Recorder* (Nov. 1924): 715; *JDYK* 23 (July 1928): 11, 21, 24, 31, 36, 52, 62; Ma Mozhen, *Dupin zai Zhongguo* (Drugs in China), pp. 105–109; Diana Lary, *Region and Nation: The Kwangsi Clique in Chinese Politics, 1925–1937,* p. 93; Hsi-sheng Ch'i, *Warlord Politics in China,* 1916–1928, p. 164; Zhang Jingru and Liu Zhiqiang, eds., *Beiyang junfa tongzhi shiqi Zhongguo shehui zhi bianqian* (Changes in Chinese Society during the Period of Beiyang Warlord Rule), pp. 73–74.

Table 18

Monopoly Opium Taxed at Hankou, 1929–1937

Year	*Dan*	Long Tons
1929	100,000	3,720
1930	117,000	4,352
1931	70,020	2,604
1932	59,860	2,227
1933	71,756	2,669
1934	126,000+	4,687+
1935	236,121	8,784
1936	210,000+	7,812+
1937	unknown	unknown

Source: United States, Department of State, *Records Relating to the Internal Affairs of China, 1930–1939,* 893.114 Narcotics/n.n., Cunningham to Sec. of State (10/25/35), Enc. 1; 893.114 Narcotics/1603, Gibbons to Sec. of State (6/4/36); 893.114 Narcotics/ 1692, Taylor to Sec. of State (9/14/36), Enc. 6. The estimates from 1929–1933 were made by the National Anti-Opium Association based on information provided by Zhong Ketuo. The data from 1934 to 1936 are based on U.S. consular information. For 1934, the amount indicated is incomplete, containing only the amount of goods shipped from Sichuan province. Similarly, the amount for 1936 is double the actual six-month figure provided by the U.S. consulates and therefore a "guesstimate."

Table 19

Statement of Deposits, Loans, and Total Assets of the Farmers Bank of China, 1933–1936 (Chinese dollars to the nearest thousand)

Year	Deposits	Loans	Total Assets
1933	8,300,000	6,200,000	—
1934	15,571,000	11,255,000	26,084,000
1935	52,989,000	25,779,000	134,678,000
1936	155,444,000	78,208,000	349,123,000

Source: Frank M. Tamagna, *Banking and Finance in China,* pp. 131–144; Zhongguo yinhang jingji yanjiushi, ed., *Quanguo yinhang nianjian* (Chinese Banks Yearbook, 1936–1937), pp. 82–84; *Chinese Year Book,* 1937, p. 529.

Table 20

Farmers Bank's Notes in Circulation, 1933–1937
(Chinese dollars to the nearest thousand)

Year	Circulation
1933	2,008,000
1934	5,633,000
1935	29,847,000
1936 to March	34,777,000
to June	92,035,000
to September	108,503,000
to December	162,014,000
1937 to March	200,053,000
to June	207,951,000

Source: Frank M. Tamagna, *Banking and Finance in China,* pp. 131–144; Zhongguo yinhang jingji yanjiushi, ed., *Quanguo yinhang nianjian* (Chinese Banks Yearbook, 1936–1937), pp. 82–84; *Chinese Year Book,* 1937, p. 529.

Notes

Abbreviations

BFOF   Great Britain, Foreign Office, British Foreign Office File 415: Confidential Print, "Opium"
CWR   *China Weekly Review*
CYB   *The China Year Book*
GCA   Guomindang Central Archives, Yangmingshan, Taiwan
GMZFGB   [*Zhonghua*] *guomin zhengfu gongbao*
Guo-260   Guoshiguan, Xindian, Taiwan, Caizhengbu: Mulu 260
JDYK   *Judu yuekan*
LHJDGB   *Luhaijun dayuanshuai dabenying gongbao*
LON   League of Nations, *League of Nations Documents and Publications, 1919–1946*
NCH   *North China Herald*
NSZFGB   *Nanjingshi zhengfu gongbao*
NTHA-3   Zhongguo di'er lishi dang'anguan (Number Two Historical Archives), Quanzonghao 3
NTHA-41   Number Two Historical Archives, Quanzonghao 41
OAWP   *Opium, A World Problem*
OCTC   *Opium Cultivation and Traffic in China*
USDS1   United States, Department of State, *Records Relating to the Internal Affairs of China, 1910–1929*
USDS2   United States, Department of State, *Records Relating to the Internal Affairs of China, 1930–1939*
ZYRB   *Zhongyang ribao*

Introduction

1. Martin Booth, *Opium: A History* (London: Simon and Schuster, 1996), pp. 103–105.
2. Jonathan Spence, "Opium Smoking in Ch'ing China," in Frederic Wakeman, Jr., and Carolyn Grant, eds., *Conflict and Control in Late Imperial China* (Berkeley: University of California Press, 1975), pp. 146–147; Booth, *Opium*, pp. 104–108.
3. Ma Mozhen, *Dupin zai Zhongguo* (Drugs in China) (Taibei: Kening chubanshe, 1994), pp. 78–79; Booth, *Opium*, pp. 109–110; Spence, "Opium Smoking in Ch'ing China," p. 148.
4. Ma, *Dupin zai Zhongguo*, p. 79; Booth, *Opium*, p. 110.
5. Dennis O. Flynn and Arturo Giráldez, "Born with a 'Silver Spoon': The Origin of World Trade in 1571," *Journal of World History* 6.2 (Fall 1995): 206–209. Before 1600, large quantities of silver circulating in China also came from Japan.
6. Frederic Wakeman, Jr., "The Canton Trade and the Opium War," in Denis Twitchett and John K. Fairbank, eds., *The Cambridge History of China*, vol. 10 (Cambridge: Cambridge University Press, 1978), pp. 178–179.
7. David E. Owen, *British Opium Policy in China and India* (New Haven: Yale University Press, 1934; reprint, New Haven: Archon Books, 1968), pp. 127–128; R. Y. Lo, *The Opium Problem in the Far East* (Shanghai: Commercial Press, 1933), p. 18; Wakeman, "The Canton Trade and the Opium War," pp. 180–181; Spence, "Opium Smoking in Ch'ing China," pp. 150–152.
8. Wakeman, "The Canton Trade and the Opium War," p. 181.
9. Ibid., pp. 182–185.
10. Lin Man-houng, "Qingmo shehui liuxing xishi yapian yanjiu, 1773–1906" (Research into the Popularity of Opium Smoking in Late Qing China, 1773–1906) (Ph.D. dissertation, National Taiwan Normal University, 1985), pp. 208, 225.
11. Lin Man-houng, "Integrating or Disintegrating the National Economy? The Opium Market within China, 1820s–1906" (unpublished paper presented at the Conference on Opium in East Asian History, 1830–1945, University of Toronto–York University, Toronto, Ontario, 9–10 May 1997).
12. Kathleen L. Lodwick, "Chinese, Missionary, and International Efforts to End the Use of Opium in China, 1890–1916" (Ph.D. dissertation, University of Arizona, 1976), pp. 36–102; Owen, *British Opium Policy*, pp. 311–354.
13. Lodwick, "Chinese, Missionary, and International Efforts," pp. 180–186; Yu Ende, *Zhongguo jinyan faling bianqianshi* (A History of the Changes in Chinese Anti-Opium Laws and Decrees) (Shanghai: Zhonghua shuju, 1934), pp. 259–263.
14. Owen, *British Opium Policy*, pp. 333–343; Lodwick, "Chinese, Missionary, and International Efforts," pp. 213–227.
15. Great Britain, Foreign Office, British Foreign Office File 415: Confidential Print, "Opium" (hereafter BFOF), in *The Opium Trade, 1911–1941*, vol. 5 (Wilmington: Scholarly Resources, 1974), F 2011/277/10, Wellesley to India Office (6/26/22).

Chapter 1: China's Narco-Economy in the 1920s and 1930s

1. Zhu Qingbao, Jiang Chiuming, and Zhang Shijie, eds., *Yapian yu jindai Zhongguo* (Opium and Modern China) (Nanjing: Jiangsu jiaoyu chubanshe, 1995), p. 152.

2. *Report of the International Opium Commission, Shanghai, China, February 1 to February 26, 1909*, vol. 2 (Shanghai: North China Daily News and Herald, 1909), p. 57. The data cited in the report are 150,000 to 585,000 piculs annually.

3. *Annual Report of the International Anti-Opium Association* 4.1 (May 1924): 1. The figure of 88 percent is based on 15,000 tons for China, 951.4 tons for India, 555.7 tons for Turkey, and 551.1 tons for Persia (Iran). The statistics for India and Turkey are located in League of Nations, *League of Nations Documents and Publications, 1919–1946 (LON)*, C.393.M.136.1926.XI, 156–165. The figure for Persia is the average of the figures for the years 1922 and 1926. The figure for 1922 was 528,241 kg (*LON*, C.393.M.136.1926.XI) and for 1926, 594,000 kg (*LON*, C.329.M.200.1932.XI, table I).

4. *Judu yuekan* (Opium, A National Issue) *(JDYK)* 23 (July 1928): 11–66; 36 (Dec. 1929): 25–56; 47 (March 1931): 2–16; *Opium Cultivation and Traffic in China (OCTC)* 4.2 (May 1924): 1–20; 5.3 (May 1925): 4–21; 6.3 (May 1926): 6–21; *The China Year Book (CYB)*, 1924, pp. 552–564; 1925, pp. 572–587; 1926, pp. 623–643; 1928, pp. 528–535. Although Yan Xishan permitted opium cultivation during the 1930s in Shanxi Province, in recognition of its excellent prohibition record up to that time, it remains blank in Map 1.

5. United States, Department of State, *Records Relating to the Internal Affairs of China, 1910–1929* (hereafter *USDS1*), microfilm, 893.114/547, "Opium Production in South Fukien" (2/10/26).

6. *USDS1*, 893.114/470, Putnam to Sec. of State (12/29/23), Enc. 6 and 7.

7. United States, Department of State, *Records Relating to the Internal Affairs of China, 1930–1939* (hereafter *USDS2*), microfilm, 893.114/419, "The Opium Problem in China" (10/3/32), 11.

8. John L. Buck, *Land Utilization in China* (Nanjing: Nanjing University, 1937; reprint, Taibei: Southern Materials Center, 1986), pp. 318–320.

9. Zhu, *Yapian yu jindai Zhongguo*, pp. 152–153.

10. Ibid.

11. *USDS1*, 893.114/591, "Opium Crop in Yunnan, China—1927" (7/14/27); Zhu, *Yapian yu jindai Zhongguo*, p. 152.

12. The figure of 50 *liang* per *mu* comes from *JDYK* 47 (March 1931): 5–6; and Zhu, *Yapian yu jindai Zhongguo*, p. 152. The high yields of over 200 *liang* per *mu* are reported in *JDYK* 36 (Dec. 1929): 48–51.

13. Zhu, *Yapian yu jindai Zhongguo*, pp. 153–154.

14. *Opium, A World Problem (OAWP)*, 2.1 (November 1928): 19–20.

15. Zhu, *Yapian yu jindai Zhongguo*, p. 152.

16. *JDYK* 47 (March 1931): 5.

17. Zhu, *Yapian yu jindai Zhongguo*, pp. 112–113.

18. *Chinese Recorder* 55.7 (July 1924): 480–481.

19. *USDS2*, 893.114 Narcotics/419, 11–13; *JDYK* 23 (July 1928): 9–62; 36 (Dec. 1929): 25–54; 47 (March 1931): 4–5.

20. *JDYK* 23 (July 1928): 13.

21. *OCTC* 5.3 (May 1925): 10; Zhu, *Yapian yu jindai Zhongguo*, p. 110; Ma, *Dupin zai Zhongguo,* pp. 106–107; *Chinese Recorder* 55.7 (July 1924): 480–481.

22. *North China Herald (NCH),* 22 Feb. 1924, 309; *JDYK* 23 (July 1928): 44–45.

23. *JDYK* 23 (July 1928): 18–20. The provisional *tankuan* was an irregular levy arbitrarily imposed on farmers by local authorities.

24. *OCTC* 6.3 (July 1926): 20.

25. Ibid., 16.

26. Lucien Bianco, "The Responses of Opium-Growers to Eradication Campaigns and Poppy Tax: China, 1900–1945" (unpublished paper presented at the Conference on Opium in East Asian History, 1830–1945, University of Toronto–York University, Toronto, Ontario, 9–10 May 1997). Bianco's earlier article focusing on Anhui province is equally enlightening. See Bianco, "Peasant Uprisings against Poppy Tax Collection in Su Xian and Lingbi (Anhui) in 1932," *Republican China* 21.1 (Nov. 1995): 93–128.

27. For the figure 7,500+ tons, see *China Christian Yearbook,* 1926, p. 326; for 11,875+ tons see *CWR,* 28 Feb. 1931, 445.

28. Sun Fengyu, "Zhong-Ri zhanzheng qijian Riben zai-Hua yapian zhengce" (Japanese Opium Policy in China during the Sino-Japanese War) (Ph.D. dissertation, National Political University, 1991), pp. 54–116; John M. Jennings, "The Opium Empire: Japan and the East Asian Drug Trade, 1895–1945" (Ph.D. dissertation, University of Hawai'i, 1995), pp. 168–189; Frederick T. Merrill, *Japan and the Opium Menace* (New York: Institute of Pacific Relations and the Foreign Policy Institute, 1942), pp. 90–110; *LON,* C.278.M.168.1936.XI, 8; *CWR,* 16 Sept. 1933, 96–101.

29. *LON,* C.290.M.176.1936.XI, 63.

30. Lynda S. Bell, "Farming, Sericulture, and Peasant Rationality in Wuxi County in the Early Twentieth Century," in Thomas G. Rawski and Lillian M. Li, eds., *Chinese History in Economic Perspective* (Berkeley: University of California Press, 1992), pp. 228–229. Net income includes the costs of fertilizer, draft animal labor, and mechanized pumping.

31. *USDS1*, 893.114/549, "The Opium Traffic and American Participation Therein" (2/9/26), 13.

32. Buck, *Land Utilization in China*, pp. 318–320; Parks Coble, Jr., *Shanghai Capitalists and the National Government, 1927–1937* (Cambridge, Mass.: Harvard University Press, 1986), pp. 84–96.

33. Buck, *Land Utilization in China*, pp. 233–237.

34. *USDS1*, 893.48/162, Mayer to Sec. of State (5/14/25), Enc. 1.

35. Edgar Snow, *Red Star over China* (New York: Random House, 1938; 1st revised and enlarged ed., Grove Press, 1968), pp. 54–55.

36. As cited in Ramon H. Myers, "The Agrarian System," in John K. Fairbank and Albert Feuerwerker, eds., *The Cambridge History of China*, vol. 13 (Cambridge: Cambridge University Press, 1986), p. 258.

37. Zhu, *Yapian yu jindai Zhongguo*, p. 161.

38. *JDYK* 36 (Dec. 1929): 32.
39. *CWR*, 24 May 1930, 493–494.
40. Zhu, *Yapian yu jindai Zhongguo*, p. 76.
41. *USDS1*, 893.114/478, Sokobin to Sec. of State (2/6/24).
42. Spence, "Opium Smoking," p. 166; *USDS1*, 893.114/493, Sokobin to Sec. of State (4/23/24).
43. Zhu, *Yapian yu jindai Zhongguo*, p. 162.
44. *USDS1*, 893.114/549, "Extracts from Article on Opium," 4.
45. Zhu, *Yapian yu jindai Zhongguo*, p. 76.
46. Ibid.
47. Ibid.
48. *JDYK* 36 (Dec. 1929): 44–45; Zhu, *Yapian yu jindai Zhongguo*, p. 79.
49. Ibid.
50. *OCTC* 6.3 (May 1926): 16.
51. *JDYK* 23 (July 1928): 23, 27, 55–56; Zhu, *Yapian yu jindai Zhongguo*, pp. 184–185.
52. Zhu, *Yapian yu jindai Zhongguo*, p. 81.
53. Ibid., p. 77.
54. *JDYK* 36 (Dec. 1929): 44–45.
55. Gretchen G. Grover, "America's Controversial Opium Carriers of the 1920s," *Sea Classics* 26:1 (Jan. 1993): 19–23; R. Y. Lo, *The Opium Problem in the Far East* (Shanghai: Commercial Press, 1933), p. 40; Percy Finch, *Shanghai and Beyond* (New York: Charles Scribner's Sons, 1953), pp. 287–288; and Merrill, *Japan and the Opium Menace*, p. 24.
56. For American consular reports on Chinese naval vessels engaged in the opium trade, see *USDS1*, 893.00/6387, MacMurray to Sec. of State (6/4/25), Enc. 1; 893.00/8906 (4/21/27), 4–5; 893.00/9514, 47–48.
57. Buck, *Land Utilization in China*, pp. 5, 89.
58. See G. William Skinner, "Regional Urbanization in Nineteenth Century China," in G. William Skinner, ed., *The City in Late Imperial China* (Stanford: Stanford University Press, 1977), pp. 211–249.
59. *USDS1*, 893.114/549, "Extracts from Article on Opium" (2/9/26), 15–17.
60. Zhu, *Yapian yu jindai Zhongguo*, p. 43.
61. *USDS1*, 893.114/549, "Extracts from Article on Opium," 7–8; Robert A. Kapp, "Chungking as a Center of Warlord Power," in Mark Elvin and G. William Skinner, eds., *The Chinese City between Two Worlds* (Stanford: Stanford University Press, 1974), pp. 143–170.
62. Apparently, in late 1923, Wang Ruqin and Yang Sen reached an understanding for splitting the revenues derived from this tax office. It later became a branch office of the Junjing Jianchachu in Hankou. BFOF, vol. 5, F 82/82/87, Macleay to Curzon (11/21/23); *OCTC* 4.2 (May 1924): 10–11; *CYB*, 1925, p. 576; *USDS1*, 893.51/4848, Adams to MacMurray (7/8/25), 1–4; *LON*, C.214.M.73.1925.XI, 3–4; Ma, *Dupin zai Zhongguo*, pp. 122–123.
63. *OCTC* 5.3 (May 1925): 7–8; BFOF, vol. 6, F 4098/184/87, Fitzmaurice to Henderson (6/14/30), Enc.
64. *JDYK* 36 (Dec. 1929): 36–37.

65. *LON*, C.214.M.73.1925.XI, 3–4.

66. *USDS1*, 893.51/4848, 1.

67. Ibid.

68. For example, in 1923 Guizhou warlord Yuan Zuming traded opium for weapons worth $500,000; and the next year Sichuan warlord Liu Chengxun sent 19,950 pounds of *chuantu* to purchase arms that he later used against rival Yang Sen. See BFOF, vol. 5, F 942/238/87, Clive to Curzon (2/12/23); *OCTC* 5.3 (May 1925): 10; *Annual Report of the IAOA* 4.1 (May 1924): 3.

69. The Gelaohui is often mistranslated as the "Elder Brother Society." There are many good books and articles on secret societies active in the late Qing and early Republican periods. Their relationship with the opium trade is covered in the following: Bao Ying, Zhang Shijie, and Hu Zhenya, eds., *Qingbang yu Hongmen dazhuan* (A Biography of the Green and Red Gangs) (Taibei: Zhouzhi wenhua, 1994), pp. 237–240; Shanghai wenshi yanjiuguan, ed., *Jiu Shanghai de yanduchang* (Opium, Gambling, and Prostitution in Old Shanghai) (hereafter *Jiu Shanghai*) (Hong Kong: Zhongyuan chubanshe, 1989), pp. 10–101; Zhu, *Yapian yu jindai Zhongguo*, 67–82; Atsushi Watanabe, "Secret Societies in Modern China: Ch'ing Pang, Hung Pang," in *Zhonghua minguo chuqi lishi yantaohui lunwenji* (Proceedings from the Conference on the Early Republic, 1912–1927), vol. 2 (Taibei: Academia Sinica, 1984), pp. 797–815; Brian G. Martin, *The Shanghai Green Gang: Politics and Organized Crime, 1919–1937* (Berkeley: University of California Press, 1996), pp. 9–63; Frederic Wakeman, Jr., *Policing Shanghai, 1927–1937* (Berkeley: University of California Press, 1995), pp. 25–39, 116–131; Jonathan Marshall, "Opium and the Politics of Gangsterism in Nationalist China, 1927–1945" *Bulletin of Concerned Asian Scholars* 8 (July–Sept. 1976): 30–38.

70. *Jiu Shanghai*, p. 95; Mei Zhenshao, *Chuanqi renwu Du Yuesheng* (The Legendary Du Yuesheng) (Taibei: Dongcha chubanshe, 1981), pp. 23–31; Wakeman, *Policing Shanghai*, pp. 116–117; Martin, *Shanghai Green Gang*, pp. 27–56.

71. Zhu, *Yapian yu jindai Zhongguo*, pp. 52, 67–82.

72. Martin, *Shanghai Green Gang*, pp. 48–63.

73. Wakeman, *Policing Shanghai*, pp. 36–37; Martin, *Shanghai Green Gang*, pp. 51–52.

74. *CWR*, 21 Feb. 1925, 333; *USDS1*, 893.00/6170, MacMurray to Sec. of State (3/18/25), 2; *Peking and Tientsin Times* (12 March 1925); Wakeman, *Policing Shanghai*, p. 38; Martin, *Shanghai Green Gang*, pp. 52–53.

75. Mei, *Chuanqi renwu Du Yuesheng*, pp. 27–31; *Jiu Shanghai*, p. 92; Wakeman, *Policing Shanghai*, pp. 120–121; Martin, *Shanghai Green Gang*, pp. 56–63. There is some confusion over the actual date of the establishment of the Sanxing Gongsi. It was probably founded after Lu Yongxiang came back in early 1925. The International Anti-Opium Association and National Anti-Opium Association commonly referred to a military syndicate in Nantong that supposedly "monopolized" the opium trade in Shanghai along with an "opium ring" operating in the French Concession. See *OCTC* 6.3 (May 1926): 19–20; *JDYK* 4 (Sept. 1926): 25; *CWR*, 23 Oct. 1926, 202–203.

76. Bao, *Qingbang yu Hongmen dazhuan*, p. 237. The authors state that "Sanxing

Gongsi" was a play on words regarding Du, Huang, and Xiao's involvement in the firm. *"San,"* which means "three," referred to the big three mobsters. The word *"xing,"* which has three "gold" characters together, symbolized the lucrative profits the three men had hoped to earn.

77. Wakeman, *Policing Shanghai*, pp. 120–121; Martin, *Shanghai Green Gang*, pp. 56–63.

78. Li Wenzhi and Zhang Youyi, comps., *Zhongguo jindai nongyeshi ziliao* (Historical Materials on Modern China's Agricultural History), vol. 2 (Beijing: Sanlian shudian, 1957), p. 621; *OCTC* 6.3 (July 1926): 19–20.

79. *USDS1*, 893.00/6387, Enc. 1; 893.00/8906, 4–5; Martin, *Shanghai Green Gang*, p. 62.

80. It should be mentioned that in 1923 the British began enforcing a total ban against opium in the International Settlement, while French authorities did not seriously undertake similar measures in their own concession until a decade later.

81. *USDS1*, 893.114/549, "Extracts from Article on Opium," 14–15.

82. Grover, "America's Controversial Opium Carriers of the 1920s," 21.

83. Kemp Tolley, *Yangtze Patrol* (Annapolis: The Naval Institute Press, 1971), p. 110; *China Critic*, 25 July 1929, 597.

84. Huang Shaoxiong, *Wushi huiyi* (Recalling the Past Fifty Years) (Shanghai: Shanghai shijie shuju, 1945), pp. 44–46; Zhongyang yanjiuyuan jindaishi yanjiusuo, *Bai Chongxi xiansheng fangwen jilu* (An Oral Interview with Mr. Bai Chongxi), vol. 1 (Taibei: Academia Sinica, 1984), pp. 15–18; Ma, *Dupin zai Zhongguo*, pp. 110–113.

85. BFOF, vol. 5, F 863/352/87, Sly to Curzon (2/6/23); J. C. S. Hall, *The Yunnan Provincial Faction, 1927–1937* (Canberra: Australian National University, 1976), p. 108.

86. British dispatches are full of reports on the Yunnan-Indochina opium trade. See BFOF, vol. 5, F 2895/175/87, Sly to Curzon (8/16/23), Enc.; F 3495/117/10, Curzon to Hardinge (11/24/22), Enc. 1–3; F 863/352/87, Sly to Curzon (2/6/23), Enc.

87. Ibid., F 863/352/87, Sly to Curzon (2/6/23).

88. BFOF, vol. 6, F 2727/244/87, Gorton to Chamberlain (4/27/28).

89. Ibid.; Ma, *Dupin zai Zhongguo*, p. 109.

90. Ma, *Dupin zai Zhongguo*, pp. 108–110.

91. Several good monographs describing the importance of Guangxi province in national politics during this era are Shi Jiashun, *Liangguang shibian zhi yanjiu* (Research into the Guangdong and Guangxi Incident) (Gaoxiong, Taiwan: Fuwen tushu chubanshe, 1992); Diana Lary, *Region and Nation: The Kwangsi Clique in Chinese Politics, 1925–1937* (Cambridge: Cambridge University Press, 1974); and Eugene W. Levich, *The Kwangsi Way in Kuomintang China, 1931–1939* (Armonk, N.Y.: M. E. Sharpe, 1993).

92. Huang, *Wushi huiyi*, pp. 154–155; Zhongyang yanjiuyuan jindaishi yanjiusuo, *Xu Qiming xiansheng fangwen jilu* (An Oral Interview with Mr. Xu Qiming) (Taibei: Academia Sinica, 1983), p. 68; *JDYK* 23 (July 1928): 52; Levich, *The Kwangsi Way*, pp. 241–246; Lary, *Region and Nation*, pp. 92–95. National Anti-Opium Association data show in *JDYK* over one-half of Guangxi's provincial revenue for 1927 coming from opium taxes.

93. This is a statement from the Kemmerer Commission's report of 1929 on China's currency crisis. See Arthur N. Young, *China's Nation-Building Effort, 1927–1937* (Stanford: Stanford University Press, 1971), p. 163.

94. *CWR*, 23 April 1927, 208.

95. Thomas G. Rawski, *Economic Growth in Prewar China* (Berkeley: University of California Press, 1989), p. 126; Young, *China's Nation-Building Effort*, p. 163.

96. *CYB,* 1925–1926, pp. 952–953.

97. Frederic E. Lee, *Currency, Banking, and Finance in China* (Washington, D.C.: Department of Commerce, 1926), p. 17.

98. Young, *China's Nation-Building Effort*, pp. 163–164; *CWR*, 26 Dec. 1925, 96.

99. *CYB,* 1925–1926, p. 949.

100. Hsi-sheng Ch'i, *Warlord Politics in China, 1916–1928* (Stanford: Stanford University Press, 1976), p. 161.

101. Frank H. H. King, *Asian Policy, History and Development* (Hong Kong: University of Hong Kong, 1979), pp. 79–80.

102. Zhu, *Yapian yu jindai Zhongguo*, pp. 179–180.

103. Andrea Lee McElderry, *Shanghai Old-Style Banks (Ch'ien-chuang), 1800–1935: a Traditional Institution in a Changing Society* (Ann Arbor: University of Michigan, 1976), pp. 10–20, 142; Frank H. H. King, *Money and Monetary Policy in China: 1845–1895* (Cambridge, Mass.: Harvard University Press, 1965), pp. 92–97; Susan Mann Jones, "Finance in Ningpo: The 'Ch'ien Chuang,' 1750–1880," in W. E. Wilmott, ed., *Economic Organization in Chinese Society* (Stanford: Stanford University Press, 1972), pp. 47–77; Frank M. Tamagna, *Banking and Finance in China* (New York: Institute of Pacific Relations, 1942), pp. 57–88; Zhu, *Yapian yu jindai Zhongguo*, pp. 123–124.

104. Zhu, *Yapian yu jindai Zhongguo*, pp. 79–80.

105. Ibid. Remittance notes from Hubei and Hunan were known as *"hanpiao,"* while those from Guangdong and Guangxi were called *"gangpiao."*

106. Zheng Yifang, *Shanghai qianzhuang, 1843–1937* (Shanghai Native Banks, 1843–1937) (Taibei: Academia Sinica, 1981), p. 36. There seems to be some dispute over the number of *qianzhuang* established during this twelve-year period. McElderry gives the total number as 105 (*Shanghai Old-Style Banks,* p. 133), while Zheng's figure is 120.

107. Hall, *Yunnan Provincial Faction*, pp. 108, 114–117; BFOF, vol. 5, F 2895/175/87, Sly to Curzon (8/16/23), Enc.; F 3495/117/10, Curzon to Hardinge (11/24/22), Enc. 1–3; F 863/352/87, Sly to Curzon (2/6/23), Enc.

108. *CWR*, 19 March 1927, 64.

109. *USDS1*, 893.114/473, Sokobin to Sec. of State (1/18/24), 1–2.

110. *OCTC* 6.3 (May 1926): 19–20. The International Anti-Opium Association misspelled the Huihai Industrial Bank as the Huai Hai Bank. See Lee, *Currency, Banking, and Finance in China*, p. 175, for identification of this bank in Nantong.

111. *USDS1*, 893.114/549, "Extracts from Article on Opium," 4–5.

112. Ibid., 5–6.

113. *USDS1*, 893.00/10000, Myers to Sec. of State (4/7/28), Enc. 3, 5–6.
114. *USDS2*, 893.114 Narcotics/419, 43.
115. *NCH*, 29 May 1926, 400.
116. *USDS2*, 893.114 Narcotics/738, "Opium Traffic in China" (4/28/34), 86. The source was reporter Wang Jingming of *Dagongbao*, in the 27 October 1933 edition.
117. Ta-chung Liu and Kung-chia Yeh, *Economy of the Chinese Mainland: National Income and Economic Development, 1933–1959* (Princeton: Princeton University Press, 1965), p. 66; Albert Feuerwerker, *Economic Trends in the Republic of China, 1912–1949* (Ann Arbor: Center for Chinese Studies, University of Michigan, 1977), p. 12; Rawski, *Economic Growth in Prewar China*, p. 15.

Chapter 2: The Effects of Opium on Chinese Society

1. Guomindang Central Archives (hereafter GCA), Yangmingshan, Taiwan, 442/54.2, "Chengban texu caiyun yantu heyue."
2. U.S. National Archives, *Shanghai Municipal Police Files, 1929–1944* (hereafter *SMPF*), microfilm, D-1456, Gerrard to Cunningham (7/23/30); Zhu, *Yapian yu jindai Zhongguo*, p. 77.
3. Finch, *Shanghai and Beyond*, p. 281.
4. The three best descriptions of the opium smoking ritual can be found in *CWR*, 28 Nov. 1936, 458; Zhu, *Yapian yu jindai Zhongguo*, pp. 162–164; and *LON*, C.635.M.254.1930.XI, vol. 1, 33. Less detailed versions are located in Lien-teh Wu, *Plague Fighter: The Autobiography of a Modern Chinese Physician* (Cambridge: W. Heffer and Sons, 1959), pp. 471–472; Lo, *The Opium Problem*, pp. 9–13; Merrill, *Japan and the Opium Menace*, pp. 10–11; and Finch, *Shanghai and Beyond*, pp. 283–286.
5. Jozsef I. Szekely, *Opioid Peptides in Substance Abuse* (Boca Raton: CRC Press, 1994), p. 195.
6. An excellent work that explores the relationship between opium use and Western literature is Alethea Hayter, *Opium and the Romantic Imagination: Addiction and Creativity in De Quincey, Coleridge, Baudelaire and Others* (Northamptonshire: Crucible, 1988).
7. Finch, *Shanghai and Beyond*, pp. 283–284.
8. *LON*, C.176.123.1937.XI, 52.
9. Wu, *Plague Fighter*, p. 477; *OCTC* 5.1 (Feb. 1925): 4.
10. I would like to thank Dr. Bengt Olausson of the Sahlgan University Hospital in Göteborg, Sweden, for explaining to me (in lay terms) the effects of morphine on the central nervous system.
11. Joel Davis, *Endorphins: New Waves in Brain Chemistry* (Garden City, N.Y.: The Dial Press, 1984), pp. 104–105.
12. Ibid., p. 3. This condition is known as "runner's high."
13. Ibid., pp. 111–112.
14. Szekely, *Opioid Peptides*, pp. 2–7, 55, 82, 161; Ronald P. Hammer, Jr., ed., *The*

Neurobiology of Opiates (Boca Raton: CRC Press, 1993), pp. 85–86, 96, 223–224, Davis, *Endorphins*, pp. 68–72.

15. Szekely, *Opioid Peptides*, pp. 205–206, 235–236; Hammer, *Neurobiology of Opiates*, pp. 148–165, 223–224, 301; Davis, *Endorphins*, pp. 124–126.

16. Lo, *Opium Problem*, pp. 11–12; Davis, *Endorphins*, pp. 73–74. The hippocampus is the brain center for emotion and memory. The degradation of mental acuity sets in only after many years of sustained opium smoking at high levels of consumption.

17. John A. Hawkins, *Opium: Addicts and Addictions* (Danville, Va.: N.p., 1937), pp. 118–128.

18. A contemporary personal account of this Dantean descent was penned by French playwright Jean Cocteau, who vividly described and sketched his hallucinatory experiences from opium withdrawal during four months of treatment in 1928–1929. See Jean Cocteau, *Opium: Journal d'une desintoxication* (Paris: Delamain et Boutelleau, 1931).

19. R. K. Newman, "Opium Smoking in Late Imperial China: A Reconsideration," *Modern Asian Studies* 29.4: 765–794.

20. *LON*, C.635.M.254.1930.XI, vol. 1, 36.

21. *USDS1*, 893.114/549, "Opium Traffic and American Participation Therein," 21.

22. *LON*, C.635.M.254.1930.XI, vol. 1, 31–32.

23. *OAWP* 3.4 (July 1930): 20–28; Hawkins, *Opium: Addicts and Addictions*, pp. 133–135.

24. Wang Qizhang, *Jieyan zhinan* (A Guidebook for Treating Opium Addiction) (Shanghai: N.p., 1936), pp. 80–82; *OAWP* 3.4 (July 1930): 20–28.

25. *OAWP* 3.4 (July 1930): 20–28; Wu, *Plague Fighter*, pp. 493–494; Wang, *Jieyan zhinan*, pp. 67–79.

26. Ibid.

27. *JDYK* 36 (Dec. 1929): 35–36, 39, 43, 47–48, 50, 53; *Jinyan zhuankan* (Special Opium Suppression Publication), 2 (June 1936): 115–118.

28. *Jinyan zhuankan* 2 (June 1936): 115–118.

29. *LON*, C.90.M.46.1926.XI, 4.

30. *JDYK* 30 (April 1929): 25; Zhongguo Guomindang zhongyang weiyuanhui dangshi shiliao bianxuan weiyuanhui, comp., *Geming wenxian* (Documents of the Revolution), vol. 71 (Taibei: Zhongguo Guomindang zhongyang weiyuanhui dangshi shiliao bianxuan weiyuanhui, 1953–), pp. 184–185.

31. *CWR*, 12 Sept. 1931, 59.

32. Zhongyang yanjiuyuan jindaishi yanjiusuo, ed., *Yu Da xiansheng fangwen jilu* (An Oral Interview with Mr. Yu Da) (Taibei: Academia Sinica, 1989), p. 75.

33. *USDS2*, 893.114 Narcotics/419, 45.

34. *JDYK* 36 (Dec. 1929): 35–36, 47, 50, 53; *CYB,* 1928, p. 525; Zhu, *Yapian yu jindai Zhongguo*, pp. 174–178.

35. *USDS2*, 893.114 Narcotics/419, "The Opium Problem in Central China," 44.

36. Zhu, *Yapian yu jindai Zhongguo*, pp. 176–177; *USDS2*, 893.114 Narcotics/419, "The Opium Problem in Central China," 6–7; Zhang Jungu, *Du Yuesheng zhuan* (A Biography of Du Yuesheng), vol. 2 (Taibei: Zhuanji wenxue chubanshe, 1967), pp. 264, 269.

37. *USDS2*, 893.114 Narcotics/419, 6–7; *CYB*, 1928, p. 525.
38. Zhongyang yanjiuyuan, *Yu Da xiansheng fangwen jilu*, pp. 74–75.
39. The National Anti-Opium Association was primarily an appendage of the National Christian Council of China.
40. These data were reprinted in Guomin zhengfu zhujichu tongjiju, ed., *Zhonghua minguo tongji tiyao* (Statistical Abstract for the Republic of China) (Nanjing: Neizhengbu, 1935), pp. 165–177.
41. *OCTC* 5.3 (May 1925): 1–21; *OCTC* 6.3 (May 1926): 1–32; *CYB*, 1928, pp. 524–539; *JDYK* 36 (Dec. 1929): 25–57; *USDS2*, 893.114 Narcotics/419, "The Opium Problem in Central China" (9/29/32), 6–7, 44–45.
42. *JDYK* 47 (March 1931): 31–34.
43. *CWR*, 5 Jan. 1935, 207.
44. *JDYK* 47 (March 1931): 40.
45. Zhu, *Yapian yu jindai Zhongguo*, p. 215.
46. *JDYK* 14 (June 1927): 18.
47. John K. Fairbank, ed., *Chinese World Order: Traditional Chinese Foreign Relations* (Cambridge, Mass.: Harvard University Press, 1968), pp. 5–6.
48. Zhu, *Yapian yu jindai Zhongguo*, p. 212.
49. Newman, "Opium Smoking in Late Imperial China," 777.
50. *JDYK* 16 (Dec. 1927): 59–60.
51. Zhu, *Yapian yu jindai Zhongguo*, p. 213.
52. Ibid., p. 214.
53. *OAWP* 3.2 (April 1930): 19.
54. Ibid.
55. *NCH*, 6 Jan. 1931, 10.
56. *CWR*, 23 May 1931, 410–411.
57. *OAWP* 3.2 (Jan. 1930): 12.
58. Wu, *Plague Fighter*, p. 495.
59. *LON*, C.635.M.254.1930.XI, vol. 1, 23–24.
60. *JDYK* 36 (Dec. 1929): 43.
61. I do not include political parties, provincial assemblies, or party-controlled labor unions in this definition.
62. David Strand, *Rickshaw Beijing: City People and Politics in the 1920s* (Berkeley: University of California Press, 1989).
63. Joseph Fewsmith, *Party, State, and Local Elites in the Republic of China: Merchant Organizations and Politics in Shanghai, 1890–1930* (Honolulu: University of Hawai'i Press, 1985).
64. Zhu, *Yapian yu jindai Zhongguo*, pp. 87–88.
65. Zhu Qihua, *Zhongguo jingji weiji jiqi qiantu* (China's Economic Crisis and Its Future) (Shanghai: Xinshengming shuju, 1932), pp. 209–210.
66. For example, the Yichang Teye Qinglihui and the Changsha Teye Qingli Gonghui. The operative word, *"qingli,"* meaning to sell off, liquidate, or clear out existing stocks of opium, was borrowed from the various *qingli teshuichu* (special tax clearance offices) within the Ministry of Finance's monopoly.

67. Zhu, *Yapian yu jindai Zhongguo*, pp. 80–88; *USDS2*, 893.114/1981, Morlock to Sec. of State (6/17/37), Enc. 2; Marshall, "Opium and the Politics of Gangsterism," p. 34.

68. Zhu, *Yapian yu jindai Zhongguo*, pp. 123–124; Edward R. Slack, Jr., "The Guomindang's Opium Policies, 1924–1937: 'Opium Suppression' in the Context of the Warlord System and the Republican Narco-Economy" (Ph.D. dissertation, University of Hawai'i, 1997), pp. 101–113; *OCTC* 6.3: 11.

69. *JDYK* 13 (July 1927): 16–17; 23 (July 1928): 46.

70. *JDYK* 21 (May 1928): 44; 23 (July 1928): 59.

71. Guoshiguan, Xindian, Taiwan, Caizhengbu: Mulu 260 (hereafter Guo-260), No. 1460, Document 7, Dan Shaofang to T. V. Soong (4/31/32). The Chinese name of this group was "Yichang gejie lizheng shouhui gong'an jiaoyu teshui fujuan weiyuanhui."

72. Ibid.

73. Zhu, *Yapian yu jindai Zhongguo*, pp. 213–214.

74. *Annual Report of the International Anti-Opium Association* 4.1 (May 1924): 18.

75. Ibid., 4–5; Yu, *Zhongguo jinyan*, pp. 193–194.

76. Yu, *Zhongguo jinyan*, pp. 184–185.

77. The first general secretary of the Antinarcotics Commission was Dr. S. H. Chüan, who was soon replaced by R. Y. Lo. See *Chinese Recorder* 55.3 (March 1924): 176–180; Lo, *The Opium Problem in the Far East*, p. 28.

78. *Chinese Recorder* 55.3 (March 1924): 176.

79. Ibid.; Yu, *Zhongguo jinyan*, p. 185.

80. *NCH*, 9 Aug. 1924, 217; 30 Aug. 1924, 337; *CWR*, 27 Sept. 1924, 138; *Hankow Herald,* 26 July 1929. Although Wu Liande and Cai Yuanpei were selected, owing to more pressing commitments, they were unable to attend.

81. *OAWP* 2.4: ii. The constituent bodies of the National Anti-Opium Association were the National Christian Council, the National Committee YMCA, the National Medical Association, the Shanghai General Chamber of Commerce, the Jiangsu Educational Association, the Shanghai Students Union, the National Women's Federation of China, the National Medical and Pharmaceutical Association, the Shanghai Medical Practitioners Union, the National Committee YWCA, the Women's Christian Temperance Union, the World Chinese Students Federation, the Red Cross Society of China, the Council of Health Education of China, the Overseas Chinese Union, the Welfare Association for Chinese Abroad, the Buddhist Association of Shanghai, the Limen Anti-Opium League, the Chinese Ratepayers Union of the International Settlement, the Newspapers Union of Shanghai, the Far East Association of Shanghai, the Vocational Educational Association of China, the China Christian Educational Association, the Libraries Union of China, the National Road Construction Association, the Streets Union of Shanghai, the Zhabei Chamber of Commerce, the Fujian Association of Shanghai, the Wenzhou Association of China, the Shanghai YMCA, the Shanghai YWCA, the Young People's Lecture Bureau of Shanghai, the Nandao Christian Institute of Shanghai, the Shanghai Preachers Union, the

Shanghai Merchants Union, the Shanghai Women's Union, the Shanghai Farmers Union, and the All-Zhejiang Association.

82. Tse-tsung Chow, *The May Fourth Movement: Intellectual Revolution in Modern China* (Cambridge, Mass.: Harvard University Press, 1960), pp. 176–182, 254–257.

83. Marie-Claire Bergère, "The Chinese Bourgeoisie, 1911–1937," in John K. Fairbank, ed., *The Cambridge History of China*, vol. 12 (Cambridge: Cambridge University Press, 1983), pp. 774–777.

84. Arne Sovik, "Church and State in Republican China: A Survey of the Relations between the Christian Churches and the Chinese Government, 1911–1945," (Ph.D. dissertation, Yale University, 1952), pp. 128–248.

85. Jessie G. Lutz, *Chinese Politics and Christian Missions: The Anti-Christian Movements of 1920–28* (Notre Dame, Ind.: Cross Cultural Publications, 1988), pp. 81–90; Kenneth S. Latourette, *History of Christian Missions in China* (New York: Macmillan, 1929), pp. 793–806; Sovik, *Church and State*, pp. 161–163.

86. *OAWP* 1.3 (March 1928): i.

87. *OAWP* 3.1 (Oct. 1929): 16–19.

88. *OAWP* 1.2 (Nov. 1927): i.

89. *OAWP* 1.3 (March 1928): 48; *Who's Who in China,* 4th ed. (Shanghai: The China Weekly Review, 1931), 445–446.

90. See *Who's Who in China,* 1931, pp. 240–241.

91. Ibid., 1933, p. 19.

92. *USDS2*, 893.114/2012, "Narcotics Traffic in Hankow" (7/3/37); Latourette, *Christian Missions*, p. 798.

93. *Who's Who in China,* 1933, p. 110.

94. The translations of the titles *Judu yuekan* and *Zhongguo yanhuo nianjian* into English are those of the National Anti-Opium Association.

95. *China Christian Yearbook,* 1926, p. 329; *NCH,* 16 May 1925, 282.

96. *JDYK* 41 (Feb. 1931): 50–52; *Chinese Recorder* 55.11 (Nov. 1924): 751.

97. *LON,* C.86.M.35.1927.XI, 130.

98. *JDYK* 4 (Sept. 1926): 24.

99. Ibid., 25; *CWR,* 3 April 1926, 110.

Chapter 3: Guomindang Opium Policy during the Height of Warlordism, 1924–1928

1. *JDYK* 23 (July 1928): 47.

2. The term "devolution of power" was coined by Philip Kuhn. See Philip Kuhn, *Rebellion and Its Enemies in Late Imperial China* (Cambridge, Mass.: Harvard University Press, 1970), pp. 211–225; Kwang-ching Liu and Richard J. Smith, "The Military Challenge: The Northwest and the Coast," in John K. Fairbank and Kwang-ching Liu, eds., *The Cambridge History of China*, vol. 11 (Cambridge: Cambridge University Press, 1980), pp. 202–273; Edward A. McCord,

The Power of the Gun: The Emergence of Modern Chinese Warlordism (Berkeley: University of California, 1993), pp. 17–45.

3. Ernest P. Young, "Politics in the Aftermath of Revolution: The Era of Yuan Shi-kai, 1912–16," in John K. Fairbank, ed., *The Cambridge History of China*, vol. 12 (Cambridge: Cambridge University Press, 1983), pp. 208–258.

4. Diana Lary, *Region and Nation*, pp. 10–20; Robert A. Kapp, *Szechwan and the Chinese Republic: Provincial Militarism and Central Power, 1911–1938* (New Haven: Yale University Press, 1973), pp. 7–33.

5. C. Martin Wilbur, "Military Separatism and the Process of Reunification under the Nationalist Regime, 1922–1937," in Ping-ti Ho and Tsou Tang, eds., *China in Crisis*, vol. 1 (Chicago: University of Chicago Press, 1968), pp. 203–204, 207; Hsi-sheng Ch'i, *The Chinese Warlord System: 1916 to 1928* (Washington, D.C.: American University, Center for Research in Social Systems, 1969), pp. 1–2; Jerome Chen, *The Military-Gentry Coalition: China under the Warlords* (Toronto: University of Toronto–York University Joint Centre on Modern East Asia, 1970), p. 7.

6. Various historians have their own periodization for "warlordism." See Hsi-sheng Ch'i, *Warlord Politics in China;* James E. Sheridan, *Chinese Warlord: The Career of Feng Yü-hsiang* (Stanford: Stanford University Press, 1966); Donald G. Gillin, *Warlord: Yen Hsi-shan in Shansi Province, 1911–1949* (Princeton: Princeton University Press, 1967); Odoric Y. K. Wou, *Militarism in Modern China: The Career of Wu P'ei-fu, 1916–1939* (Folkstone, England: Dawson, 1978); Ch'en, *The Military-Gentry Coalition*; Diana Lary, "Warlord Studies," *Modern China* 6.4 (Oct. 1980): 439–470.

7. Sheridan, *Chinese Warlord*, pp. 14–15; Gillin, *Warlord: Yen Hsi-shan in Shansi Province*, pp. 1–15; J. C. S. Hall, *The Yunnanese Provincial Faction, 1927–1937* (Canberra: Australian National University, 1976), pp. 4–9; Diana Lary, "Warlord Studies," 442–444.

8. Ch'i, *Warlord Politics*, p. 1; James Sheridan, *China in Disintegration: The Republican Era in Chinese History, 1912–1949* (New York: The Free Press, 1975), p. 58.

9. Wilbur, "Military Separatism and the Process of Reunification," p. 214.

10. Mao Tse-tung, *Selected Works*, vol. 2 (New York: International Publishers, 1954), p. 272.

11. Ch'en, *Military-Gentry Coalition*, p. 6.

12. Lloyd Eastman, "The May Fourth Movement as a Historical Turning Point," in Kenneth Lieberthal, Joyce Kallgren, Roderick MacFarquhar, and Frederic Wakeman, Jr., eds., *Perspectives on Modern China* (Armonk: M. E. Sharpe, 1991), p. 131.

13. Hung-mao Tien, *Government and Politics in Kuomintang China, 1927–1937* (Stanford: Stanford University Press, 1972), p. 43.

14. Ibid.

15. Ch'i Hsi-sheng was the first scholar to look at this period using systems theory to analyze the separate but related categories that constituted what he first termed the "Chinese Warlord System" in 1969 and later termed the "Chinese Political

System" in 1976. I am essentially using his terminology to describe the framework within which all political matters were resolved on the national and local levels. My focus, however, is on how various warlords (including Chiang Kai-shek) financed their armies to compete within this system and their relationship to the opium trade. Furthermore, I do not agree with Ch'i that this system ended with the culmination of the Northern Expedition in 1928; rather, I think it continued through the Nanjing Decade and finally terminated with the Communist victory in 1949.

16. Sun, "Zhong-Ri zhanzheng qijian Riben zai-Hua yapian zhengce," pp. 54–116; Jennings, "The Opium Empire: Japan and the East Asian Drug Trade, 1895–1945," pp. 168–189; Merrill, *Japan and the Opium Menace*, pp. 90–110; *LON*, C.278.M.168.1936.XI, 8; *CWR*, 16 Sept. 1933, 96–101.

17. *USDS1*, 893.00/5332, Putnam to Sec. of State (12/12/23).

18. *USDSI*, 893.00/5962, "Political Conditions, North Fukien" (12/22/24), 7, Enc. 2, 2; Li Guoqi, ed., *Minguoshi lunji* (A Collection of Articles on the History of Republican China) (Taibei: Nantian shuju, 1990), pp. 161–162, 193–194.

19. *USDS1*, 893.512/232, "Taxation in Amoy" (1/23/24).

20. Ibid., Enc. 1.

21. Ibid. According to this report, the estimated revenue per year garnered from these taxes was $38,490, or about 40 percent of actual collections, based on information supplied by the Xiamen consulate.

22. Ibid.

23. *USDSI*, 893.114/476, Carleton to Schurman (1/21/24).

24. *Peking and Tientsin Times,* 18 Feb. 1924; *OCTC*, 4.2 (May 1924): 6; *LON*, A.32.1924.XI, 13.

25. *Annual Report of the International Anti-Opium Association* 4.1 (May 1924): 2.

26. *USDS1*, 893.114/485, Heintzelman to Schurman (3/25/24), Enc. 1, 2; *OCTC* 5.3 (May 1925): 14–15.

27. *USDS1*, 893.114/619, Sokobin to Sec. of State.

28. Herbert L. May, *Survey of Smoking Opium Conditions in the Far East* (New York: Foreign Policy Association, 1928), p. 25.

29. Sun Wen, *Guofu quanji bubian* (Supplementary Volume to the Collected Works of Sun Wen, Father of the Nation) (Taibei: Zhongguo Guomindang zhongyang zhixing weiyuanhui, 1981), p. 298; Guoli bianyiguan sanmin zhuyi dacidian bianshen weiyuanhui, comp., *Sanmin zhuyi dacidian* (Encyclopedia of the Three Principles of the People), vol. 2 (Taibei: Youshi wenhua shiye gongsi, 1993), p. 1571.

30. Zhongguo Guomindang zhongyang zhixing weiyuanhui xuanchuanbu, ed., *Jinyan xuanchuan huikan* (A Compendium of Anti-Opium Literature) (Nanjing: Guomindang zhongyang zhixing weiyuanhui xuanchuanbu, 1929), pp. 3–4.

31. Ibid., 4–5; *Sanmin zhuyi dacidian*, pp. 1571–1572.

32. Sun Wen, *Guofu quanji* (The Collected Works of Sun Wen, Father of the Nation), vol. 2 (Taibei: Zhongguo Guomindang zhongyang zhixing weiyuanhui, 1961), pp. 881–883; *Dongfang zazhi* (Eastern Miscellany), 21.2:154; *OAWP* 1.1 (July 1927), 3–5.

33. Sun's first government was established in 1917–1918 with the ostensible blessings of Yunnan and Guangxi warlords Tang Jiyao and Lu Rongting. When native Guangdong warlord Chen Jiongming captured Canton in 1920, he too sought the legitimacy that Sun's presence accrued. Once again in 1922, Sun and his civil government were displaced by so-called loyal warlord Chen Jiongming. In early 1923, Chen was himself routed from Canton by Yunnanese and Guangxi warlords who invited Sun back to head the government in February 1923, completing the vicious warlord cycle. See Ssu-yü Teng, "Introduction/A Decade of Challenge," in F. Gilbert Chan and Thomas H. Etzold, eds., *China in the 1920s: Nationalism and Revolution* (New York: New Viewpoints, 1976), pp. 4–5.

34. *Luhaijun dayuanshuai dabenying gongbao* (Bulletin of the Commander in Chief of the Armed Forces Headquarters; hereafter *LHJDGB*), 2 (20 Jan. 1924): Zhiling; *Guangzhoushi shizheng gongbao* (Canton Municipal Government Bulletin), 115 (11 Feb. 1924): 20–22; 117 (25 Feb. 1924): 11–13; Lai Shuqing, ed., *Guomin zhengfu liunian jinyan jihua jiqi chengxiao, 1935–1940* (The Nationalist Government's Six-Year Opium Suppression Plan and Its Results) (Taibei: Guoshiguan, 1986), pp. 13, 20. Although the regulations were promulgated on this date, Yang Xiyan was appointed *jinyan duban* on 5 December 1923.

35. *NCH*, 12 Jan. 1924, 45. Yang Xiyan was the minister of finance for the Canton government (24 January to 11 June 1923). See Lai Zehan, "Guangzhou geming zhengfu de jianli, 1917–1926" (Foundation of the Canton Revolutionary Government, 1917–1926), in *Zhonghua minguo chuqi lishi yantaohui lunwenji, 1912–1917* (Proceedings from the Conference on the Early Republic, 1912–1927), vol. 1 (Taibei: Academia Sinica, 1984), p. 386.

36. *LHJDGB* 1 (10 Jan. 1924): Dayuanshuai ling; 2 (20 Jan. 1924): Dayuanshuai ling; *OCTC* 4.2 (May 1924): 3.

37. *LHJDGB* 4 (10 Feb. 1924): Zhiling 102, Zhiling 120; Sun, *Guofu quanji*, vol. 4, 1063.

38. *LHJDGB* 5 (20 Feb. 1924): Zhiling 138; BFOF, vol. 5, F 2576/82/87, Foreign Office to Secretary General, League of Nations (8/9/24).

39. *NCH*, 26 Jan. 1924, 127; BFOF, F 2576/82/87, Foreign Office to Secretary General, League of Nations (8/9/24).

40. *LHJDGB* 8 (20 April 1924): Xunling 103; 9 (30 April 1924): Xunling 118; *CWR*, 12 April 1924, 239.

41. *Zhongguo Guomindang zhoukan* (National Party Weekly) (Canton) 35 (24 Aug. 1924); BFOF, vol. 5, F 2576/82/87, Foreign Office (8/9/24); *LON*, C.214.M.73.1925.XI, 1–2; *LHJDGB* 9 (30 April 1924): Xunling 120.

42. *CWR*, 9 Feb. 1924, 394; 2 Aug. 1924, 312.

43. *NCH*, 15 April 1924, 6; *CWR*, 20 March 1924, 176.

44. *LON*, C.214.M.73.1925.XI, 1–2.

45. *NCH*, 26 July 1924, 131; *CWR*, 2 Aug. 1924, 312; *OCTC* 5.3 (May 1925): 9.

46. Richard C. DeAngelis, "Jacob Gould Schurman, Sun Yat-sen, and the Canton Customs Crisis," *Jindaishi yanjiusuo jikan* (Institute of Modern History Quarterly), 8 (Oct. 1979): 253–293; C. Martin Wilbur, *Sun Yat-sen: Frustrated Patriot* (New York: Columbia University Press, 1976), pp. 167–190.

47. Li Guoqi, "Song Ziwen dui Guangdong de caizheng gexin" (T. V. Soong's Reform of Guangdong's Financial Administration), in *Zhonghua minguo chuqi lishi yantaohui lunwenji, 1912–1927* (Proceedings from the Conference on the Early Republic: 1912–1927), vol. 2 (Taibei: Academia Sinica, 1984), p. 483.

48. *USDS1*, 893.00/7416, "Situation in China" (4/29/26), Enc. 7; Wilbur, *Sun Yat-sen*, pp. 212–223; Li, "Song Ziwen dui Guangdong caizheng de gexin," pp. 476–482; Donald A. Jordan, *The Northern Expedition: China's National Revolution of 1926–1928* (Honolulu: University of Hawai'i Press, 1976), pp. 13–20.

49. *USDS1*, 893.00/5650, Jenkins to Bell (9/20/24), Enc. 1 and 2; Li, "Song Ziwen dui Guangdong caizheng de gexin," p. 483; Bergère, "The Chinese Bourgeoisie, 1911–1937," pp. 795–796.

50. Hsi-sheng Ch'i, "Financial Constraints on the Northern Expedition," in *Proceedings of the Conference on the Early Republic, 1912–1927*, vol. 1 (Taibei: Academia Sinica, 1984), pp. 250–253; Li, "Song Ziwen dui Guangdong caizheng de gexin," pp. 482–493.

51. The preamble *(liyou)* of these regulations is quite interesting. After blaming the proliferation of narcotics in China on the Beiyang warlords and the British (customs officials), and enumerating the difficulties of opium suppression in Guangdong province, it compares the new system to the Japanese opium monopoly on Taiwan. Ironically, the Guomindang dispatched personnel to Taiwan to study this system in a failed attempt to legalize the trade in 1931. The revised Opium Suppression Regulations can be found in *Zhonghua guomin zhengfu gongbao* (hereafter *GMZFGB*), 3:17–24; May, *Survey of Smoking Opium Conditions*, annex 3, pp. 46–48.

52. *GMZFGB* 3:17–24; May, *Survey of Smoking Opium Conditions,* annex 3, pp. 46–48.

53. Ibid.

54. GCA, Document No. 442/54.2.

55. *LON*, C.214.M.73.1925.XI, 1–2; *CWR*, 20 March 1924, 176.

56. *GMZFGB* 51 (Jan. 1926): 64.

57. Ibid. The first head of the Jinyan Zongchu was Chen Fu. See *Shenbao*, 26 Nov. 1925, 4.

58. *CWR*, 1 Nov. 1925, 287.

59. *GMZFGB* 51 (Jan. 1926): 64; Li, "Song Ziwen dui Guangdong caizheng de gexin," p. 491. The new monopoly instituted under T. V. Soong in late November 1925 farmed out the opium business to the Gongcheng Gongsi. It is not clear what compensation, if any, was paid to the Anhua Gongsi when the Nationalist government canceled its contract.

60. *USDS1*, 893.00/7416, "Situation at Canton" (4/29/26), Enc. 7.

61. Ibid.; Li, "Song Ziwen dui Guangdong caizheng de gexin," p. 487. George Sokolsky states that Cantonese were paying "a hundred-odd taxes," while Li says "over 70."

62. *GMZFGB* 51 (Nov. 1926): 62–63; *USDS1*, 893.00/7416, Enc. 7; Zhongguo Guomindang, *Geming wenxian*, vol. 26, pp. 5412–5413; Caizhengbu caizheng nianjian bianzuanchu, ed., *Caizheng nianjian* (Ministry of Finance Yearbook), vol. 1 (Shanghai: Shangwu yinshuguan, 1935), pp. 16–17.

63. *GMZFGB* 51 (Nov. 1926): 64.

64. Ibid. Before this time, Guomindang monopolies regulated only sales of opium paste and not of raw opium.

65. Ibid. Soong's predictions proved true, for revenues hovered between the $8 million and the $10 million mark for the years 1927 to 1929. See Guangdongsheng caizhengting, ed., *Guangdongsheng caizheng jishi* (A Veritable Record of Financial Administration in Guangdong Province) (Canton: Guangdongsheng caizheng ting, 1933), pp. 26–28.

66. *GMZFGB* 51 (Nov. 1926): 64; *OCTC* 6.3 (May 1926): 23.

67. Liu, *A Military History of Modern China*, pp. 26, 72–73.

68. Liu Jizeng, Mao Lei, and Yuan Jicheng, eds., *Wuhan guomin zhengfushi* (A History of the Nationalist Government in Wuhan) (Wuhan: Hubei renmin chubanshe, 1986), pp. 200–210; Zhongyang yanjiuyuan jindaishi yanjiusuo, ed., *Zhou Yongneng xiansheng fangwen jilu* (An Oral Interview with Mr. Zhou Yongneng) (Taibei: Academia Sinica, 1984), pp. 94–104; *USDS1*, 893.00/7721, 4–5; Jordan, *Northern Expedition*, pp. 104–105.

69. Lai, *Guomin zhengfu*, p. 15; *CYB*, 1928, pp. 524–525; *OAWP* 1.2 (Nov. 1927): 1.

70. *JDYK* 23 (July 1928): 27–29; *CYB*, 1928, pp. 524–525.

71. Liu, *Wuhan guomin zhengfushi*, p. 205.

72. Ibid., p. 204. Military expenditures accounted for over 80 percent of total outlays.

73. Deng Qingyou, comp., *Junzheng zhiguanzhi* (A Compilation of Officials during the Period of Military Rule), vol. 1 (Lanzhou: Gansu renmin chubanshe, 1985), pp. 500–501. This volume notes the establishment of an opium suppression office in Hankou in early April.

74. Zhongyang yanjiuyuan, *Zhou yongneng xiansheng fangwen jilu*, p. 98.

75. *CWR*, 9 July 1927, 135; Parks M. Coble, *The Shanghai Capitalists and the Nationalist Government, 1927–1937* (Cambridge, Mass.: Harvard University Press, 1986), pp. 40–41.

76. *JDYK* 13 (July 1927): 1, 15.

77. BFOF, vol. 6, F 522/127/87, Lampson to Chamberlain (12/20/27), Annex 1.

78. *Shenbao*, 26 July 1927, 9.

79. BFOF, vol. 6, F 522/127/87, Lampson to Chamberlain (12/20/27), Enc. 1, Annexes 4, 5, 7, 9; *CWR*, 30 July 1927, 211; 6 Aug. 1927, 259; *JDYK* 23 (July 1928): 35; *USDS1*, 893.00/9514, 47–48; *LON*, C.557.M.199.1927.XI, Annex 4, 107–108.

80. BFOF, vol. 6, F 522/127/87, Lampson to Chamberlain (12/20/27), Enc. 1.

81. *USDSI*, 893.00/9660, 11–12.

82. BFOF, vol. 6, F 522/127/87, Enc. 1; Martin, *Shanghai Green Gang*, 136–139.

83. BFOF, vol. 6, F 522/127/87, Enc. 1; *CWR*, 19 Nov. 1927, 297; *USDS1*, 893.114/ 602, 12.

84. *NCH*, 26 Nov. 1927, 360; *USDS1*, 893.114/602, Enc. 2; BFOF, vol. 6, F 522/127/87, Enc. 1, Annexes 10, 11. The official explanation for terminating the Zhongxing Gongsi's contract was that the company actively promoted the sale of opium despite the announced intention of Nanjing to reduce the volume of trade and sold opium of such a high potency that those who smoked it could not break the habit.

85. *USDS1*, 893.00/9481 (893.00/P. R. Shanghai/2), 11; Martin, *Shanghai Green Gang*, p. 137.
86. *JDYK* 16 (Dec. 1927): 15–17; *USDS1*, 893.114/608, Enc. 1; 893.114/604, 12; 893.114/597, 4.
87. *JDYK* 23 (July 1928): 9–10.
88. Ibid,. 9-53; *USDS1*, 893.00/7319, 2–3; 893.114/606, 1–4; 893.00/7391, 2.
89. *CYB*, 1928, pp. 524–525.
90. *Shenbao*, 10 Jan. 1928, 5; *CWR*, 14 Jan. 1928, 178–179.
91. Yu, *Zhongguo jinyan*, pp. 288–299. A total of eleven different regulations regarding the Guomindang's opium centralization scheme were issued within a twenty-two-day period.
92. Soong was serving as minister of finance under the Wuhan government when Chiang Kai-shek broke with the Communist-influenced regime there in March 1927. Relations between the two men were somewhat distant immediately thereafter. As a consequence, the first minister of finance in Nanjing was Gu Yingfen, followed by Sun Fo. During Chiang Kai-shek's "retirement," he married Soong's sister, and when the generalissimo emerged from retirement, his new brother-in-law was rehabilitated as well.
93. Copies of these regulations can been found in *GMZFGB* 46:6–10; Yu, *Zhongguo jinyan*, pp. 286–288.
94. *GMZFGB* 46:6–10; Yu, *Zhongguo jinyan*, pp. 286–288.
95. *GMZFGB* 46:6–10; Yu, *Zhongguo jinyan*, pp. 286–288.
96. *LON*, C.328.M.88.1928.XI, 90–91.

Chapter 4: Nanjing's Response to Attacks on Opium Policy, 1924–1937

1. Sun, *Guofu quanji*, vol. 2, pp. 881–883; *Dongfang zazhi* 21.2: 154; *OAWP* 1.1 (July 1927): 3–5.
2. Sovik, "Church and State," pp. 161–162, 198–200.
3. Alan Baumler, "Playing with Fire: The Nationalist Government and Popular Anti-Opium Agitation in 1927–28," *Republican China* 21.1 (Nov. 1995): 57.
4. Fewsmith, *Party, State, and Local Elites*, pp. 89–166, 194.
5. *CYB*, 1928, pp. 524–539; *JDYK* 16 (Dec. 1927): 5, 15–22; 23 (July 1928): 9–53.
6. Yu, *Zhongguo jinyan*, pp. 190–191; *CWR*, 14 May 1927, 288–289; *NCH*, 23 April 1927, 155; *OAWP* 1.1 (July 1927): 7–8.
7. Yu, *Zhongguo jinyan*, p. 191.
8. *CWR*, 3 Sept. 1927, 485; *OAWP* 1.2 (Nov. 1927): 46–52.
9. Yu, *Zhongguo jinyan*, p. 192.
10. *NCH*, 17 Dec. 1927, 485.
11. *JDYK* 16 (Dec. 1927): 32; Yu, *Zhongguo jinyan*, p. 193.
12. *OAWP* 1.3 (March 1928): 29–33, 36; *JDYK* 17 (Jan. 1928): 7; *JDYK* 18 (Feb. 1928): 11.
13. *Shenbao*, 7, Feb. 1928; Yu, *Zhongguo jinyan*, p. 201; *CWR*, 31 March 1928, 151; *NCH*, 31 March 1928, 522.

14. *JDYK* 22 (June 1928): 7; Yu, *Zhongguo jinyan*, p. 202.
15. *NCH*, 14 July 1928, 64.
16. Yu, *Zhongguo jinyan*, pp. 202–205; *OAWP* 2.1 (Nov. 1928): 5–18.
17. *NCH*, 31 Jan. 1925, 181.
18. Copies of these laws can be found in the following sources: Yu, *Zhongguo jinyan*, pp. 203, 302–304; *Jinyan xuanchuan huikan*, pp. 59–62; Lai, *Guomin zhengfu*, pp. 372–376; *OAWP* 2.1 (Nov. 1928): 13–18.
19. Zhang Zhijiang, ed., *Quanguo jinyan huiyi huibian* (Proceedings from the National Opium Prohibition Conference) (Nanjing: Executive Yuan, 1929), "Diyi lei," pp. 29–40; *OAWP* 2.2 (Jan. 1929): 7–20.
20. *China Critic*, 15 Nov. 1928, 495; *NCH,* 17 Nov. 1928, 250; *CWR* 17 Nov. 1928, 393; BFOF, vol. 6, F 441/69/87, Lampson to Chamberlain (12/4/28).
21. Zhang, *Quanguo jinyan huiyi huibian*, "Yanjiang," p. 40.
22. *OAWP* 2.2 (Jan. 1929): 1, 12.
23. Yu, *Zhongguo jinyan*, pp. 300–301; Min Ch'ien T. Z. Tyau, *Two Years of Nationalist China* (Shanghai: Kelly and Walsh, 1930), pp. 305–309.
24. *Shibao*, 30 Jan. 1929; *GMZFGB* 177:203. A set of regulations governing official commemoration of the holiday included the following protocol: memorial flags and banners flown by all military and government agencies, schools, factories and shops; speeches in schools about the Opium War; commemorative ceremonies that included singing the Guomindang anthem, saluting the images of Sun and Lin Zexu, and a reading of Sun's "Judu yixun"; and public burnings of confiscated opium, heroin, morphine, and associated paraphernalia to climax the ceremonies.
25. See Tyau, *Two Years of Nationalist China*, p. 309.
26. *Dongfang zazhi* 27.13: 127.
27. *JDYK* 41 (July 1930): 10; 42 (August 1930): 33.
28. *China Critic*, 15 May 1930, 472; *OAWP* 3.4 (July 1930): 19–20.
29. *NCH*, 20 May 1930, 304.
30. Estimates for the actual amount of opium vary. See *Dongfang zazhi* 26.5:126; *NCH*, 1 Dec. 1928, 354.
31. See various issues of *Shenbao*, *CWR*, *NCH*, and the *China Critic* from December 1928 to February 1929; and *USDS1*, 893.114 Kiangan/1 (12/10/28) and 2 (2/8/29).
32. *China Critic*, 20 Dec. 1928, 584.
33. *NCH*, 22 Dec. 1928, 480; 12 Jan. 1929, 68; *CWR,* 29 Dec. 1928, 194; *USDS1*, 893.114 N 16 Kiangan/2, Cunningham to MacMurray (2/8/29).
34. In November 1930, Zhang was appointed superintendent *(duban)* of the Jiangsu Suiqing Duban Gongshu (Superintendent's Office for Pacification in Jiangsu). See Xu Youchun, ed., *Minguo renwu dacidian* (Encyclopedia of Personalities in the Republic of China) (Beijing: Hebei rennin chubanshe, 1991), p. 902.
35. Leang-li T'ang, *The Inner History of the Chinese Revolution* (London: George Routledge and Sons, 1930), pp. 354–355; Lary, *Region and Nation*, pp. 37–38; and *USDS1*, 893.114 Kiangan/1 and 2. An interesting story about this incident was related by Zhou Yongneng, who at that time was chief secretary for the Shang-

hai Special Municipality government, working directly under Mayor Zhang Dingfan. According to an interview with Zhou by scholars from the Academia Sinica, right after the National Opium Prohibition Conference had ended, Zhang Zhijiang had been informed of a large shipment of opium en route from Hankou to Shanghai and asked Zhang Dingfan to investigate the matter secretly with him. Zhang related the information to Dai Shifu, who dispatched roving patrols along the wharfs to intercept the shipment. The outnumbered policemen were kidnaped and locked inside a temple near Longhua. When the police freed themselves and reported back to Dai Shifu, the incident was leaked to the press and the city was in an uproar. A meeting between leading party, municipal and central government personnel, and military staff was held to discuss the matter. Several days later, it was disclosed that the Guangxi Clique had intentionally shipped the opium to destroy public confidence in the central government but that Zhang and the others were ordered to keep this information in strict confidence. See Zhongyang yanjiuyuan, *Zhou Yongneng xiansheng fangwen jilu*, pp. 125–126.

36. *CWR*, 20 July 1929, 5; 3 August 1929, 448; 9 Nov. 1929, 390; *China Critic*, 31 Oct. 1929, 875; *NCH*, 12 Oct. 1929, 43; 2 Nov. 1929, 164. For a detailed exposé of the facts of this case, see *JDYK* 32 (August 1929): 43–45; 35 (Nov. 1929): 12–17.

37. *USDS1*, 893.114 Narcotic Laws/30, Adams to MacMurray (10/31/29); *CWR*, 16 Nov. 1929, 426; *China Critic*, 21 Nov. 1929, 934.

38. Coble, *The Shanghai Capitalists*, pp. 86–94.

39. Department of Agriculture and Economics, College of Agriculture and Forestry, University of Nanking, and The National Flood Relief Commission, eds., *The 1931 Flood in China* (Nanking: University of Nanking, 1931), pp. 10–12; National Flood Relief Commission, ed., *Report of the National Flood Relief Commission* (Shanghai: National Flood Relief Commission, 1933), pp. 1–10.

40. Howard L. Boorman and Richard C. Howard, eds., *Biographical Dictionary of Republican China*, vol. 5 (New York: Columbia University Press, 1971), p. 402. Liu's contribution in spreading Western medical practices and techniques in China were second only to Wu Liande. Under his direction, the Central Hospital in Nanjing became the most modern medical facility in Republican China. He published national sanitary codes in 1928, fought plagues alongside Wu Liande, and helped to raise the standards of modern Chinese medicine.

41. BFOF, vol. 6, F 1698/22/87, Ingram to Henderson (1/22/31), Enc. 2.

42. *NCH*, 20 Jan. 1931, 76.

43. Wu Liande, Zhong Ketuo, and Luo Yunyan (R. Y. Lo) were all important members of the National Anti-Opium Association hierarchy.

44. Lai, *Guomin zhengfu*, pp. 76–77; *CWR*, 14 Feb. 1931, 394.

45. *CWR*, 28 Feb. 1931, 444–445, 450–452.

46. *Shenbao*, 20 Feb. 1931; *NCH*, 24 Feb. 1931, 259; *CWR*, 28 Feb. 1931, 444–452; *OAWP* 4.3 (April 1931): 1–32. Before this meeting on 19 February, an eight-point declaration of the National Anti-Opium Association's intentions to deal with this matter was issued to the press that, among other things, proposed the

restriction on executive members serving concurrently on the National Opium Prohibition Committee. Apparently, the proposal was rejected. See *Shenbao*, 14 Feb. 1931; *NCH*, 17 Feb. 1931, 219.

47. Annual receipts from customs yielded an average of $121 million during 1924 to 1928, but after agreements reached between Nanjing and the foreign powers over China's recovering import tariff autonomy, collection rose dramatically to $244 million in 1929, $290 million in 1930, and $385 million in 1931. Abolition of the *lijin* and native customs duties were necessary sacrifices in the name of "unequal treaty" revision. See Young, *China's Nation-Building Effort*, pp. 17–20, 37–54, 65–66; Paul K. T. Sih, ed., *The Strenuous Decade: China's Nation-Building Efforts, 1927–1937* (New York: St. John's University, 1970), pp. 87–101; *CYB*, 1933, pp. 476–477.

48. *USDS2*, 893.114 Narcotics/625, "Strictly Confidential" (1/29/34), 3–4; Martin, *Shanghai Green Gang*, pp. 39–40.

49. Number Two Historical Archives, Nanjing, People's Republic of China, Quanzonghao 3: Caizhengbu (hereafter NTHA-3), No. 882, Li Muqing to T. V. Soong (2/16/31). Nine sets of regulations were drafted by Li for the purpose.

50. Ibid.

51. Ibid., No. 882, Li Muqing to T. V. Soong (2/12/31). *Jizhengsuo* (examination and tax collection departments) were established at the following locations: Lingbao (which also doubled as the Shanzhou Branch Henan Special Tax Clearance Office), Wendizhen, Xuchang, Zhoujiakou, Xinyang, Xixiakou, Huangchuan (Huangzhou Examination and Tax Collection Department), Luba (Luzhe Examination and Tax Collection Department), Yongcheng (Yongxia Examination and Tax Collection Department), Nanyang, Dengxian (Xindeng Examination and Tax Collection Department), Luoyang, Guide (Guiyu Examination and Tax Collection Department), and Jinziguan. *Jianchasuo* (inspection posts) were established in Kaifeng (inside the Provincial General Affairs Office), Tahe, Wu'an (Wushe Inspection Post), Mengxian (Wenmeng Inspection Post), Madian, Daokou, Xinxiang (Xinpo Inspection Post), and Anyang (Anlin Inspection Post).

52. *CWR*, 11 April 1931, 290; *China Critic*, 16 April 1931, 383; *OAWP* 4.4 (July 1931): 29.

53. *China Critic*, 26 March 1931, 290.

54. *OAWP* 4.4 (July 1931): 33.

55. This whole unsavory affair is described in the *China Critic*, 7 May 1931, 438–439.

56. *CWR*, 20 June 1931, 120; Lai, *Guomin zhengfu*, pp. 33–34.

57. *CWR*, 23 May 1931, 408. Ellen La Motte wrote several books on opium, including *The Ethics of Opium* and *The Opium Monopoly*.

58. Lai, *Guomin zhengfu*, pp. 33–34; *OAWP* 4.4 (July 1931): 1–2.

59. *Guowen zhoubao* (National Literature Weekly), 8.26 (1931): 6; *Zhonghua minguo shishi jiyao*, July–Dec. 1931, 5–6.

60. *CWR*, 11 July 1931, 240; 18 July 1931, 282; *NCH*, 7 July 1931, 3; *Zhonghua minguo shishi jiyao*, July–Dec. 1931, 5–6.

61. *CWR*, 11 July 1931, 240; *OAWP* 4.4 (July 1931): 2–3; *Zhonghua minguo shishi jiyao*, July–Dec. 1931, 5–6. It was reported in the *China Weekly Review* that "the

National Government, suffering an economic strain, has decided to float a loan of $400,000,000 in the form of 'opium suppression' bonds. Opium smoking dens are to be prohibited unless they register with the bureau and buy bonds ranging from $1,000 to $10,000 in proportion with their scales of business. In addition to the 'license fees,' a tax of 30 cents will be levied on each ounce of opium or opium substitutes."

62. *CWR,* 11 July 1931, 240; *OAWP* 4.4 (July 1931): 2–3; *Zhonghua minguo shishi jiyao,* July–Dec. 1931, 5–6.

63. The forces of public opposition were the National Anti-Opium Association, Ma Yinchu, the Shanghai Municipal Guomindang Headquarters, as well as various labor unions. See *CWR,* 27 June 1931, 136; 4 July 1931, 178; 18 July 1931, 282; 1 August 1931, 349; *NCH,* 7 July 1931, 3; *OAWP* 4.4 (July 1931): 2–4. Li Muqing played a major role in creating the Opium Smuggling Prevention Department headquarters in Hankou. His involvement in this ill-fated monopoly venture is detailed in NTHA-3, No. 875, Li Muqing to T. V. Soong (6/18/31), Li Muqing to T. V. Soong (6/30/31); No. 1121, Li Muqing to T. V. Soong (7/1/31). Li was charged by the Control Yuan with violating prohibition and promoting the sale of opium in Henan province at the time. See *CWR,* 11 July 1931, 240.

64. *CWR,* 1 Aug. 1931, 334–335; *NCH,* 28 July 1931, 120–121, 11 Aug. 1931, 192.

65. Marshall, "Opium and the Politics of Gangsterism," 33; Seagrave, *Soong Dynasty,* pp. 332–333.

66. Martin, *Shanghai Green Gang,* pp. 140–141.

67. Those arrested for the assassination attempt were linked to Guangdong and Guangxi separatists who were at odds with Nanjing over Hu Hanmin's house arrest. See *NCH,* 11 Aug. 1931, 192; Coble, *Shanghai Capitalists,* pp. 114–115.

68. *USDS2,* 893.114 Narcotics/1992, Enc. 1.

69. *USDS2,* 893.114 Narcotics/625, "Strictly Confidential" (1/29/34), 6–7.

70. *USDS2,* 893.114 Narcotics/1992, Enc. 1. This document was sent by Treasury Attaché M. R. Nicholson on 7 June 1937 to the Commissioner of Customs in Washington, D.C. The enclosure was titled "National Anti-Opium Association's Future and Its Problems."

71. Zhongguo Guomindang, *Geming wenxian,* vol. 76, pp. 137–140. The resolution read: "The National Government heretofore has been unable to link its determination for suppressing opium with the methods implemented. Each province deals with this matter in its own way, and there still exist the so-called Special Tax Offices, Clearance Offices, Reconstruction Offices, Minority Affairs Offices, numerous organizations with bizarre names that are only agencies that collect opium taxes or sell opium. In Gansu province . . . and Yunnan province . . . poppies are planted everywhere, and [provincial governments] use opium taxes as their largest source of administrative funding."

72. *USDS2,* 893.114 Narcotics/370, Johnson to Secretary of State (7/6/32), Enc. 1; *China Critic,* 26 May 1932, 524. Liu Ruiheng was also brought up on charges of neglect of duty and disregard for human life by the Control Yuan in 1934 and

for embezzling funds earmarked for the Central Hospital in 1936. See *CWR*, 7 July 1934, 238; 21 Dec. 1934, 88; 1 Aug. 1936, 325.

73. *USDS2*, 893.114 Narcotics/354, Adams to Secretary of State (6/4/32), Enc.
74. *GMZFGB* 11 (Luoyang) (20 June 1932); *USDS2*, 893.114 Narcotics/358, Peck to Secretary of State (6/24/32), Enc. 2.
75. *USDS2*, 893.114 Narcotics/625, "Strictly Confidential" (1/29/34), 6–7.
76. The National Anti-Opium Association offices were originally located in the headquarters of the National Christian Council, 23 Yuanmingyuan Road, from August 1924 to July 1927. Their second location was at the Shanghai Bankers Association, 4 Hong Kong Road, until early 1933. The final address was 128 Museum Road. All of these addresses were within the British-administered International Settlement.
77. *USDS2*, 893.114 Narcotics/625, "Strictly Confidential" (1/29/34), 6–7.
78. Wu, *Plague Fighter*, pp. 471–499.
79. *OAWP* 4.4 (July 1931): 32–33.
80. *USDS2*, 893.114 Narcotics/625, "Strictly Confidential" (1/29/34), 5–7; *CWR*, 3 Dec. 1932, 16.
81. *CWR*, 6 May 1933, 368.
82. Zhongyang ribao (Central Daily News) *(ZYRB)*, 2 Sept. 1932; Lai, *Guomin zhengfu*, pp. 46–47.
83. *Dagongbao*, 25 Sept. 1932; *ZYRB*, 21 Oct. 1932; Central Commission for Opium Suppression, *Traffic in Opium and Other Dangerous Drugs, Annual Report 1932*, 1–5; Lai, *Guomin zhengfu*, pp. 390–392.
84. Lai, *Guomin zhengfu*, pp. 47–51, 390–408; Central Commission for Opium Suppression, *Traffic in Opium and Other Drugs, Annual Report 1933*, 1–10.
85. *ZYRB*, 25 June 1934, 2; *Zhongyang zhoubao* 317, 2 July 1934; *Shenbao*, 23 June 1934, 4; *NCH*, 4 July 1934, 8.
86. *Shenbao*, 28 May 1934, 7.
87. Lai, *Guomin zhengfu*, pp. 56–57; *Guomin zhengfu junshi weiyuanhui weiyuanhuizhang Nanchang xingying chuli jiaofei shengfen zhengzhi gongzuo baogao* (A Report by the Chairman of the National Government's Military Affairs Commission at Nanchang on Political Work in the Bandit Suppression Zones) (Nanchang, 1934), 91.
88. For reactions of various countries to the six-year plan, see *LON*, C.530.M.241.1934.XI, 4; C.33.M.14.1935.XI, 59.
89. Huang's italics. *China Christian Yearbook,* 1934–1935, p. 351.
90. I have found no substantive discussion of this link in any present-day works, despite it's being mentioned in several contemporary sources. See *CWR*, 15 Dec. 1934, 98; *NCH*, 4 July 1934, 8; *LON*, C.256.M.105.1934.XI, 11; *Jinyan zhuankan* 2 (June 1936): 2–3.
91. For sources concerning the New Life Movement, see Zhongguo Guomindang, *Geming wenxian*, vol. 68, "Xinshenghuo yundong shiliao"; Wei, *Counterrevolution in China*, pp. 76–81; Eastman, *The Abortive Revolution*, pp. 13–14, 66–70; T'ang, *Reconstruction in China*, pp. 33–46; Arif Dirlik, "The Ideological Foun-

dations of the New Life Movement: A Study in Counterrevolution," *Journal of Asian Studies* 34.4 (Aug. 1975): 945–980.

92. James C. Thomson, Jr., *While China Faced West: American Reformers in Nationalist China, 1928–1937* (Cambridge, Mass.: Harvard University Press, 1969), pp. 158.

93. Xinshenghuo yundong cujin zonghui, ed., *Minguo ershisannian xinshenghuo yundong zongbaogao* (General Report on the New Life Movement for 1934) (Nanchang, 1935), p. 363.

94. *ZYRB*, 17 March 1934, 2; *Nanjingshi zhengfu gongbao* (Nanjing Municipal Government Bulletin) (hereafter *NSZFGB*) 139 (31 March 1934): 10–12. According to a press report in May 1930, the capital was designated as a model area for opium suppression. The Central Hospital was ordered to create a model opium treatment facility but inexplicably waited four years to do so. See *NCH*, 20 May 1930, 304.

95. *ZYRB*, 6 April 1934, 3; *NSZFGB* 140 (30 April 1934): 75; Eastman, *The Abortive Revolution*, p. 67; Wei, *Counterrevolution in China*, p. 78.

96. *ZYRB*, 17 April 1934, 2; 2 May 1934, 2.

97. *ZYRB*, 2 May 1934, 2. The titles of these two pieces of antinarcotics literature were *Qing guoren jichu yapiandu* (An Appeal to Citizens to Urgently Eradicate the Opium Poison) and *Yapian mafei baimian hongwan weifa qiangshen wangguo miezhong chedi saochu* (Opium, Morphine, White Powder [Heroin], and Red Pills Are Illegal and Kill the Body, Subjugate the Nation and Destroy the Race, and Must Be Thoroughly Eradicated).

98. *NSZFGB* 141 (31 May 1934): 79–81.

99. *ZYRB*, 4 May 1934, 2; 6 May 1934, 2; *NSZFGB* 141 (31 May 1934): 79–97.

100. *Zhongyang zhoubao* 312 (28 March 1934); *ZYRB*, 4 June 1934, 2; *Shenbao*, 4 June 1934, 3.

101. *Shenbao*, 6 Dec. 1934, 3; *CWR*, 15 Dec. 1934, 98. Members of the emergency conference included Gu Zhenglun (Nanjing Garrison commander), Shi Ying, Chen Zhuo (chief of police), Liu Ruiheng (director of public health and National Opium Prohibition Committee chairman), Zhang Wangzhao (chief judge of the Nanjing District Court), and Wang Zuxiang (director of the Municipal Department of Public Health).

102. *Shenbao*, 8 Dec. 1934, 3; *ZYRB*, 8 Dec. 1934, 2; *CWR*, 15 Dec. 1934, 98; *NSZFGB* 148 (31 Dec. 1934): 105–108.

103. Ibid.

104. Xinshenghuo yundong cujin zonghui, *Minguo ershisannian xinshenghuo yundong zonggongbao*, p. 370.

105. Hu Shize used these words when explaining the six-year plan before the League of Nations Opium Advisory Committee in 1934. See *LON*, C.530.M.241.1934.XI, 4.

106. Lai, *Guomin zhengfu*, pp. 55–57, 415–421.

107. Ibid.

108. *LON*, C.277.M.144.1935.XI, 80–88.

109. *Guowen zhoubao* 12.21:4; *Dagongbao*, 7 June 1935; 4; *CWR*, 1 June 1935, 28.

110. *Junshi weiyuanhui weiyuanhuizhang xingying zhengzhi gongzuo baogao*, pp. 91–92; Zhongguo Guomindang, *Geming wenxian*, vol. 29, pp. 6349–6350; *Shenbao*, 30 May 1935, 3; *NCH*, 5 June 1935, 370; Lai, *Guomin zhengfu*, pp. 122–125.

111. *LON*, C.82.M.41.1925.XI, "Protocol," 1.

112. *Shenbao*, 4 June 1935, 3; *CWR*, 8 June 1935, 5; *NCH*, 12 June 1935, 424.

113. On 15 June 1935, Chiang issued the Organizational Regulations for the General Commission for Opium Suppression, the Measures for the Registration of Opium Smokers within a Definite Time Period, and the Regulations for the Organization of Opium Suppression Committees of Provinces-Municipalities and Branch Opium Suppression Sub-Committees of Districts. See Central Commission for Opium Suppression, *Annual Report*, 1935, 6–12, appendixes 13–17; *Chinese Year Book*, 1936–1937, pp. 439–442; Lai, *Guomin zhengfu*, pp. 129–134, 427–435.

114. Lai, *Guomin zhengfu*, pp. 422–424; NTHA-41 (2), No. 72, Chiang Kai-shek to Opium Suppression Supervisory Bureau (1/21/36), Military Affairs Commission General Order 149 (2/1/36).

115. A list of members appears in Zhang Pengyuan and Chen Huaiyu, comps., *Guomin zhengfu zhiguan nianbiao* (Yearly Tables of Officials in the National[ist] Government), vol. 1, (Taibei: Academia Sinica, 1987), pp. 345–347.

116. *Jinyan zhuankan* 1 (Dec. 1935): 1–2; *NCH*, 3 July 1935, 15; *CWR*, 6 July 1935, 202; *USDS2*, 893.114 Narcotics/1308, 108; *SMPF*, D-7138, "Extract from Daily Report." The journal *Jinyan zhuankan* was published by the Shanghai Municipal Opium Suppression Committee. In the preface to its first issue, the photographs of all seven members, their assistants, Mayor Wu Tiecheng, and even Chiang Kai-shek are featured.

117. Marshall, "Opium and the Politics of Gangsterism," 19–48; Wakeman, *Policing Shanghai*, pp. 260–275.

118. *USDS2*, 893.114 Narcotics/1981, Treasury Dept. to Morlock (6/17/37), Enc. 2. Under the Special Tax Clearance Office monopoly, the transport and wholesale merchants had formed business associations called Qingli Teyehui, or Qingli Teye Gonghui. After 1934, they dropped the "Qingli" from their name. See NTHA-41, No. 389 (11), Xiao Zizhen to Huang Weicai (9/28/36).

119. Zhang, *Du Yuesheng zhuan*, vol. 2 pp. 264–269. Others, such as Ilona Ralf Sues and Sterling Seagrave, have stated that although Du had been cured of opium smoking, he merely exchanged one vice for another and became hooked on heroin pills. See Seagrave, *Soong Dynasty*, p. 335; Ilona Ralf Sues, *Shark's Fins and Millet* (Garden City, N.Y.: Garden City Publishing Co., 1945), pp. 77, 81.

120. For a copy of this speech, see *Jinyan zhuankan* 1 (Dec. 1935): 3–7.

121. See Lai, *Guomin zhengfu*, pp. 424–476; *LON*, C.176(a).M.123(a).1937.XI, 1–77; C.127.M.79.1939.XI, 1–2; C.76.M.31.1938.XI, 1–4.

122. The general commission moved out of Chiang's Military Affairs Commission field headquarters to Nanjing after changing its name to the Central Commission for Opium Suppression. See NTHA-41 (2), No. 72, Chiang Kai-shek to Opium Suppression Supervisory Bureau (1/21/36); Military Affairs Commission General Order 149 (2/2/36).

123. *Zhonghua minguo shishi jiyao,* Jan.–June 1936, 293–296; *ZYRB,* 7 Feb. 1936, 2; *NCH,* 12 Feb. 1936, 257; *CWR,* 22 Feb. 1936, 425, 432.
124. *LON,* C.290.M.176.1936.XI, 52–76.
125. *CWR,* 6 June 1936, 26.
126. *CWR,* 4 July 1936, 161.
127. *China Christian Year Book,* 1934–1935, p. 349.
128. See Thomson, *While China Faced West*, pp. 151–195.
129. *USDS2,* 893.114 Narcotics/1992, Treasury Department to Morlock (6/30/37), Enc. 1.
130. Ibid. Among those listed as attending the meeting were Bishop L. H. Roots, R. R. Millican (secretary of the Christian Literature Society of China), Paul Yen (executive secretary of the New Life Movement), J. L. Huang (general secretary of the Officers Moral Endeavor Association), and Li Denghui of the National Anti-Opium Association.
131. For copies of Chiang's speech, see *ZYRB,* 4 June 1937, 1; *Zhonghua minguo shishi jiyao,* Jan.–June 1937, 525–527; *LON,* C.127.M.79.1939.XI, Annex, 31–32.
132. *ZYRB,* 4 June 1937, 1; *Zhonghua minguo shishi jiyao,* Jan.–Jun. 1937, 525–527; *LON,* C.127.M.79.1939.XI, Annex, 31–32.
133. See *Chinese Recorder* 68.8 (Aug. 1937): 533–534; and *CWR,* 14 Aug. 1937, 385, for announcements of the National Anti-Opium Association's dissolution. For the opium prophecy, see *USDS2,* 893.114/625, "Strictly Confidential."

Chapter 5: Practical Determinants of Guomindang Opium Policy

1. Wilbur, "Military Separatism and the Process of Reunification," pp. 239–241, 259–260.
2. Documents concerning the two Military Reorganization and Disbandment conferences can be found in Zhongguo Guomindang, *Geming wenxian*, vol. 24, pp. 4839–5024.
3. Dau-lin Hsü, "Chinese Local Administration under the National Government" (unpublished papers, University of Washington, 1967–1972), chapter 1, "National Unification and War Preparation," p. 9.
4. For a solid yet not overly tedious account of the Guomindang's anti-Communist campaigns, see Zhu Houde, ed., *Jiaofei jianshi* (A Concise History of Bandit Suppression) (Taibei: Guofangbu shizheng bianyinju, 1976). For a more detailed account, see Guofangbu shizhengju, comp., *Jiaofei zhanshi* (A History of Military Actions against the Communist Rebellion, 1930–1945), 6 vols. (Taibei: Zhonghua dadian bianyinhui, 1967).
5. Tien, *Government and Politics in Kuomintang China,* pp. 73–82, 151–170.
6. Soong arrived in Hankou on 10 April 1929 and on 15 April officially opened the Hankou Branch Central Bank, which was housed in the building formerly occupied by the Russo-Asiatic Bank. See *Shenbao,* 13 April 1929, 6–7; 14 April 1929, 4; 16 April 1929, 6; *CWR,* 18 April 1929, 316; 2 May 1929, 358.

7. *Shenbao*, 15 April 1929, 5; 17 April 1929, 4. Shen Qingyi was appointed the first director of the Lianghu Special Tax Clearance Office.

8. The first extension was granted in July 1929 for three additional months to the end of October 1929. A second extension of six months was granted for the period October 1929 to April 1930, followed by a third (May–August 1930) and fourth extension (September–December 1930). The final requests to prolong its life were dated 29 December 1930 and 7 January 1931 in the Ministry of Finance records and came at the behest of Hunan provincial government chairman He Jian, who stated that "the liquidation of existing stocks of opium is the lifeline of our military rations. Naturally, we must expend every effort to help get this source of revenues for our armies." See *Shenbao*, 22 July 1929, 4; NTHA-3, No. 934, Shen Gongli to T. V. Soong (3/26/30), Li Muqing to T. V. Soong (8/25/30), He Jian to T. V. Soong (1/7/31); No. 1011, Shen Gongli to T. V. Soong (5/10/30).

9. NTHA-3, No. 934, Shen Gongli to T. V. Soong (3/26/30).

10. *USDS2*, 893.114 Narcotics/419 (10/3/32), "The Opium Problem in Central China," 46.

11. For locations of the Hubei Special Tax Clearance Office branches, see NTHA-3, No. 1011, Shen Gongli to T. V. Soong (1/7/30), Shen Gongli to T. V. Soong (5/10/30); No. 952, Chen Shaogui to T. V. Soong (4/18/30), Xie Fencheng to T. V. Soong (7/24/30). The *North China Herald* reported these branch offices were created in June 1930. See *NCH*, 17 June 1930, 454.

12. NTHA-3, No. 1013 (n.d.), "Qingli Hunan teshuichu Zhonghua minguo ershinian geyuefen zhifu yusuanshu" (Hunan Special Tax Clearance Office Budget of Monthly Expenditures for 1931). According to this document, the Hunan Special Tax Clearance Office was created sometime in 1930.

13. Steamships mentioned in the Ministry of Finance records were the *Poshi*, the *Fuyang*, the *Shudu*, the *Yuchuan*, the *Chuying*, the *Puquan,* and the *Wanhe*. See NTHA-3, No. 941 (3/22/31), No. 950 (11/22/30), No. 991 (5/27/30), No. 1011 (5/10/30), No. 1039 (9/29/30), No. 1051 (11/18/30); Guo-260, No. 1460, Document 8 (5/5/31).

14. NTHA-3, No. 1057, Yang Tong to T. V. Soong (3/31/31). This document stated that each member drew a monthly salary of $300.

15. NTHA-3, No. 1011, Shen Gongli to T. V. Soong (4/16/30); No. 1030, He Zongliang to T. V. Soong (11/11/31).

16. NTHA-3, No. 934, Shen Gongli to T. V. Soong (3/26/30).

17. NTHA-3, No. 882, Li Muqing to T. V. Soong (2/16/31); No. 907, Directive 33463 (10/31/31); No. 1030, He Zongliang to T. V. Soong (11/11/31), Liu Xiang to T. V. Soong (11/16/31).

18. NTHA-3, No. 907, Li Muqing to T. V. Soong (10/31/31). Following the Yangtze flood of 1931 and the Shanghai Incident of early 1932, these amounts were lowered to $50,000 and $30,000, respectively.

19. NTHA-3, No. 882, Li Muqing to T. V. Soong (2/16/31); No. 1030 He Zongliang to T. V. Soong (11/11/31), Liu Xiang to T. V. Soong (11/16/31).

20. NTHA-3, No. 882, Li Muqing to T. V. Soong (2/16/31).

21. NTHA-3, No. 941, He Chengjun to T. V. Soong (1/22/31), He Baohua to T. V. Soong (1/24/31), Yang Tong/He Baohua to T. V. Soong (1/25/31), Special Business Merchants in Hankou to T. V. Soong (2/14/31); No. 1015, Huang Zhenxing to H. H. Kung (4/13/33); No. 1042, Central Bank to T. V. Soong (12/18/31); Guo-260, No. 1459, Documents 4, 7, 10.

22. NTHA-3, No. 1012, Chiang Kai-shek to H. H. Kung (4/14/34), H. H. Kong to Chiang Kai-shek (4/16/34). This official correspondence was initiated by Chiang from his Nanchang Military Affairs Commission field headquarters regarding the amount of revenue generated by the Lianghu (later Hubei) Special Tax Clearance Office during the tenures of Li Muqing and Xiong Zijia, who were directors of the Hankou Main Office during 1930–1932.

23. See *CYB*, 1932, p. 428; *CYB*, 1933, pp. 474–477; Young, *China's Nation-Building Effort*, appendix 1, pp. 433–440. Opium from Hankou's Special Tax Clearance Office earned $17.5 million in 1929 and $13.5 million in 1930.

24. Guo-260, No. 1460, Document 1, He Chengjun to T. V. Soong (11/11/31). This revenue-sharing agreement was also reported in *USDS2*, 893.114 Narcotics/738, "Opium Traffic in China" (4/28/34), 42–43.

25. Guo-260, No. 1459, Document 4, He Chengjun to T. V. Soong (3/10/32), Enc.

26. NTHA-3, No. 883, Shen Gongli to T. V. Soong (1/5/30); No. 1011 Shen Gongli to T. V. Soong (5/10/30); No. 1039 Li Muqing to T. V. Soong (9/29/30).

27. *NCH*, 29 April 1930, 172; 17 June 1930, 454; 17 July 1930, 482; 9 December 1930, 334; *USDS2*, 893.114 Narcotics/738, "Opium Traffic in China," 43. It appears that the Hubei Bureau of Finance farmed out the collection of taxes on the wholesale and retail trade (including licensing opium dens) to the so-called Forty-eight Houses (forty-eight opium transport and wholesale firms). According to an article in the Chinese monthly *New Hankou*, the four principal sources of municipal revenue came from the house tax, the deed transfer tax, the water and light utilities tax, and the special goods tax, the latter of which accounted for one-third of the total monthly sum.

28. NTHA-3, No. 1052, Li Muqing to T. V. Soong (9/5/30).

29. NTHA-3, No. 1011, Yang Tong/He Baohua to T. V. Soong (5/4/31). The tenures for directors of the Hankou Main Office were as follows: Shen Qingyi (4/17/29–12/27/29), Shen Gongli (12/28/29–7/10/30), Li Muqing (7/11/30–1/10/31), Yang Tong/He Baohua (1/11/31–7/?/31), Li Muqing (7/?/31–12/2/31), Xiong Zijia (12/2/31–8/3/32), Huang Zhenxing (8/3/32–3/?/34), and Li Jihong (3/?/34–10/?/34).

30. BFOF, vol. 6, F 4098/184/87, Fitzmaurice to Henderson (6/14/30), Enc. Another $5 was presumably the "procedural fee."

31. NTHA-3, No. 1023, Assistant Minister of Finance to Generalissimo's Headquarters (2/27/30); BFOF, vol. 6, F 3485/184/87, Toller to Henderson (5/26/30), Enc. 2.

32. NTHA-3, No. 1023, Assistant Minister of Finance to Generalissimo's Headquarters (2/27/30), "Qingli lianghu teshuichu micheng Chen tepaiyuan ruchuan jiehe teshui gaijin zhengshou qingxing zhaiyao" (Summary of the Lianghu Spe-

cial Tax Clearance Office Secret Report Detailing the Dispatch of Special Agent
Chen to Sichuan to Negotiate the Improvement of Special Tax Collection Procedures) (hereafter Secret Report) (3/22/30), Shen Gongli to T. V. Soong (3/25/
30). The *dan* of opium in this system weighed 1,000 *liang* or 83.3 pounds. See
NTHA-3, No. 952, Xie Fencheng to T. V. Soong (7/24/30).

33. NTHA-3, No. 991, Shen Gongli to T. V. Soong (5/27/30).
34. NTHA-3, No. 1023, "Secret Report" (3/22/30); BFOF, vol. 6, F 3466/184/87,
Phillips to Henderson (5/16/30); *USDS2*, 893.114 Narcotics/n.n., "Kwangsi's
Opium Revenue" (4/12/35).
35. NTHA-3, No. 1023, Shen Gongli to T. V. Soong (3/25/30).
36. NTHA-3, No. 991, Shen Gongli to T. V. Soong (5/27/30).
37. NTHA-3, No. 1023, He Chengjun to T. V. Soong (3/27/30), He Chengjun to
T. V. Soong (6/5/30).
38. NTHA-3, No. 1023, He Chengjun to T. V. Soong (6/5/30).
39. NTHA-3, No. 1023, He Chengjun to T. V. Soong (7/21/30), Li Muqing to
T. V. Soong (8/19/30). The vouchers were in denominations of $100 and $1,000,
and became valid on 1 October 1930.
40. BFOF, vol. 6, F 4098/184/87, Fitzmaurice to Henderson (6/14/30), Enc.; F 5262/
184/87, Lampson to Henderson (6/20/30), Enc. 1; F 3485/184/87, Toller to Henderson (5/26/30), Enc. 2.
41. NTHA-3, No. 1023, Chen Shaogui to T. V. Soong (6/10/30).
42. BFOF, vol. 6, F 3570/184/87, Brenan to Lampson (5/29/30), Enc.; F 3634/184/87,
Brenan to Lampson (5?/31/30); F 5008/792/87, Brenan to Henderson (7/30/30).
43. Guo-260, No. 1460, Document 8, He Chengjun to T. V. Soong (5/5/32).
44. NTHA-3, No. 1011, Shen Gongli to T. V. Soong (4/16/30), Shen Gongli to
T. V. Soong (5/10/30); BFOF, vol. 6, F 4098/184/87, Fitzmaurice to Henderson
(6/14/30), Enc.
45. NTHA-3, No. 941, He Chengjun to T. V. Soong (1/22/31), He Baohua to
T. V. Soong (1/24/31), Yang Tong to T. V. Soong (1/25/31), Li Muqing to T. V.
Soong (2/3/31), Hankou Special Business Merchants to T. V. Soong (2/14/31).
The letter from the Hankou Special Business Clearance Association is the most
informative of the lot in terms of describing the total monetary losses, the number of attacks, and the responsible military units.
46. NTHA-3, No. 991, Shen Gongli to T. V. Soong (5/27/30), T. V. Soong to
Chiang Kai-shek (5/29/30). The actual amount was 820,282 *liang*.
47. Ibid., Shen Gongli to T. V. Soong (5/27/30); Sichuan, Yunnan, and Guizhou
Special Business Merchants to T. V. Soong (6/6/30).
48. This entire episode was covered in the local press as well as recorded by the British and American consulates. See NTHA-3, No. 991, He Yingqin to T. V.
Soong (6/13/30); No. 1026 He Yingqin to T. V. Soong (6/30/30); *USDS2*, 893.114
Narcotics/135, Lockhart to Johnson (6/26/30); BFOF, vol. 6, F 5262/184/87,
Lampson to Henderson (7/20/30), Enc. 3; *JDYK* 42 (Aug. 1930): 33–34; *NCH*, 15
July 1930, 84; 22 July 1930, 125.
49. NTHA-3, No. 1027, Yang Tong/He Baohua to T. V. Soong (2/19/31), Yang

Tong/He Baohua to T. V. Soong (3/14/31), Yang Tong to T. V. Soong (4/10/31); *USDS2*, 893.114 Narcotics/419, "The Opium Problem in Central China" (10/3/32), 22.

50. NTHA-3, No. 1058, T. V. Soong to Long Yun and Mao Guangxiang (6/8/31).
51. Ibid.
52. NTHA-3, No. 1058, Long Yun to T. V. Soong (7/8/31).
53. NTHA-3, Ma Kongfan to T. V. Soong (8/29/31); Ma, *Dupin zai Zhongguo*, pp. 109–110.
54. Guo-260, No. 1459, Document 2, He Chengjun to T. V. Soong (2/11/32), and Enc. from Xiong Zijia to Soong.
55. Ibid., Document 7, Xiong Zijia to T. V. Soong (3/25/32).
56. NTHA-3, No. 1011, Yang Tong/He Baohua to T. V. Soong (5/4/31).
57. Ibid.
58. Coble, *Shanghai Capitalists*, pp. 109–115.
59. Ibid.
60. *USDS2*, 893.114 Narcotics/738, "The Opium Traffic in China" (4/28/34), 46–57; Martin, *Shanghai Green Gang*, p. 157. For reports in the press concerning the expansion of the unofficial monopoly into Jiangsu, Jiangxi, and Anhui provinces, see *CWR*, 30 July 1932, 338; 3 Sept. 1932, 34; 17 Sept. 1932, 87; 1 Oct. 1932, 213; 19 Nov. 1932, 518; 3 Dec. 1932, 16; 24 Dec. 1932, 175; *NCH*, 28 Sept. 1932, 100; 30 Nov. 1932, 336; 14 Dec. 1932, 426. As occurred in previous attempts by Nanjing to implement a monopoly, the National Anti-Opium Association led the charge against this plan. However, with most of the population in China distracted by the Japanese problem, there was little public sympathy for National Anti-Opium Association criticism.
61. *USDS2*, 893.114 Narcotics/419, "The Opium Traffic in Central China" (10/3/32), 26; 893.114 Narcotics/738, "The Opium Traffic in China" (4/28/34), 75. The U.S. consuls in Hankou had very detailed and accurate information concerning the traffic passing through the main office, and apparently, their source was a person who had access to such records within the opium tax agency.
62. The actual figure was $3,938,600. See NTHA-3, No. 1042, Li Muqing to T. V. Soong (7/24/31), Central Bank to T. V. Soong (12/18/31).
63. Ibid., Central Bank to T. V. Soong (4/29/32).
64. *USDS2*, 893.114 Narcotics/738, "The Opium Traffic in China" (4/28/34), 56; *SMPF*, D-3648, "Public Sale of Opium in Shanghai" (12/31/32); Martin, *Shanghai Green Gang*, pp. 156–157; Marshall, "Opium and the Politics of Gangsterism," pp. 33–34.
65. Guo-260, No. 1457, Document 6, Huang Zhenxing to T. V. Soong (10/8/32).
66. *USDS2*, 893.114 Narcotics/528, Cunningham to Sec. of State (7/31/33), Enc. 1–3; 893.114 Narcotics/738, "The Opium Traffic in China" (4/28/34), 51; *SMPF*, D-4028 (9/17/32), D-3648 (12/31/32).
67. Zhongguo Guomindang zhongyang weiyuanhui dangshi shiliao bianxuan weiyuanhui, comp., *Zhonghua minguo zhongyao shiliao chubian—dui-Ri kangzhan shiqi* (Preliminary Compilation of Important Historical Materials on the Chinese

Republic—the Period of the War of Resistance against Japan) (Taibei, 1981), vol. 3, 440.

68. Guo-260, No. 1460, Document 16, Huang Zhenxing to T. V. Soong (9/5/32); No. 1457, Document 6, Huang Zhenxing to T. V. Soong (10/8/32), Document 1, Huang Zhenxing to T. V. Soong (9/28/32), Document 5, Order from Bandit Suppression Headquarters to Hubei Special Tax Clearance Office (10/12/32).

69. Guo-260, No. 1460, Document 17, Tang Hai'an to T. V. Soong (9/27/32). Tang Hai'an was at that time superintendent of Maritime Customs at Shanghai. Included in this letter was a copy of regulations titled "Simplified Regulations for Special Agents Stationed Outside of the Hubei Special Tax Clearance Office," indicating that other Maritime Customs stations along the Yangtze had similar agents stationed there as well. Article 1 stated, "As a means to put an end to smuggling, this bureau has already reached an agreement with the high-ranking administrative officials in various provinces and municipalities that our office must dispatch special agents to these important places to work with them in all anti-smuggling related matters."

70. NTHA-3, No. 1015, Huang Zhenxing to T. V. Soong (10/28/32); No. 1042, Central Bank to T. V. Soong (10/28/32); No. 1038, Chen Zhaonian to T. V. Soong (11/12/32).

71. Except for a few items dated from 1933 and 1934 pertaining to affairs before 31 December 1932, the connection between the Ministry of Finance and the unofficial opium monopoly agencies was formally terminated.

72. NTHA-3, No. 875, Li Muqing to T. V. Soong (6/18/31). At the end of this set of documents along with several others preserved in Nanjing is a sheet of paper mentioning a fire in the Ministry of Finance that broke out on 12 December 1932. Given the lucrative nature of the Special Tax Clearance Office operation and numerous instances of embezzlement and other acts of corruption committed at all levels, it seems more than a coincidence.

73. NTHA-3, No. 1011, Yang Tong/He Baohua to T. V. Soong (5/4/31).

74. *Shenbao*, 19 March 1933, 9; 20 March 1933, 7; Tan Yuzuo, *Zhongguo zhongyao yinhang fazhanshi* (A History of the Development of Leading Chinese Banks) (Taibei: Zhongguo xinwen chuban gongsi, 1961), pp. 281–282; Sun Xiufu, "Jiang Jieshi yu Zhongguo nongmin yinhang" (Chiang Kai-shek and the Farmers' Bank), *Minguo dang'an* (Republican Archives), 1 (1996): 91–98. Nanjing provided $3 million; $500,000 each was put up by the provinces of Henan, Hubei, Anhui, and Jiangxi; and $5 million was provided by opium merchants.

75. When Li Muqing established the Henan Special Tax Clearance Office in early 1931, Zhengzhou was its main office, with branches at Kaifeng (*jianchasuo*) and Huangchuan (*jizhengsuo*). In February 1932, Xiong Shihui petitioned T. V. Soong to establish a branch (*jianchasuo*) in Jiujiang. When the monopoly was extended during mid-late 1932, other offices were opened in Jiangxi at Nanchang, Hukou, and the Niuhang Railway Station; and in Anhui at Anqing, Wuhu, and Datong. See NTHA-3, No. 883, Li Muqing to T. V. Soong (2/12/31); Guo-260, No. 1459, Document 6, Xiong Shihui to T. V. Soong (2/6/32);

USDS2, 893.114 Narcotics/738, "The Opium Traffic in China" (4/28/34), 49–51. The locations of the Four Provinces Agricultural Bank in 1933–1934 were Hankou, Yichang, Shashi, Anqing, Zhengzhou, Huangchuan, Kaifeng, and Jiujiang. See *CYB*, 1934, p. 413; Tan, *Zhongguo zhongyao yinhang*, p. 282.

76. *USDS2*, 893.114 Narcotics/656, Adams to Sec. of State (2/7/34). See also *USDS2*, 893.114 Narcotics/738, "The Opium Traffic in China" (4/28/34), 67, 79–80; Marshall, "Opium and the Politics of Gangsterism," 35; Coble, *Shanghai Capitalists*, pp. 114, 195–197; *Shenbao*, 1 Jan. 1934, 13.

77. NTHA-3, No. 941, Special Business Merchants in Hankou to T. V. Soong (2/14/31). In this letter to Soong, Hankou special merchants stated that they collected taxes in Sichuan, Hankou, Shanghai, and other places in order to "suppress through taxation," on the one hand, and to offset military expenditures, on the other.

78. NTHA-3, No. 1023, Shen Gongli to T. V. Soong (3/25/30); No. 1030, He Zongliang to T. V. Soong (11/11/30), Liu Xiang to T. V. Soong (11/16/31), Ministry of Finance Order No. 34368 to the Hubei Special Tax Clearance Office (12/4/31); No. 1011, Yang Tong/He Baohua to T. V. Soong (5/4/31); Guo-260, No. 1460, Document 7, Dan Shaofang to T. V. Soong (4/31/32); *USDS2*, 893.114 Narcotics/738, "The Opium Trade in China" (4/28/34). Such abuses by merchants who reported taxes for the transport merchants in the Special Tax Clearance Office included stealing opium from these merchants, underreporting the taxes owed in exchange for bribes, abusing their authority to collect extortionate procedural fees for their services, and collusion with directors of the Special Tax Clearance Office to embezzle tax monies and smuggle opium.

79. *USDS2*, 893.114 Narcotics/738, "The Opium Traffic in China" (4/28/34), 58–68.

80. Ibid.

81. Ibid., 67–68.

82. NTHA-3, No. 1030, He Zongliang to T. V. Soong (11/11/31), Liu Xiang to T. V. Soong (11/16/31).

83. NTHA-41, No. 263, Opium Suppression Supervisory Bureau Warehouse (3/24/36), Enc. "Youhan yunmin shuihuo banfa" (Regulations for Transporting Taxable Goods from Hankou to Fujian). Article 2 of the regulations describes how local merchants in the Government Warehouse set prices at the Pingjia Weiyuanhui. Article 4 describes how the merchants paid the Farmers Bank the taxes that it collected on behalf of the Opium Suppression Supervisory Bureau. The main document also describes how the Farmers Bank assessed a procedural fee for collecting taxes based on each *dan* of opium taxed. Although this document was from 1936, the procedures it describes were most likely implemented in 1933.

84. Ibid.; *USDS2*, 893.114 Narcotics/644, "December 1933 Monthly Compilation," 2.

85. *Shenbao*, 1 Nov. 1933, 11.

86. *USDS2*, 893.114 Narcotics/701, "February 1934 Monthly Report," 2.

87. *USDS2*, 893.114 Narcotics/738, "The Opium Traffic in China" (4/28/34), 75.

88. For information regarding Japanese smuggling operations, see Lin Mingde,

"Riben dui Huabei de jingji qinlue" (The Japanese Economic Invasion of North China), *Zhongyang yanjiuyuan jindaishi yanjiu jikan* 9 (June 1990): 421–444; *CWR*, 28 April 1934, 332; 14 July 1934, 281; 1 Dec. 1934, 15; *Chinese Year Book,* 1936–1937, pp. 891–927; Coble, *Facing Japan*, pp. 302–309; T. A. Bisson, *Japan in China* (New York: The MacMillan Company, 1938), pp. 129–135.

89. *CWR*, 3 March 1934, 35; Coble, *Shanghai Capitalists*, pp. 146–147; Young, *China's Nation-Building Effort*, p. 173; W. Y. Lin, *The New Monetary System in China* (Chicago: University of Chicago Press, 1936), pp. 13–17.

90. Young, *China's Nation-Building Effort*, p. 173; Coble, *Shanghai Capitalists*, pp. 146–147.

91. Coble, *Shanghai Capitalists*, pp. 163–172.

92. In late 1931, the agency changed its name from the Qingli Lianghu Teshuichu to the Qingli Hubei Teshuichu, because the Hunan offices were being run by He Jian and his provincial government.

93. See *USDS2*, 893.114 Narcotics/729, "March 1934 Monthly Compilation", 3; *China Christian Year Book,* 1934–1935, p. 345.

94. Neizhengbu, comp., *Neizheng nianjian* (Ministry of the Interior Yearbook), vol. 2 (Shanghai: Shangwu yinshuguan, 1935), pp. 574–577; *Guomin zhengfu junshi weiyuanhui weiyuanhuizhang Nanchang xingying chuli jiaofei shengfen zhengzhi gongzuo baogao,* 91; *USDS2*, 893.114 Narcotics/729, 3–4; *LON*, C.299.M.182.1936.XI, 90; Lai, *Guomin zhengfu*, pp. 52–53; *Chinese Christian Year Book,* 1934–1935, pp. 347–348. The translation of Jinyan Duchachu as the Opium Suppression Supervisory Bureau appears in Nationalist English-language publications.

95. *Neizheng nianjian*, vol. 2, pp. 574–577.

96. NTHA-41, No. 225 (3), No. 241, Xue Zhendong to Huang Weicai (9/30/34). No. 471 (5) Wu Hefu to Huang Weicai (5/1/37); *Neizheng nianjian*, vol. 2, p. 576; *USDS2*, 893.114 Narcotics/1819, Gray to Sec. of State (1/5/37).

97. Lai, *Guomin zhengfu*, pp. 410–414.

98. For an enlightening discussion of bureaucratic irregularities, see Eastman, *The Abortive Revolution*, pp. 14–20, 299–303.

99. *USDS2*, 893.00/12948, McHugh to Sec. of State, 14; 893.00/12617, Peck to Sec. of State, 3; Eastman, *The Abortive Revolution*, p. 19.

100. These irregularities are discussed in NTHA-3, No. 1030, He Zongliang to T. V. Soong (11/11/31), Liu Xiang to T. V. Soong (11/16/31).

101. NTHA-41, No. 317, Xiao Juetian to Huang Weicai (10/29/35); No. 263, "Yunmin qianyun tehuo jiakuan jiyiqie yongfei niju yusuan liebiao" (A Table of Rates and Fees for Shipments of Guizhou and Yunnan Special Goods to Fujian) (3/24/36).

102. *USDS2*, 893.114 Narcotics/738, "Opium Traffic in China" (4/28/34), 67.

103. *CYB,* 1934, p. 413; *Chinese Year Book,* 1937, pp. 526–527; Zhongguo yinhang jingji yanjiushi, ed., *Quanguo yinhang nianjian* (Chinese Banks Yearbook, 1936–1937) (Shanghai: Zhongguo yinhang yanjiushi, 1937; reprint, Washington, D.C.: Center for Chinese Research Materials, 1971), pp. 80–81; Tan, *Zhongguo zhongyao yinhang*, p. 286.

104. NTHA-41, No. 263, "Yunmin qianyun tehuo jiakuan jiyiqie yongfei niju yusuan liebiao" (3/24/36).
105. Ibid., Enc.
106. Ibid., No. 317, "Tongzhi Guizhousheng jinzheng banfa" (Regulations for Controlling the Administration of Opium Suppression in Guizhou) (9/30/35).
107. Tan, *Zhongguo zhongyao yinhang*, pp. 283–285.
108. *LON*, C.290.M.176.1936.XI, 65; *Jinyan huikan* 1 (3 June 1937): "Baogao," 30–31; Tamagna, *Banking and Finance in China*, pp. 129–130.
109. Tamagna, *Banking and Finance in China*, p. 130; Tan, *Zhongguo zhongyao yinhang*, p. 285; *Shenbao*, 7 Feb. 1936, 3.
110. Zhonguo yinhang jingji yanjiushi, *Quangguo yinhang nianjian*, p. 80.
111. Young, *China's Nation-Building Effort*, pp. 239–261, 412–413.
112. Zhonguo yinhang jingji yanjiushi, *Quangguo yinhang nianjian*, pp. 80–81; Tan, *Zhongguo zhongyao yinhang*, pp. 281–285. H. H. Kung was appointed chairman of the board on 26 March 1935. The other board members during 1933–1937 were Ye Qiutang, Zhou Peizhen, Guo Waifang, Xu Jizhuang, Xu Fu, Zhou Cangbo, Mai Shigu, Zhou Xingtang, Pu Zhengdong, Mao Bingli, Zhu Kongyang, and Zhao Jiyan.
113. For documents written by Wang Chengying as director of the Guizhou Branch Opium Suppression Supervisory Bureau to the Hankou Main Bureau, see NTHA-41, No. 356 (3), Wang Chengying to Huang Weicai (5/5/36); and No. 356 (4), Wang Chengying to Huang Weicai (6/17/36). Li Jihong served as director of the Opium Suppression Office in Nanjing in 1927 and as a National Opium Prohibition Committee member from 1928 to 1935; he was dispatched to Taiwan to study the Japanese opium monopoly in 1931; and he was director of the failed Opium Smuggling Prevention Department monopoly, director of the Hankou Main Bureau in 1934–1935, a member of the Central Commission for Opium Suppression in 1935–1937, and finally resident supervisor of the Guangdong Opium Suppression Committee in 1936–1937.
114. His predecessors were Yuan Zuming (1922–1925), Peng Hanzhang (1925–1929), and Mao Guangxiang (1929–1932). See Ma, *Dupin zai Zhongguo*, pp. 109–110.
115. Marshall, "Opium and the Politics of Gangsterism," 26; Hall, *Yunnan Provincial Faction*, p. 172. Hall quotes from a *Zhongyang ribao* article that stated that Wang Jialie was flown out of Guiyang in Zhang Xueliang's personal aircraft to Hankou, while Marshall claims that Wang fled south with his armies. However, it appears that a good number of Wang's troops (not Wang himself) under warlord Yu Guozhai moved into the Guizhou-Guangxi border area and most likely allied with the forces of the Southwest Political Council following the reorganization of the provincial government. See *USDS2*, 893.114 Narcotics/1100, "RE: Opium Revenue of Kweichow Province" (3/19/35); 893.114/1139, "RE: Opium Situation in Kwangsi Province" (4/26/35). For Li Zhonggong's tenure on the General/Central Commission for Opium Suppression, see Zhang, *Guomin zhengfu zhiguan nianbiao*, pp. 345–346.

116. *NCH*, 10 April 1935, 53.
117. *Zhonghua minguo shishi jiyao* (Jan.–June 1935), 345.
118. NTHA-41, No. 231 (4), Xiao Juetian to Huang Weicai (12/7/35); No. 197, Xiao Juetian to Li Jihong (10/28/35); No. 317, Xiao Juetian to Huang Weicai (10/29/35). The main bureau was located at Guiyang; an agency at Anshun; several general affairs departments at Bijie, Xingyi, Zhuofeng, Dushan, Zhenyuan, Tongren, and Zunyi; plus a supervised transport substation at Xiasi.
119. NTHA-41, No. 196, Xiao Juetian to Li Jihong (10/12/35).
120. Although two brigades of smuggling prevention soldiers were ordered by Chiang, by mid-December they had still not been deployed. According to Xiao Juetian, the local Baoantuan (Peace Preservation Corps) were supposed to have assumed these duties until the units could be assembled. But owing to mopping-up operations being conducted against the Communists, they were unable to comply with this order, and smuggling was a big problem until early 1936. See NTHA-41, No. 146, Xiao Juetian to Huang Weicai (12/13/35).
121. Marshall, "Opium and the Politics of Gangsterism," 26–27; Ma, *Dupin zai Zhongguo*, pp. 130–131; Eastman, *The Abortive Revolution*, pp. 252–262; Lary, *Region and Nation*, pp. 197–198; Hall, *Yunnan Provincial Faction*, pp. 136–140, 179–180.
122. NTHA-41, No. 317, "Tongzhi Guizhousheng Jinzheng Banfa."
123. Three Cantonese merchants named Yong Anli, Guang Rongtai, and Wan Xiangzhuang made all purchases in Guizhou. See NTHA-41, No. 356 (3), Wang Chengying to Huang Weicai (5/5/36). American consular reports from mid-1936 likewise indicate that Guizhou opium exported to Guangxi was only 15 percent of its former volume. See *USDS2*, 893.114 Narcotics/1683, Bodre to Sec. of State (9/2/36), Enc. 8.
124. *USDS2*, 893.114 Narcotics/1598, Johnson to Sec. of State (4/30/36).
125. Levich, *The Kwangsi Way*, p. 243; *CWR*, 13 June 1936, 41, 45–46.
126. *CWR*, 13 June 1936, 41, 45–46.
127. For an informative survey of Guomindang road construction, see Wang Qinyu, *Jindai Zhongguo de daolu jianshe* (Railroad and Highway Construction in Modern China) (Hong Kong: Longmen shudian, 1969); Leang-li T'ang, *Reconstruction in China: A Record of Progress and Achievement in Facts and Figures* (Shanghai: China United Press, 1935), pp. 217–236. Pertinent telegrams from Chiang Kai-shek to various military and civil officials concerning the massive highway construction project can be found in Zhongguo Guomindang, *Zhonghua minguo zhongyao shiliao chubian*, vol. 3, pp. 328–329.
128. Eastman, *The Abortive Revolution*, pp. 251-262; Young, *China's Nation-Building Effort*, pp. 254-256.
129. *USDS2*, 893.114 Narcotics/1547, "Stilwell Report" (3/5/35); Marshall, "Opium and the Politics of Gangsterism," 25.
130. *Jinyan huikan* 1 (3 June 1937): "Baogao," 12; *Chinese Year Book*, 1937, p. 1165; *CWR*, 15 August 1936, 394–395.
131. NTHA-41, No. 225 (3); No. 241, Xue Zhendong to Huang Weicai (9/30/36); No. 471 (5) Wu Hefu to Huang Weicai (5/1/37).

132. *Jinyan huikan* 1 (3 June 1937): "Zhuanzai," 9–13; *NCH*, 13 Jan. 1937, 70; *CWR*, 3 April 1937, 175–176.

133. NTHA-41, No. 164, "Nanyang reyapian zhuanmai zhidu diaocha" (Investigation of the Boiled-Opium Monopoly Systems in Southeast Asia) (10/9/37); *LON*, C.127.M.79.1939.XI, 3–4; *USDS2*, 893.114 Narcotics/2085, Treasury Dept. to Fuller (10/5/37), Enc. 1.

134. NTHA-41, No. 247, Huang Weicai to Shanghai, Anhui, Jiangxi, and Henan Agencies, Jiujiang, Anqing, and Datong General Affairs Departments (9/7/36), Huang Jiming to Huang Weicai (9/14/36).

135. *USDS2*, 893.114 Narcotics/2012, "Narcotics Traffic in Hankow" (7/3/37), 8.

136. LON, C.277.M.144.1935.XI, 85; C.76.M.31.1938.XI, 11–12, C.127.M.79.1939.XI; *USDS2*, 893.114 Narcotics/2012, "Narcotics Traffic in Hankow" (7/3/37). The figure for 1937 was a guess from Zhong Ketuo and about one-half of the actual total (he was estimating the amount that went directly to Chiang).

137. *China Christian Year Book*, 1934–1935, p. 349; *USDS2*, 893.114 Narcotics/2012, "Narcotics Traffic in Hankow" (7/3/37), 8.

138. Merrill, *Japan and the Opium Menace*, p. 33.

139. Young, *China's Nation-Building Effort*, appendix 1, pp. 433–435.

Conclusion

1. *LON*, C.176.M.123.1937.XI, 12.

2. *LON*, C.127.M.79.1939.XI, Annex, 31–32.

3. *CWR*, 24 April 1934, 340. The Red Spears were a village self-defense militia association that had branches throughout Anhui, Henan, Shandong, and Jiangsu. See Elizabeth J. Perry, *Rebels and Revolutionaries in North China, 1845–1945* (Stanford, Calif.: Stanford University Press, 1980), pp. 152–207.

4. *LON*, C.76.M.31.1938.XI, 11; C.127.M.79.1939.XI, 3, 15; *USDS2*, 893.114 Narcotic/1147, Josselyn to Sec. of State (5/7/35), 2.

5. *Dagongbao*, 26 April 1935; *USDS2*, 893.114 Narcotics/1147, Josselyn to Sec. of State (5/7/35), Enc.

6. *LON*, C.277.M.144.1935.XI, 85–87; C.315.M.211.1937.XI, 54–56.

7. NTHA-41 *(2)*, No. 75, "Jinyan nianjian 1937," 58; Lai, *Guomin zhengfu*, p. 237; Zhu, *Yapian yu jindai Zhongguo*, p. 386.

8. *LON*, C.290.M.176.1936.XI, 63.

9. NTHA-41, No. 196, Xiao Juetian to Li Jihong (10/12/35); NTHA-41 *(2)*, No. 75, "Jinyan nianjian 1937," 58; Lai, *Guomin zhengfu*, p. 237; Zhu, *Yapian yu jindai Zhongguo*, p. 386.

10. The actual figure was at least 80,000 *dan*. See NTHA-41, No. 197, Zhong Boyi/Liu Xiang to Chiang Kai-shek (7/9/37); NTHA-41 *(2)*, No. 75, "Jinyan nianjian 1937," 58; Lai, *Guomin zhengfu*, p. 237; Zhu, *Yapian yu jindai Zhongguo*, p. 386.

11. *LON*, C.127.M.79.1939.XI, 12.

12. *LON*, C.249.M.147.1938.XI, 55; Zhu, *Yapian yu jindai Zhongguo*, pp. 419–440;

Merrill, *Japan and the Opium Menace*, pp. 100–110; Thomas D. Reins, "China and the International Politics of Opium, 1900–1937: The Impact of Reform Revenue, and the Unequal Treaties" (Ph.D. dissertation, Claremont Graduate School, 1981), pp. 265–268; Sun Bang, Yu Haiying, and Li Shaobo, eds., *Weiman shiliao congshu* (A Collection of Historical Materials on Manchukuo), vol. 4 (Changchun: Jilin renmin chubanshe, 1993), pp. 681–732.

13. *LON*, C.277.M.144.1935.XI, 82; C.176.M.123.1937.XI, 43; C.78.M.31.1938.XI, 20; C.127.M.79.1939.XI, 24–25; Zhu, *Yapian yu jindai Zhongguo*, pp. 390–397; Lai, *Guomin zhengfu*, pp. 270–300.

14. Lai, *Guomin zhengfu*, p. 145; Zhu, *Yapian yu jindai Zhongguo*, p. 392.

15. *LON*, C.277.M.144.1935.XI, 82; C.176.M.123.1937.XI, 43; C.78.M.31.1938.XI, 20; C.127.M.79.1939.XI, 24–25; Zhu, *Yapian yu jindai Zhongguo*, pp. 390–397; Lai, *Guomin zhengfu*, pp. 270–300.

16. Ibid.

17. Zhongguo Guomindang, *Geming wenxian*, vol. 93, pp. 70–73.

18. Wang Zuxiang, *Weisheng xingzheng sanshinian suoyi* (Fragmentary Recollections from Thirty Years of Public Health Administration) (Taibei: Academia Sinica, 1953), pp. 36–39.

19. Lai, *Guomin zhengfu*, pp. 165–169, 339–341; *USDS2*, 893.114 Narcotics/2217, Josselyn to Sec. of State (3/8/38); Gao Yingdu, ed., *Zhonghua minguo neizhengzhi* (A Record of Internal Affairs in the Republic of China), vol. 2 (Taibei: Zhonghua wenhua chubanshe, 1957), pp. 263–272.

20. Sun Fengyu, "Zhong-Ri zhanzheng qijian Riben zai-Hua yapian zhengce," pp. 104–150; Merrill, *Japan and the Opium Menace*, pp. 158–161; Sun Bang, et al., *Weiman shiliao congshu*, vol. 4, pp. 681–731.

21. Chen Yongfa, "Hongtaiyang xiade yingsuhua: Yapian maoyi yu Yan'an moshi" (Poppies under a Red Sun: The Opium Trade and the Yan'an Way), *Xinshixue* 1.4 (Dec. 1990): 41–117; *idem*, "Between Survival and Ideology: The CCP Commercial Experience in Yan'an" (unpublished paper, 1996).

22. Yongming Zhou, "Nationalism, Identity, and State Building: Anti-Drug Crusades in Communist China, 1949–1952" (unpublished paper presented at the Conference on Opium in East Asian History, 1830–1945, University of Toronto–York University, Toronto, Ontario, 9–10 May 1997); Ronald D. Renard, *The Burmese Connection: Illegal Drugs and the Making of the Golden Triangle* (Boulder: Lynne Rienner Publishers, 1996), pp. 53–56.

23. Fo Shih, *An Exposure of Chinese Communist Drug Dealing in the "Golden Triangle"* (Taibei: Hsueh Hai Publishers, 1978), p. 34; Renard, *The Burmese Connection*, p. 71.

24. Ibid., *Honolulu Advertiser*, 21 July 1996, A-11.

25. *International Herald Tribune*, 28 May 1997, 4; *New Straits Times*, 5 June 1997, 22.

Glossary

Anhua Gongsi 安華公司
annei rangwai 安內攘外

Bai Chongxi 白崇禧
baidikuan 白地款
Bai Zhiying 白芝英
Banshichu 辦事處
baoshang 包商
baozhengjin 保證金
Ba-Zi yundan 巴秭運單
Beifa 北閥
biantu 邊土
buzheng chuanshui 補征川稅

Cai Yuanpei 蔡元培
Caizheng Tongchouchu 財政統籌處
Cang Zhiping 藏之平
Cao Rulin 曹汝霖
changji 娼妓
Changjiang 長江
Chao Dianzhi 超典之
"Chengban texu caiyun yantu heyue" 承辦特許採運煙土合約
Chen Lifu 陳立夫
Chen Shaogui 陳紹嫣

Chen Shaokuan 陳紹寬
Chiang Kai-shek (Jiang Jieshi) 蔣介石
Chuan-E Lianyun Banfa 川鄂聯運辦法
Chuan-Qian-E Lianyun Banfa 川黔鄂聯運辦法
chuantu 川土
cungen 存根

Dagongbao 大公報
dan 石, 擔
Daoguang 道光
datu 大土
Deng Xiaoping 鄧小平
diaochafei 調查費
Duan Qirui 段棋瑞
dubo 賭博
duikan 對勘
dushen 賭神
Du Yuesheng 杜月笙

fabi 法幣
fakuan 罰款
Fakuanju 罰款局
fangqu 防區
Fan Qiwu 范其務

213

fangzhao lianghu banfa 仿照兩湖辦法

fatuan 法團

fengtiao 封條

Feng Yuxiang 馮玉祥

fenhao 分號

fenqi jinzhong shengfen 分期禁種省份

fenzhuang 分庄

Fudian Yinhang 富滇銀行

fujiashui 附加稅

Fuzhoushi Jinyanju 福州市禁煙局

fuzhuangfei 服裝費

gantu 甘土

gao 膏

gaoliang 高粱

gaoliangjiu 高粱酒

Gao Liaoshi 高廖氏

Gao Ying 高瑛

geda 各答

Gelaohui 哥老會

gongan jiaoyu teshui fujuan 公安教育特稅附捐

Gongcheng Gongsi 公誠公司

Gonggu Xi'nanji 鞏固西南計

gongyun 公運

gongzhan 公棧

guandu shangban 官督商辦

Guangyun Gongsi 廣運公司

gunzishang 滾子商

guofu 國父

guohua 國花

guojia zhongyao zhi xiangyuan 國家重要之餉源

Guomindang 國民黨

Guo Rudong 郭汝棟

Gu Ziren 顧子仁

hang 行

hangshang 行商

Hankou Teye Gonghui 漢口特業公會

Hankou Teye Qinglihui 漢口特業清理會

He Baohua 何葆華

He Chengjun 何成濬

He Jian 何鍵

heimi 黑米

He Yingqin 何應欽

Hongbang 紅幫

hongtu 紅土

Hu Hanmin 胡漢民

Hu Shize 胡世澤

hua 花

Huanghe 黃河

Huang Jiahui 黃嘉惠

Huang Jiechu 黃傑初

Huang Jinrong 黃金榮

Huang Juezi 黃爵滋

Huang Weicai 黃爲材

Huang Yaoting 黃耀廷

Huang Zhenxing 黃振興

huasi weigong 化私爲公

Huihai Shiye Yinhang 匯海實業銀行

huipiao 匯票

huishui 匯水

hujidui 護緝隊

huodan 貨單

huzhao 護照

jianchasuo 檢查所

Jiandu Weiyuanhui 監督委員會

Jiang'an 江安

Jiangsu Quansheng Teshuiju 江蘇全省特稅局

Jianguansuo 監管所

jianshang 奸商

jiaofei shengfen 剿匪省份

jiaohe　繳核

Jiaqing　嘉慶

jieyansuo　戒煙所

jieyan yaopin　戒煙藥品

jieyanyuan　戒煙院

Jindu Shishi Banfa　禁毒實施辦法

jinjue　禁絕

jinyan　禁煙

Jinyan Chajichu　禁煙查緝處

Jinyanchu　禁煙處

jinyan duban　禁煙督辦

Jinyan Dubanshu　禁煙督辦署

Jinyan Duchachu　禁煙督察處

Jinyanfa　禁煙法

Jinyanfa Shixing Tiaoli　禁煙法施行條例

jinyan fensuo　禁煙分所

Jinyan gongbao　禁煙公報

Jinyan Jinianri　禁煙紀念日

Jinyanju　禁煙局

Jinyan Shishi Banfa　禁煙實施辦法

Jinyan Tiaoli　禁煙條例

Jinyan Weiyuanhui　禁煙委員會

Jinyan weiyuanhui gongbao　禁煙委員會公報

Jinyan Weiyuanhui Zongchu　禁煙委員會總處

Jinyan Zongchu　禁煙總處

jinyan zongjian　禁煙總監

Jinyan Zongju　禁煙總局

Jin Yapianyan Ling　禁鴉片煙令

jisibing　緝私兵

Jiyi Zhuanyun Gongsi　濟宜專運公司

jizhengsuo　稽徵所

Judu Weiyuanhui　拒毒委員會

"Judu yixun"　拒毒遺訓

juedui jinyan　絕對禁煙

juedui jinyan qucheng　絕對禁煙區城

juedui jinzhong qucheng　絕對禁種區城

Jufeng Maoyi Gongsi　聚豐貿易公司

junfa　軍閥

Junjing Jianchachu　軍警檢查處

junyongpiao　軍用票

juzishu　橘子樹

keshang　客商

Kong Xiangxi　孔祥熙

Kwantung (Guandong)　關東

lanjuan　懶捐

li　禮

liandan　聯單

liang　兩

Liangguang Yapian Zhuanmaiju　兩廣鴉片專賣局

Lianghu　兩湖

liaozi　料子

Li Denghui　李登輝

Li Hongzhang　李鴻章

Li Jihong　李基鴻

Li Jichen　李濟琛

lijin　釐金

Li Liejun　李烈鈞

Li Muqing　李慕青

Li Yuanhong　黎元洪

Li Zhonggong　李仲公

Li Zongren　李宗仁

lingjianshang　零剪商

lingshoushang　零售商

Lin Zexu　林則徐

Liu Chengxun　劉成勳

Liu Zhenhuan　劉震寰

liudong yanguan　流動煙館

Liunian jinjue yapian zhi jueyian　六年禁絕鴉片之決議案

Liunian Jinyan Jihua　六年禁煙計劃

Liu Ruiheng 劉瑞恒
Liu Wenhui 劉文輝
Liu Xiang 劉湘
Long Yun 龍雲
Lu Diping 魯滌平
Lu Yongxiang 盧永祥
Luo Jialun 羅家倫
Luo Yunyan 羅運炎

Ma Kongfan 馬空凡
Mao Guangxiang 毛光翔
Mao Zedong 毛澤東
miaojuan 苗捐
Minsheng Shiye Gongsi 民生實業公司
mu 畝

Niu Yongjian 紐永建
Nongmin Yinhang 農民銀行

Paogehui 袍哥會
Peng Hanzhang 彭漢章
pifashang 批發商
Pingjia Weiyuanhui 平價委員會
pingyuanyan 平原煙
pinyin 拼音

qian 錢
qiantu 黔土
qianzhuang 錢莊
Qingbang 青幫
Qinghongbang 青紅幫
qingjie yundong 清潔運動
qingli 清理
Qingli Lianghu Teshuichu 清理兩湖特稅處
Qingli Hubei Teshuichu 清理湖北特稅處
Qingli Teyehui 清理特業會
Qingmiaohui 青苗會

Quansheng Jinyan Zongju 全省禁煙總局

regao 熱膏
regaoshang 熱膏商
Regao Tongyehui 熱膏同業會

Sanxing Gongsi 三鑫公司
Shanghai Gonganju 上海公安局
Shanghaishi Jinyan Weiyuanhui 上海市禁煙委員會
Shanghai Teye Gonghui 上海特業公會
shangren caituan 商人財團
shanyan 山煙
Shenbao 申報
shengguan facai 生官發財
Shen Gongli 沈公儷
shengtu 生土
Shisheng Jinyan Duchachu 十省禁煙督察處
Shi Ying 石瑛
Shi Zhaoji 施肇基
Shoudu Suqing Yanduchang Sanhai Yundong 首都肅清煙賭娼三害運動
Shoudu Suqing Yanduchang Lianhe Xuanchuan Dahui 首都肅清煙賭娼聯合宣傳大會
Shoudu Suqing Yandu Weiyuanhui 首都肅清煙毒委員會
shouxufei 手續費
shuangqiangbing 雙槍兵
Shuichehui 水車會
shuidan 稅單
siliandan 四聯單
sishiba jia 四十八家
Song Ziliang 宋子良
Soong, T. V. (Song Ziwen) 宋子文
Sun Chuanfang 孫傳芳

Sun Ke　孫科
Sun Wen (Sun Yat-sen)　孫文 (中山)
Sun Yuan　孫垣

Tang Jiyao　唐繼堯
Tang Shaoyi　唐紹儀
Tang Shengzhi　唐生智
tankuan　攤款
tanxinchu　談心處
Tan Yankai　譚延闓
tehuo　特貨
tehuo fashousuo　特貨發售所
Teshe Zhuanju　特設專局
teshui　特稅
Teshui Zongju　特稅總局
texu zhengfei　特許證費
teye gongsi　特業公司
teye shangren　特業商人
Teye Qinglihui　特業清理會
tianfushui　田附稅
tidan　提單
tong　桐
Tongzhi Guizhousheng Jinzheng
　　Banfa　統制貴州省禁政辦法
tu　土
tuanti　團體
tugao　土膏
tugaodian　土膏店
tuhao lieshen　土豪劣紳

waisheng　外省
Wang Chengying　王澂瑩
Wang Jialie　王家烈
Wang Jingqi　王景歧
Wang Jingwei　王精衛
Wang Quanlin　王泉麟
Wang Zhongshi　王鐘氏
Wang Zuxiang　王祖祥
wannong　玩弄
wanquan jinjue　完全禁絕

Wanxian Chajichu　萬縣查緝處
Weijin Wupin Chajichu　違禁物品
　　查緝處
Wen Qun　文群
Wu Chaoshu　伍朝樞
wugu　五穀
Wu Liande　伍連德
Wu Peifu　吳佩孚
wuquan　物權
wushang bujian　無商不奸

Xia Douyin　夏斗寅
xian　縣
Xiao Juetian　蕭覺天
xiaoqian　消遣
xiaotu　小土
xiehui　協會
Xijiang　西江
Xingyuan Gongsi　興源公司
Xinhankou ribao　新漢口日報
Xinhua Shiye Gongsi　新華實業公司
Xinshenghuo Yundong　新生活運動
Xinshenghuo Yundong Cujinhui　新
　　生活運動促進會
Xinwenbao　新聞報
Xinyuan Gongsi　信遠公司
Xiong Shihui　熊式輝
Xiong Zijia　熊子嘉
Xiyapian hui shangyin, chouyapianshui
　　yehui shangyin; yapian yanyin yijie,
　　yapian shuiyin nanjie　吸鴉片會
　　上癮抽鴉片稅也會上癮鴉片
　　煙癮易戒鴉片稅癮難戒
Xu Naiji　許乃濟
Xu Shichang　徐世昌
Xue Dubi　薛篤弼

yamen　衙門
yanbang　煙幫
yanduchang　煙賭娼

Yan Baohang　閻寶航
Yan Xishan　閻錫山
Yang Hu　楊虎
Yang Shuzhuang　楊樹莊
Yang Tong　楊同
Yangtze (Yangzi)　揚子
yanguan　煙館
yangui　煙鬼
Yang Ximin　楊希閔
Yang Xiyan　楊西巖
Yang Yongtai　楊永泰
yanhao　煙號
yanmiao fajin　煙苗罰金
yanqiang　煙槍
yanshang　煙商
yanyaosuo　煙藥所
yanzhen　煙針
yanzhuang　煙庄
yanziwo　燕子窩
yaopin　藥品
Yaopinshang Keyou Gonghui　藥品
　商客友公會
yapian　鴉片
yapian dawang　鴉片大王
yashi　雅室
Ye Chucang　葉楚傖
yideng yipiao　一燈一票
yingchoupin　應酬品
yingsuhua　罌粟花
Yongding Gongsi　永定公司
Yongzheng　雍正
Youjiang　右江
yuan　圓
Yuan Shikai　袁世凱
Yuan Zuming　袁祖銘
Yuchuan　裕川
Yu Da　於達
Yu-E-Wan-Gan Sisheng Nongmin
　Yinhang　豫鄂晚贛四省農民
　銀行

yujin yuzheng　寓禁於征
yunshang　運商
yuntu　雲土
yuzhengjuan　預征卷

Zeng Guofan　曾國藩
Zhang Fakui　張發奎
Zhang Xiaolin　張嘯林
Zhang Xueliang　張學良
Zhang Zhijiang　張之江
Zhang Zongchang　張宗昌
Zhang Zuolin　張作霖
zhaoshang　招商
Zhao Xi'en　趙錫恩
zhekou　折扣
Zheng Hongnian　鄭洪年
Zhenjiang Baoandui　鎮江保安隊
zhizi　枳子
Zhonghua Guomin Juduhui　中華國
　民拒毒會
Zhong Ketuo　鐘可託
Zhongxing Gongsi　中興公司
Zhongyang Jinyan Weiyuanhui　中央
　禁煙委員會
Zhongyang ribao　中央日報
zhongyan paizhaoshui　重煙牌照
　稅
Zhou Enlai　周恩來
Zhou Lisheng　周利生
Zhou Yinren　周蔭人
Zhou Yongneng　周雍能
Zhuanmai Zongju　專賣總局
zhuanyunsuo　專運所
Zhu Zhaoxin　朱兆莘
zonghui　總會
Zongli yixun jinjue yapian'an　總理遺
　訓禁絕鴉片案
Zuojiang　左江
zuozhuang　坐庄
Zuo Zongtang　左宗堂

Bibliography

The Annual Report of the International Anti-Opium Association. 4.1 (May 1924). Beijing: International Anti-Opium Association, 1924.

Arnold, Julean. *China, A Commercial and Industrial Handbook*. Washington, D.C.: Department of Commerce, 1926.

Bao Ying, Zhang Shijie, and Hu Zhenya, eds. *Qingbang yu Hongmen dazhuan* (Biography of the Green and Red Gangs). Taibei: Zhouzhi wenhua, 1994.

Baumler, Alan. "Playing with Fire: The Nationalist Government and Opium in China, 1927–1941." Ph.D. dissertation, University of Illinois at Urbana-Champaign, 1997.

———. "Playing with Fire: The Nationalist Government and Popular Anti-Opium Agitation in 1927–28." *Republican China* 21.1 (Nov. 1995): 43–91.

Bedeski, Robert E. *State-Building in Modern China: The Kuomintang in the Prewar Period*. Berkeley: Institute of East Asian Studies, University of California, 1981.

Bell, Lynda S. "Farming, Sericulture, and Peasant Rationality in Wuxi County in the Early Twentieth Century." In *Chinese History in Economic Perspective*, edited by Thomas G. Rawski and Lillian M. Li, pp. 207–242. Berkeley: University of California Press, 1992.

Bergère, Marie-Claire. "The Chinese Bourgeoisie, 1911–1937." In *The Cambridge History of China*, vol. 12, edited by John K. Fairbank, pp. 722–825. Cambridge: Cambridge University Press, 1983.

Bianco, Lucien. "Peasant Uprisings against Poppy Tax Collection in Su Xian and Lingbi (Anhui) in 1932." *Republican China* 21.1 (Nov. 1995): 93–128.

———. "The Responses of Opium-Growers to Eradication Campaigns and Poppy Tax: China, 1900–1945." Unpublished paper presented at the Conference on Opium in East Asian History, 1830–1945, University of Toronto–York University, Toronto, Ontario, 9–10 May 1997.

Bisson, T. A. *Japan in China*. New York: The MacMillan Company, 1938.

Boorman, Howard L., and Richard C. Howard, eds. *Biographical Dictionary of Republican China*. 5 vols. New York: Columbia University Press, 1967–1971.

Booth, Martin. *Opium: A History*. London: Simon and Schuster, 1996.

Buck, John L. *Land Utilization in China: A Study of 16,786 Farms in 168 Localities, and 38,256 Farm Families in Twenty-Two Provinces in China, 1929–1933*. Nanjing: Nanjing University, 1937; reprint, Taibei: Southern Materials Center, 1986.

Caizhengbu caizheng nianjian bianzuanchu, comp. *Caizheng nianjian* (Ministry of Finance Yearbook). 2 vols. Shanghai: Shangwu yinshuguan, 1935.

Central Commission for Opium Suppression, ed. *Traffic in Opium and Other Dangerous Drugs, Annual Report*. Nanjing: Central Commission for Opium Suppression, 1935–1939.

Ch'en, Jerome. "The Communist Movement, 1927–1937." In *The Cambridge History of China*, vol. 13, edited by John K. Fairbank and Albert Feuerwerker, pp. 168–229. Cambridge: Cambridge University Press, 1986.

———. *The Military-Gentry Coalition: China under the Warlords*. Toronto: University of Toronto–York University Joint Centre on Modern East Asia, 1979.

Chen Yongfa. "Between Survival and Ideology: The CCP Commercial Experience in Yan'an." Unpublished paper, 1996.

———. "Hongtaiyang xiade yingsuhua: Yapian maoyi yu Yan'an moshi" (Poppies under a Red Sun: The Opium Trade and the Yan'an Way). *Xinshixue* (New Studies in History), 1.4 (Dec. 1990): 41–117.

Ch'i, Hsi-sheng. *The Chinese Warlord System: 1916–1928*. Washington, D.C.: Center for Research in Social Systems, American University, 1969.

———. "Financial Constraints on the Northern Expedition." In *Zhonghua minguo chuqi lishi yantaohui lunwenji, 1912–1927* (Proceedings from the Conference on the Early Republic, 1912–1927), edited by Zhongyang yanjiuyuan jindaishi yanjiusuo, vol. 1, pp. 249–269. Taibei: Academia Sinica, 1984.

———. *Warlord Politics in China, 1916–1928*. Stanford, Calif.: Stanford University Press, 1976.

The China Christian Yearbook. Edited by Rev. Frank Rawlinson. Shanghai: Christian Literature Society, 1924–1937.

China Critic. Shanghai, 1928–1937.

China Weekly Review. Shanghai, 1924–1937.

The China Year Book. Edited by H. G. W. Woodhead. Tianjin: The Tientsin Press, 1924–1930; Shanghai: North China Daily News and Herald, 1931–1937.

Chinese Recorder. Shanghai, 1924–1937.

The Chinese Year Book. Edited by Gui Zhongshu. Shanghai: The China Critic, 1936–1939.

Chow, Tse-tsung. *The May Fourth Movement: Intellectual Revolution in Modern China*. Cambridge, Mass.: Harvard University Press, 1960.

Coble, Parks M., Jr. *Facing Japan: Chinese Politics and Japanese Imperialism, 1931–37*. Cambridge, Mass.: Harvard University Press, 1991.

———. *The Shanghai Capitalists and the Nationalist Government, 1927–1937*. Cambridge, Mass.: Harvard University Press, 1986.

Cocteau, Jean. *Opium: Journal d'une desintoxication.* Paris: Delamain et Boutelleau, 1931.

Crop Reports. Nanjing, 1931–1937.

Dagongbao (L'Impartial). Tianjin, 1928–1937.

Davis, Joel. *Endorphins: New Waves in Brain Chemistry.* Garden City, N.Y.: The Dial Press, 1984.

DeAngelis, Richard C. "Jacob Gould Schurman, Sun Yat-sen, and the Canton Customs Crisis." *Jindaishi yanjiusuo jikan* (Institute of Modern History Quarterly), 8 (Oct. 1979): 253–293.

Deng Qingyou, comp. *Junzheng zhiguanzhi* (A Compilation of Officials during the Period of Military Rule). 2 vols. Lanzhou: Gansu renmin chubanshe, 1985.

Department of Agriculture and Economics, College of Agriculture and Forestry, University of Nanking, and the National Flood Relief Commission, eds. *The 1931 Flood in China.* Nanking: University of Nanking, 1931.

Dirlik, Arif. "The Ideological Foundations of the New Life Movement: A Study in Counterrevolution." *Journal of Asian Studies* 34.4 (August 1975): 945–980.

Dongfang zazhi (Eastern Miscellany). Shanghai, 1924–1937.

Duara, Prasenjit. *Culture, Power, and the State: Rural North China, 1900–1942.* Stanford, Calif.: Stanford University Press, 1988.

Eastman, Lloyd E. *The Abortive Revolution: China under Nationalist Rule, 1927–1937.* Cambridge, Mass.: Harvard University Press, 1974.

————. *Family, Fields and Ancestors: Constancy and Change in China's Social and Economic History, 1550–1949.* Oxford: Oxford University Press, 1988.

————. "The May Fourth Movement as a Historical Turning Point." In *Perspectives on Modern China*, edited by Kenneth Lieberthal, Joyce Kallgren, Roderick MacFarquhar, and Frederic Wakeman, Jr., pp. 123–138. Armonk, N.Y.: M. E. Sharpe, 1991.

————. "Nationalist China during the Nanking decade." In *The Nationalist Era in China, 1927–1949*, edited by Lloyd E. Eastman, Jerome Ch'en, Suzanne Pepper, and Lyman P. Van Slyke, pp. 1–52. Cambridge: Cambridge University Press, 1991.

Eisenlohr, L. E. S. *International Narcotics Control.* London: George Allen and Unwin, 1934.

Fairbank, John K., ed. *Chinese World Order: Traditional Chinese Foreign Relations.* Cambridge, Mass.: Harvard University Press, 1968.

Feuerwerker, Albert. *Economic Trends in the Republic of China, 1912–1949.* Ann Arbor: Center for Chinese Studies, University of Michigan, 1977.

Fewsmith, Joseph. *Party, State, and Local Elites in Republican China: Merchant Organizations and Politics in Shanghai, 1890–1930.* Honolulu: University of Hawai'i Press, 1985.

Finch, Percy. *Shanghai and Beyond.* New York: Charles Scribner's Sons, 1953.

Flynn, Dennis O., and Atruro Giráldez. "Born with a 'Silver Spoon': The Origin of World Trade in 1571." *Journal of World History* 6.2 (Fall 1995): 201–221.

Gao Yingdu, ed. *Zhonghua minguo neizhengzhi* (A Record of Internal Affairs in the Republic of China). Taibei: Zhonghua wenhua chubanshe, 1957.

Giles, Herbert G. *Some Truths about Opium.* Cambridge: W. Heffer and Sons, 1923.

Gillin, Donald G. *Warlord: Yen Hsi-shan in Shansi Province, 1911–1949*. Princeton, N.J.: Princeton University Press, 1966.

Great Britain, Foreign Office. British Foreign Office File 415: Confidential Print, "Opium." In *The Opium Trade, 1910–1941*. Facsimile reprint. 6 vols. Wilmington: Scholarly Resources, 1974.

Grover, Gretchen G. "American's Controversial Opium Carriers of the 1920s." *Sea Classics* 26.1 (Jan. 1993): 18–24, 77.

Guangdongsheng caizhengting, ed. *Guangdongsheng caizheng jishi* (A Veritable Record of Financial Administration in Guangdong Province). Guangzhou: Guangdongsheng caizhengting, 1933.

Guangzhoushi shizheng gongbao (Canton Municipal Government Bulletin). Canton, 1924–1927.

Guofangbu shizhengju, comp. *Beifa jianshi* (A Concise History of the Northern Expedition). 2nd ed. Taibei: Zhengzhong shuju, 1970.

———. *Jiaofei zhanshi* (A History of Military Actions against the Communist Rebellion, 1930–1945). 6 vols. Taibei: Zhonghua dadian bianyinhui, 1967.

Guoli bianyiguan sanmin zhuyi dacidian bianshen weiyuanhui, comp. *Sanmin zhuyi dacidian* (Encyclopedia of the Three Principles of the People). Taibei: Youshi wenhua shiye gongsi, 1993.

Guomin zhengfu junshi weiyuanhui weiyuanhuizhang Nanchang xingying chuli jiaofei shengfen zhengzhi gongzuo baogao (A Report by the Chairman of the National Government's Military Affairs Commission at Nanchang on Political Work in the Bandit Suppression Zones). Nanchang, 1934.

Guomin zhengfu zhujichu tongjiju, ed. *Zhonghua minguo tongji tiyao* (Statistical Abstract for the Republic of China). Nanjing: Neizhengbu, 1935.

Guoshiguan (Repository of National History). Xindian, Taiwan. Caizhengbu: Mulu 260 (Ministry of Finance: Index 260). File numbers 1457–1460.

Guowen zhoubao (National Literature Weekly). Tianjin, 1931.

Hall, J. C. S. *The Yunnan Provincial Faction, 1927–1937*. Canberra: Australian National University, 1976.

Hammer, Ronald P., Jr., ed. *The Neurobiology of Opiates*. Boca Raton: CRC Press, 1993.

Hankow Herald. Hankou, 1926–1929.

Hawkins, John A. *Opium: Addicts and Addictions*. Danville, Va.: N.p., 1937.

Hayter, Alethea. *Opium and the Romantic Imagination: Addiction and Creativity in De Quincey, Coleridge, Baudelaire and Others*. Northamptonshire: Crucible, 1988.

The Honolulu Advertiser. Honolulu, 1996.

Hsü, Dau-lin. "Chinese Local Administration under the National Government." Unpublished papers, University of Washington, 1967–1972.

Huang Kewu. "Cong Shenbao yiyao guanggao kan minchu Shanghai de yiliao wenhua yu shehui shenghuo, 1912–26" (Viewing the Medical Culture and Society of Early Republican Shanghai from the Medicinal Advertisements in *Shenbao*). *Jindaishi yanjiusuo jikan* (Institute of Modern History Quarterly), 17 (Dec. 1988): 183–185.

Huang Shaoxiong. *Wushi huiyi* (Recalling the Past Fifty Years). Shanghai: Shanghai shijie shuju, 1945.

International Herald Tribune. Singapore, 1998.

Jennings, John M. "The Opium Empire: Japan and the East Asian Drug Trade, 1895–1945." Ph.D. dissertation, University of Hawai'i, 1995.

Jinyan banyuekan (Opium Suppression Fortnightly). Nanjing, 1936–1937.

Jinyan gongbao (Opium Prohibition Bulletin). Nanjing, 1929–1930.

Jinyan huikan (Collection of Opium Suppression Literature in Commemoration of Opium Prohibition Memorial Day). Nanjing, 1937.

Jinyan weiyuanhui gongbao (National Opium Prohibition Committee Bulletin). Nanjing, 1931.

Jinyan zhuankan (Special Opium Suppression Publication). Shanghai, 1936–1937.

Johnstone, Jr., William C. *The Shanghai Problem.* Stanford, Calif.: Stanford University Press, 1937; reprint, Westport, Conn.: Hyperion Press, 1973.

Jones, Susan Mann. "Finance in Ningpo: The 'Ch'ien Chuang,' 1750–1880." In *Economic Organization in Chinese Society*, edited by W. E. Wilmott, pp. 47–78. Stanford, Calif.: Stanford University Press, 1972.

Jordan, Donald A. *The Northern Expedition: China's National Revolution of 1926–1928.* Honolulu: University of Hawai'i Press, 1976.

Judu yuekan (Opium, A National Issue). Shanghai, 1926–1936.

Kapp, Robert A. "Chungking as a Center of Warlord Power." In *The Chinese City between Two Worlds*, edited by Mark Elvin and G. William Skinner, pp. 143–170. Stanford, Calif.: Stanford University Press, 1974.

———. *Szechwan and the Chinese Republic: Provincial Militarism and Central Power, 1911–1938.* New Haven: Yale University Press, 1973.

Kennedy, Thomas L. "Mausers and the Opium Trade: The Hupeh Arsenal, 1895–1911." In *Perspectives on a Changing China*, edited by Joshua A. Fogel and William T. Rowe, pp. 113–135. Boulder: Westview Press, 1979.

King, Frank H. H. *Asian Policy, History and Development.* Hong Kong: University of Hong Kong, 1979.

———. *Money and Monetary Policy in China: 1845–1895.* Cambridge, Mass.: Harvard University Press, 1965.

Kuhn, Philip A. *Rebellion and Its Enemies in Late Imperial China: Militarization and Social Structure, 1796–1864.* Cambridge, Mass.: Harvard University Press, 1970.

Lai Shuqing, ed. *Guomin zhengfu liunian jinyan jihua jiqi chengxiao, 1935–1940* (The National Government's Six-Year Opium Suppression Plan and Its Results, 1935–1940). Taibei: Guoshiguan, 1986.

Lai Zehan. "Guangzhou geming zhengfu de jianli, 1917–1926" (Foundation of the Canton Revolutionary Government, 1917–1926). In *Zhonghua minguo chuqi lishi yantaohui lunwenji, 1912–1927* (Proceedings from the Conference on the History of the Early Republic, 1912–1927), vol. 1, pp. 363–394. Taibei: Academia Sinica, 1984.

La Motte, Ellen N. *The Ethics of Opium.* New York: The Century Co., 1924.

Lary, Diana. *Region and Nation: The Kwangsi Clique in Chinese Politics, 1925–1937.* Cambridge: Cambridge University Press, 1974.

———. *Warlord Soldiers: Chinese Common Soldiers, 1911–1937.* Cambridge: Cambridge University Press, 1985.

————. "Warlord Studies." *Modern China* 6.4 (Oct. 1980): 439–470.

Latourette, Kenneth S. *History of Christian Missions in China*. New York: Macmillan, 1929.

League of Nations. *League of Nations Documents and Publications, 1919–1946*. Category XI: Traffic in Opium and Other Dangerous Drugs. Microfilm. New Haven, Conn.: Research Publications Inc., 1970–1972.

Lee, Frederic E. *Currency, Banking, and Finance in China*. Washington, D.C.: Department of Commerce, 1926.

Levich, Eugene W. *The Kwangsi Way in Kuomintang China, 1931–1939*. Armonk, N.Y.: M. E. Sharpe, 1993.

Li Guoqi. *Minguoshi lunji* (A Collection of Articles on National History). Taibei: Nantian shuju, 1990.

————. "Song Ziwen dui Guangdong caizheng de gexin" (T. V. Soong's Reform of Guangdong's Financial Administration). In *Zhonghua minguo chuqi lishi yantaohui lunwenji, 1912–1927*, vol. 2, pp. 475–502, Taibei: Academia Sinica, 1989.

Li Wenzhi and Zhang Youyi, comps. *Zhongguo jindai nongyeshi ziliao* (Source Materials on Modern China's Agricultural History). 3 vols. Beijing: Sanlian shudian, 1957.

Lin, Man-houng. "Integrating or Disintegrating the National Economy? The Opium Market within China, 1820s–1906." Unpublished paper presented at the Conference on Opium in East Asian History, 1830–1945, University of Toronto–York University, Toronto, Ontario, 9–10 May 1997.

————. "Qingmo shehui liuxing xishi yapian yanjiu, 1773–1906" (Research into the Popularity of Opium Smoking in Late Qing China, 1773–1906). Ph.D. dissertation, National Taiwan Normal University, 1985.

Lin Mingde. "Riben dui Huabei de jingji qinlue" (The Japanese Economic Invasion of North China). *Zhongyang yanjiuyuan jindaishi yanjiu jikan* 9 (June 1990): 421–444.

Lin, W. Y. *The New Monetary System in China*. Chicago: Chicago University Press, 1936.

Liu, F. F. *A Military History of China: 1924–1929*. Princeton, N.J.: Princeton University Press, 1956.

Liu Jizeng, Mao Lei, and Yuan Jicheng, eds. *Wuhan guomin zhengfushi* (A History of the Wuhan National Government). Wuhan: Hubei renmin chubanshe, 1986.

Liu, Kwang-ching, and Richard R. Smith. "The Military Challenge: The Northwest and the Coast." In *The Cambridge History of China*, edited by John K. Fairbank and Kwang-ching Liu, vol. 11, pp. 202–273. Cambridge: Cambridge University Press, 1980.

Liu, Ta-chung, and Kung-chia Yeh. *The Economy of the Chinese Mainland: National Income and Economic Development, 1933–1959*. Princeton, N.J.: Princeton University Press, 1965.

Lo, R. Y. *The Opium Problem in the Far East*. Shanghai: Commercial Press, 1933.

Lodwick, Kathleen L. "Chinese, Missionary, and International Efforts to End the Use of Opium in China, 1890–1916." Ph.D. dissertation, University of Arizona, 1976.

Luhaijun dayuanshuai dabenying gongbao (Bulletin of the Commander in Chief of the Armed Forces Headquarters). Canton, 1924–1925.

Lutz, Jessie Gregory. *Chinese Politics and Christian Missions: The Anti-Christian Movements of 1920–28*. Notre Dame, Ind.: Cross Cultural Publications, 1988.

Ma Mozhen. *Dupin zai Zhongguo* (Drugs in China). Taibei: Kening chubanshe, 1994.

Mann, Susan M. *Local Merchants and the Chinese Bureaucracy, 1730–1950*. Stanford, Calif.: Stanford University Press, 1987.

Mao Tse-tung. *Selected Works*. 5 vols. New York: International Publishers, 1954.

Marshall, Jonathan. "Opium and the Politics of Gangsterism in Nationalist China, 1927–1945." *Bulletin of Concerned Asian Scholars* 8 (July–Sept. 1976): 19–48.

Martin, Brian G. *The Shanghai Green Gang: Politics and Organized Crime, 1919–1937*. Berkeley: University of California Press, 1996.

May, Herbert L. *Survey of Smoking Opium Conditions in the Far East*. New York: Foreign Policy Association, 1928.

McCord, Edward A. *The Power of the Gun: The Emergence of Modern Warlordism*. Berkeley: University of California Press, 1993.

McCoy, Alfred W. *The Politics of Heroin: CIA Complicity in the Global Drug Trade*. New York: Lawrence Hill Publishers, 1991.

McElderry, Andrea L. *Shanghai Old-Style Banks (Ch'ien-Chuang), 1800–1935: A Traditional Institution in a Changing Society*. Ann Arbor: University of Michigan, 1976.

Mei Zhenshao. *Chuanqi renwu Du Yuesheng* (The Legendary Du Yuesheng). Taibei: Dongcha chubanshe, 1981.

Merrill, Frederick T. *Japan and the Opium Menace*. New York: Institute of Pacific Relations and the Foreign Policy Institute, 1942.

Meyer, Kathryn, and Terry Parsinnen. *Webs of Smoke: Smugglers, Warlords, Spies, and the History of the International Drug Trade*. New York: Rowman and Littlefield Publishers, 1998.

Ministry of Finance. *Report for the 21st and 22nd Fiscal Years, July 1932 to June 1934*. Nanjing: Ministry of Finance, 1935.

Myers, Ramon H. "The Agrarian System." In *The Cambridge History of China*, edited by John K. Fairbank and Albert Feuerwerker, vol. 13, pp. 230–269. Cambridge: Cambridge University Press, 1986.

Nanjingshi zhengfu gongbao (Nanjing Municipal Government Bulletin). Nanjing, 1928–1937.

National Flood Relief Commission, ed. *Report of the National Flood Relief Commission*. Nanking: University of Nanking, 1931.

Neizhengbu, comp. *Neizheng nianjian* (Ministry of the Interior Yearbook). 2 vols. Shanghai: Shangwu yinshuguan, 1935.

Newman, R. K. "Opium Smoking in Late Imperial China: A Reconsideration." *Modern Asian Studies* 29.4 (1995): 765–794.

New Straits Times. Singapore, 1998.

North China Herald. Shanghai, 1924–1937.

Opium, A World Problem. Shanghai, 1927–1931.

Opium Cultivation and Traffic in China. Beijing, 1924–1926.

Owen, David E. *British Opium Policy in China and India*. New Haven: Yale University Press, 1934; reprint, New Haven: Archon Books, 1968.

Peking and Tientsin Times. Beijing, 1925–1934.

Perkins, Dwight H. *Agricultural Development in China, 1368–1968*. Chicago: Aldine Publishing Co., 1969.

Perry, Elizabeth J. *Rebels and Revolutionaries in North China, 1845–1945.* Stanford, Calif.: Stanford University Press, 1980.

Quanguo caizheng huiyi mishuchu, ed. *Quanguo caizheng huiyi huibian* (Proceedings from the National Financial Conference). Nanjing: Caizhengbu, 1928.

Quanguo jingji huiyi mishuchu, ed. *Quanguo jingji huiyi zhuankan* (A Special Publication of the National Economic Conference). Shanghai: Caizhengbu, 1928.

Rawski, Thomas G. *Economic Growth in Prewar China.* Berkeley: University of California Press, 1989.

Reins, Thomas D. "China and the International Politics of Opium, 1900–1937: The Impact of Reform, Revenue, and the Unequal Treaties." Ph.D. dissertation, Claremont Graduate School, 1981.

Renard, Ronald D. *The Burmese Connection: Illegal Drugs and the Making of the Golden Triangle.* Boulder: Lynne Rienner Publishers, 1996.

Report of the International Opium Commission, Shanghai, China. February 1 to February 26, 1909. 2 vols. Shanghai: North China Daily News and Herald, 1909.

Rush, James R. *Opium to Java: Revenue Farming and Chinese Enterprise in Colonial Indonesia, 1860–1910.* Ithaca, N.Y.: Cornell University Press, 1990.

Seagrave, Sterling. *The Soong Dynasty.* New York: Harper and Row, 1985.

Selden, Mark. *The Yenan Way in Revolutionary China.* Cambridge, Mass.: Harvard University Press, 1971.

Shanghai wenshi yanjiuguan, ed. *Jiu Shanghai de yanduchang* (Opium, Gambling, and Prostitution in Old Shanghai). Hong Kong: Zhongyuan chubanshe, 1989.

Shenbao (Truth Post). Shanghai, 1924–1937.

Sheridan, James E. *China in Disintegration: The Republican Era in Chinese History, 1912–1949.* New York: The Free Press, 1975.

———. *Chinese Warlord: The Career of Feng Yü-hsiang.* Stanford, Calif.: Stanford University Press, 1966.

Shi Jiashun. *Liangguang shibian zhi yanjiu* (Research into the Guangdong-Guangxi Incident). Gaoxiong, Taiwan: Fuwen tushu chubanshe, 1992.

Shibao (Times). Shanghai, 1928–1937.

Shih, Fo. *An Exposure of Chinese Communist Drug Dealing in the "Golden Triangle."* Taibei: Hsueh Hai Publishers, 1978.

Sih, Paul K. T., ed. *The Strenuous Decade: China's Nation-Building Efforts, 1927–1937.* New York: St. John's University Press, 1970.

Skinner, G. William. "Regional Urbanization in Nineteenth Century China." In *The City in Late Imperial China*, edited by G. William Skinner, pp. 211–249. Stanford, Calif.: Stanford University Press, 1977.

Slack, Edward R., Jr. "The Guomindang's Opium Policies, 1924–1937: Understanding 'Opium Suppression' in the Context of the Warlord System and the Republican Narco-economy." Ph.D. dissertation, University of Hawai'i, 1997.

Snow, Edgar. *Red Star over China.* New York: Random House, 1938; 1st revised and enlarged edition., Grove Press, 1968.

Sovik, Arne. "Church and State in Republican China: A Survey of the Relations between the Christian Churches and the Chinese Government, 1911–1945." Ph.D. dissertation, Yale University, 1952.

Spence, Jonathan D. "Opium Smoking in Ch'ing China." In *Conflict and Control in Late Imperial China*, edited by Frederic Wakeman, Jr., and Carolyn Grant, pp. 143–173. Berkeley: University of California Press, 1975.

Strand, David. *Rickshaw Beijing: City People and Politics in the 1920s*. Berkeley: University of California Press, 1989.

Su Zhongbo and Yang Zhenya, eds. *Guo-Gong liangdang guanxishi* (History of the Relationship between the National and Communist Parties). Nanjing: Jiangsu renmin chubanshe, 1990.

Sues, Ilona Ralf. *Shark's Fins and Millet*. Garden City, N.Y.: Garden City Publishing Co., 1945.

Sun Bang, Yu Haiying, and Li Shaobo, eds. *Weiman shiliao congshu* (A Collection of Historical Materials on Manchukuo). 10 vols. Changchun: Jilin renmin chubanshe, 1993.

Sun Fengyu. "Zhong-Ri zhanzheng qijian Riben zai-Hua yapian zhengce (1931–1945)" (Japanese Opium Policy in China during the Sino-Japanese War [1931–1945]). Ph.D. dissertation, National Political University (Taiwan), 1991.

Sun Wen (Sun Yat-sen). *Guofu quanji* (The Collected Works of Sun Wen, Father of the Nation). 6 vols. Revised edition. Taibei: Zhongguo Guomindang zhongyang zhixing weiyuanhui, 1961.

———. *Guofu quanji bubian* (Supplementary Volume to the Collected Works of Sun Wen, Father of the Nation). Taibei: Zhongguo Guomindang zhongyang zhixing weiyuanhui, 1981.

Sun Xiufu. "Jiang Jieshi yu Zhongguo nongmin yinhang" (Chiang Kai-shek and the Farmers Bank). *Minguo dang'an* (Republican Archives), 1 (1996): 91–98.

Sze, Alfred Sao-ke. *Geneva Opium Conferences*. Baltimore: Johns Hopkins Press, 1926.

Szekely, Jozsef I. *Opioid Peptides in Substance Abuse*. Boca Raton: CRC Press, 1994.

Tamagna, Frank M. *Banking and Finance in China*. New York: Institute of Pacific Relations, 1942.

Tan Yuzuo. *Zhongguo zhongyao yinhang fazhanshi* (A History of the Development of Important Chinese Banks). Taibei: Zhongguo xinwen chuban gongsi, 1961.

T'ang, Leang-li. *The Inner History of the Chinese Revolution*. London: George Routledge and Sons, 1930.

———. *Reconstruction in China: A Record of Progress and Achievement in Facts and Figures*. Shanghai: China United Press, 1935.

———. *Suppressing Communist Banditry in China*. Shanghai: China United Press, 1934.

Teng, Ssu-yü. "Introduction/A Decade of Challenge." In *China in the 1920s: Nationalism and Revolution*, edited by F. Gilbert Chan and Thomas H. Etzhold, pp. 1–14. New York: New Viewpoints, 1976.

Thomson, James C., Jr. *While China Faced West: American Reformers in Nationalist China, 1928–1937*. Cambridge, Mass.: Harvard University Press, 1969.

Tien, Hung-mao. *Government and Politics in Kuomintang China, 1927–1937.* Stanford, Calif.: Stanford University Press, 1972.

Tolley, Kemp. *Yangtze Patrol.* Annapolis: The Naval Institute Press, 1971.

Tyau, Min Ch'ien T. Z. *Two Years of Nationalist China.* Shanghai: Kelly and Walsh, 1930.

United States, Department of State. *Records Relating to the Internal Affairs of China, 1910–1929.* Washington, D.C.: National Archives Microfilm Publications, Series 893.

————. *Records Relating to the Internal Affairs of China, 1930–1939.* Washington, D.C.: National Archives Microfilm Publications, Series 893.

U.S. National Archives. *Shanghai Municipal [International Settlement] Police Files, 1929–1944.* Microfilm. Wilmington, Del.: Scholarly Resources, 1990.

van de Ven, Hans J. "Public Finance and the Rise of Warlordism." In *Minguo yanjiu* (Studies on Republican China), edited by Zhang Xianwen, vol. 1, pp. 89–137. Nanjing: Nanjing daxue chubanshe, 1994.

Walker, William O., III. *Opium and Foreign Policy.* Chapel Hill: University of North Carolina Press, 1991.

Wakeman, Frederic, Jr. "The Canton Trade and the Opium War." In *The Cambridge History of China,* edited by Denis Twitchett and John K. Fairbank, vol. 10, pp. 163–212. Cambridge: Cambridge University Press, 1978.

————. *Policing Shanghai, 1927–1937.* Berkeley: University of California Press, 1995.

Wang Qinyu. *Jindai Zhongguo de daolu jianshe* (Railroad and Highway Construction in Modern China). Hong Kong: Longmen shudian, 1969.

Wang Qizhang. *Jieyan zhinan* (A Guidebook for Treating Opium Addiction). Shanghai: N.p., 1936.

Wang Zuxiang. *Weisheng xingzheng sanshinian suoyi* (Fragmentary Recollections from Thirty Years of Public Health Administration). Taibei: Academia Sinica, 1953.

Watanabe, Atsushi. "Secret Societies in Modern China: Ch'ing Pang, Hung Pang— Late Ch'ing and Early Republic of China." In *Zhonghua minguo chuqi lishi yantaohui lunwenji* (Proceedings from the Conference on the Early Republic, 1912–1927), vol. 2, pp. 797–815. Taibei: Academia Sinica, 1984.

Watson, Andrew, ed. *Mao Zedong and the Political Economy of the Border Region.* Cambridge: Cambridge University Press, 1980.

Wei, William. *Counterrevolution in China: The Nationalists in Jiangxi during the Soviet Period.* Ann Arbor: University of Michigan Press, 1985.

Who's Who in China. 3d ed. Shanghai: The China Weekly Review, 1925.

————. 4th ed. Shanghai: The China Weekly Review, 1931.

————. 5th ed. Shanghai: The China Weekly Review, 1936.

Wilbur, C. Martin. "Military Separatism and the Process of Reunification under the Nationalist Regime, 1922–1937." In *China's Heritage and the Communist Political System.* Vol. 1, Book 1, of *China in Crisis,* edited by Ping-ti Ho and Tang Tsou, pp. 203–263. Chicago: University of Chicago Press, 1968.

————. "The Nationalist Revolution: From Canton to Nanking, 1923–28." In *The Cambridge History of China,* edited by John K. Fairbank, vol 12, pp. 527–621. Cambridge: Cambridge University Press, 1983.

———. "Problems of Starting A Revolutionary Base: Sun Yat-sen and Canton, 1923." *Jindaishi yanjiusuo jikan* 4.2 (Oct. 1978): 665–727.

———. *Sun Yat-sen: Frustrated Patriot.* New York: Columbia University Press, 1976.

Wou, Odoric Y. K. *Militarism in Modern China: The Career of Wu Peifu.* Folkstone, England: Dawson, 1978.

Wu, Lien-teh. *Plague Fighter: The Autobiography of a Modern Chinese Physician.* Cambridge: W. Heffer and Sons, 1959.

Wu, Wen-tsao. *The Chinese Opium Problem and Public Opinion and Action.* New York: The Academy Press, 1928.

Xinshenghuo yundong cujin zonghui, ed. *Minguo ershisannian xinshenghuo yundong zongbaogao* (General Report on the New Life Movement in 1934). Nanchang, 1935.

Xu Youchun, ed. *Guomin renwu dacidian* (Encyclopedia of Personalities in the Republic of China). Beijing: Hebei renmin chubanshe, 1991.

Young, Arthur N. *China's Nation-Building Effort, 1927–1937.* Stanford, Calif.: Stanford University Press, 1971.

Young, Ernest P. "Politics in the Aftermath of Revolution: The Era of Yuan Shikai, 1912–16." In *The Cambridge History of China*, edited by John K. Fairbank, vol. 12, pp. 208–258. Cambridge: Cambridge University Press, 1983.

Yu Ende. *Zhongguo jinyan faling bianqianshi* (A History of the Changes in China's Anti-Opium Laws and Decrees). Shanghai: Zhonghua shuju, 1934.

Zhang Jingru and Liu Zhiqiang, eds. *Beiyang junfa tongzhi shiqi Zhongguo shehui zhi bianqian* (Changes in Chinese Society during the Period of Beiyang Warlord Rule). Beijing: Zhongguo renmin daxue chubanshe, 1992.

Zhang Jungu. *Du Yuesheng zhuan* (A Biography of Du Yuesheng). 4 vols. Taibei: Zhuanji wenxue chubanshe, 1967.

Zhang Pengyuan and Chen Huaiyu, comps. *Guomin zhengfu zhiguan nianbiao* (Yearly Tables of Officials in the National Government). Taibei: Academia Sinica, 1987.

Zhang Xianwen, ed. *Minguo yanjiu* (Studies on Republican China). 2 vols. Nanjing: Nanjing daxue chubanshe, 1994.

Zhang Zhijiang, ed. *Quanguo jinyan huiyi huibian* (Proceedings from the National Opium Prohibition Conference). Nanjing: Executive Yuan, 1929.

Zheng Yifang. *Shanghai qianzhuang, 1843–1937* (Shanghai Native Banks, 1843–1937). Taibei: Academia Sinica, 1981.

Zhongguo di'er lishi dang'anguan (Number Two [Second] Historical Archives of China). Nanjing, People's Republic of China. Quanzonghao 3: Caizhengbu (Ministry of Finance). File numbers 875–1121. Quanzonghao 41: Neizhengbu jinyan weiyuanhui (Opium Suppression Committee of the Ministry of the Interior). File numbers 1–731.

Zhongguo Guomindang zhongyang dangshihui (Guomindang Central Archives). Yangmingshan, Taiwan. Zhongguo guomindang shiqi 2, January 1924–July 1937 (Chinese National Party Period, Part 2). File numbers 442/54.1, 442/54.2.

Zhongguo Guomindang zhongyang weiyuanhui dangshi shiliao bianxuan weiyuanhui, comp. *Geming wenxian* (Documents of the Revolution). Series. Taibei, 1953–.

————. *Zhonghua minguo zhongyao shiliao chubian—dui-Ri kangzhan shiqi* (Preliminary Compilation of Important Historical Materials on the Chinese Republic— the Period of the War of Resistance against Japan). 3 vols. Taibei, 1981.

Zhongguo Guomindang zhongyang zhixing weiyuanhui xuanchuanbu, ed. *Jinyan xuanchuan huikan* (A Compendium of Anti-opium Literature). Nanjing: Guomindang zhongyang zhixing weiyuanhui xuanchuanbu, 1929.

Zhongguo Guomindang zhoukan (National Party Weekly). Canton, 1924.

Zhongguo nongcun (Village Agriculture). Shanghai, 1935.

Zhongguoshi xuehui, ed. *Beiyang junfa, 1912–1928* (Beiyang Warlords, 1912–1928). 6 vols. Wuhan: Wuhan chubanshe, 1990.

Zhongguo yinhang jingji yanjiushi, ed. *Quanguo yinhang nianjian* (Chinese Banks Yearbook, 1936–1937). Shanghai: Zhongguo yinhang jingji yanjiushi, 1937; reprint, Washington, D.C.: Center for Chinese Research Materials, 1971.

Zhonghua guomin zhengfu gongbao (National Government Bulletin). Canton, 1925–1927; Nanjing, 1927–1937.

Zhonghua minguo shishi jiyao bianji weiyuanhui, comp. *Zhonghua minguo shishi jiyao* (Essential Historical Events in the Republic of China). Series 1894–. Taibei: Guoshiliao yanjiu zhongxin, 1974–.

Zhongyang ribao (Central Daily News). Nanjing, Shanghai, 1928–1937.

Zhongyang yanjiuyuan jindaishi yanjiusuo, ed. *Bai Chongxi xiansheng fangwen jilu* (An Oral Interview with Mr. Bai Chongxi). 2 vols. Taibei: Academia Sinica, 1984.

————. *Xu Qiming xiansheng fangwen jilu* (An Oral Interview with Mr. Xu Qiming). Taibei: Academia Sinica, 1983.

————. *Yu Da xiansheng fangwen jilu* (An Oral Interview with Mr. Yu Da). Taibei: Academia Sinica, 1989.

————. *Zhou Yongneng xiansheng fangwen jilu* (An Oral Interview with Mr. Zhou Yongneng). Taibei: Academia Sinica, 1984.

Zhongyang zhoubao (Central Weekly). Nanjing, 1934.

Zhou Yongming. "Nationalism, Identity, and State Building: Anti–Drug Crusades in Communist China, 1949–1952." Unpublished paper presented at the Conference on Opium in East Asian History, 1830–1945, University of Toronto–York University, Toronto, Ontario, 9–10 May 1997.

Zhu Hanguo, ed. *Nanjing guomin zhengfu jishi* (A Veritable Record of the National Government at Nanjing). Beijing: Anhui renmin chubanshe, 1993.

Zhu Houde, ed. *Jiaofei jianshi* (A Concise History of Bandit Suppression). 6 vols. Taibei: Zhonghua dadian bianyinhui, 1967.

Zhu Qihua. *Zhongguo jingji weiji jiqi qiantu* (China's Economic Crisis and Its Future). Shanghai: Xinshengming shuju, 1932.

Zhu Qingbao, Jiang Chiuming, and Zhang Shijie, eds. *Yapian yu jindai Zhongguo* (Opium and Modern China). Nanjing: Jiangsu jiaoyu chubanshe, 1995.

INDEX